KEORAPETSE KGOSITSILE & THE BLACK ARTS MOVEMENT

AFRICAN ARTICULATIONS

ISSN 2054-5673

SERIES EDITORS
Ranka Primorac, Madhu Krishnan & Edgar Nabutanyi

EDITORIAL ADVISORY BOARD
Akin Adesokan (Indiana University)
James Ferguson (Stanford University)
Simon Gikandi (Princeton University)
Stefan Helgesson (Stockholm University)
Isabel Hofmeyr (University of the Witwatersrand)
Lydie E. Moudileno (University of Southern California, Dornsife)
Upamanyu Pablo Mukherjee (University of Oxford)
Grace A. Musila (University of the Witwatersrand)
Stephanie Newell (Yale University)
Caroline Rooney (University of Kent)
Meg Samuelson (University of Adelaide)
Jennifer Wenzel (Columbia University)

African Articulations showcases cutting-edge research into African literary and performance cultures, broadly understood to include written and oral literatures, theatre, film, music, social media creativity and digital arts. It aims to make available new perspectives on the complex relationships between Africa's cultural producers, texts, consumers, geographies and aesthetic or critical discourses. Books in the series focus on the ways in which African texts and practices are articulated – how they are connected, spoken about, and speak for themselves – in relation to local, regional and global networks and histories. With cultural production from the continent at its core, the series challenges scholarship that uncritically privileges the internationally visible above the supposedly ephemeral and local. African Articulations provides indispensable resources for scholars and students of modern and contemporary African cultures.

Please contact the series editors with an outline, or download the proposal form https://boydellandbrewer.com/african-articulations/. Only send a full manuscript if requested to do so.

Ranka Primorac, University of Southampton, r.primorac@soton.ac.uk

Madhu Krishnan, University of Bristol, madhu.krishnan@bristol.ac.uk

Edgar Nabutanyi, Makere University, enabutanyi@chuss.mak.ac.ug

Previously published volumes are listed at the back of this volume.

KEORAPETSE KGOSITSILE & THE BLACK ARTS MOVEMENT

Poetics of Possibility

Uhuru Portia Phalafala

© Uhuru Portia Phalafala 2024

All Rights Reserved. Except as permitted under current legislation
no part of this work may be photocopied, stored in a retrieval system,
published, performed in public, adapted, broadcast,
transmitted, recorded or reproduced in any form or by any means,
without the prior permission of the copyright owner

The right of Uhuru Portia Phalafala to be identified as
the author of this work has been asserted in accordance with
sections 77 and 78 of the Copyright, Designs and Patents Act 1988

First published 2024
James Currey
Paperback edition 2026

ISBN 978-1-84701-277-7 (Hardback)
ISBN 978-1-84701-467-2 (Paperback)

James Currey is an imprint of Boydell & Brewer Ltd
www.jamescurrey.com
and of Boydell & Brewer Inc.
www.boydellandbrewer.com

Our Authorised Representative for product safety in the EU is Easy Access
System Europe – Mustamäe tee 50, 10621 Tallinn,
Estonia, gpsr.requests@easproject.com

A CIP catalogue record for this book is available
from the British Library

The publisher has no responsibility for the continued existence or accuracy of URLs for
external or third-party internet websites referred to in this book, and does not guarantee
that any content on such websites is, or will remain, accurate or appropriate

for mma (1956–2023) le papa
koko le rakgolo babina-tšhwene
koko le rakgolo babina-tlou
bokoko-khukhu le borakgolo-khukhu

Contents

List of Illustrations	viii
Acknowledgements	ix
List of Abbreviations	xi
Introduction: Elsewhere	1
1 A Writing Life – A Riting Life – A Rioting Life	33
2 Names: Mother, What is My Name?	61
3 Songs: Native Sons Dancing Like Crazy	91
4 Spaces: Twenty-First-Century Suns/Sons Must Rise Again	117
5 Places: Black Consciousness Ecologies of Futurity	147
Coda	173
Bibliography	191
Index	203

List of Illustrations

1	Jamal Cyrus' 'Towards a Walk in the Sun'	133
2	Robert Pruitt's comic cover	136
3	Robert Pruitt's comic interior	140
4	Robert Pruitt's comic interior ii	142
5	Lefifi Tladi's 'Mosima Motlhaela Thupa'	165
6	Lefifi Tladi's 'Mosima Motlhaela Thupa' ii	167

All images are reproduced by kind permission of the artists.

Acknowledgements

Gratitude to the guiding spirits of my ancestors who bestowed upon me the gift of healing through words. I am from a lineage of storytellers, healers, and teachers whose gift I carry forward through this work. I thank them for guiding this journey with their gruelling and exacting guidance, and with their divine light. I am honoured to be and walk with the memory keepers: ditšhwene le ditlou. Thobela.

My parents modelled dreaming, hard work, resilience, and leisure for us, under a deadly regime. They were community builders who parented, birthed (my mother as midwife), fed, and loved black people in all the communities we lived in. Their communitarian spirit makes this book possible. Thank you Matee and Sebone Phalafala.

This book is also dedicated to my siblings who are my greatest loves and who continue to teach me, ground me, see and affirm me. I love you so much.

During the research and writing of this book, I was broken open by the loss of my mentors and teachers Keorapetse Kgositsile, Bhekizizwe Peterson, Onako Nokhanyo Mhlana, Lerato Khanye, Jabulani Tsambo, Noemi Gonzales, and Noji Matutu – and as such have gained powerful ancestors. I love you always.

I wrote this book on various prestigious fellowships where I was hosted generously and enjoyed intellectual enrichment, in Michigan (University of Michigan African Presidential Scholars), Ghana (African Humanities Program), Senegal (West Africa Research Center) and at the Stellenbosch Institute for Advanced Studies (STIAS).

Librarians at various Special Collections holdings and research centres supported the development of this book: Schomburg Center for Research in Black Culture, University of California Berkley's Bancroft Library, University of Kwa-Zulu Natal's Howard's Center for African Literary Studies, Northwestern University's Melville J. Herskovits Library of African Studies, University of Botswana. A special mention to Andrew Martin at Amazwi in Grahamstown, and librarians at the Amistad Special Collections Library in New Orleans, without whose steady and unwavering commitment this book would not have come together.

In 2014 I took a leap of faith and travelled to the States for the first time to interview Kgositsile's contemporaries who organised, wrote, and made community with him. Without them there was no point of departure: Rashida Ismaili who opened the door to everybody else – Sam Anderson, Amina

Baraka, Reginald Gibbons, Evelyn Neal, Quincy Troupe, Gloria House, Ipeleng Kgositsile, A.B and Karen Spellman. And the eldership modelled by Sterling Plumpp who offered me more than an interview but also gentle mentorship. In South Africa and Botswana, I interviewed Baleka Mbete, Gwen Ansell, Mongane Serote, Muxe Nkondo, Baleka Mbete, Lefifi Tladi, Tshidi Moagi, Thulaganyo Mogobe, and Victor Mtubani. Thank you all for holding the dream with me, for energizing my research with stories. Thank you for welcoming me in your homes and offices, for feeding me and praying for me.

This book is also dedicated to my mentors, whom I know are proud: Bhekizizwe Peterson, Harry Garuba, Meg Samuelson, Grace Musila, and Chris Ouma. To my colleagues who make the world of ideation and pedagogy magical, thank you for seeing and trusting me. Thank you zethu matebeni. Stephane Robolin: how do I begin to express my gratitude? Ke a leboga Tsitsi Jaji, Stefan Helgesson, Brent Edwards, and Carter Mathes for motivating me, for scanning and sending me chapters, for inviting me to your classrooms, for your solidarity. I am grateful to Margo Crawford for her rich reader's report that opened the way to the book's methodology. Brenda Cooper and Andrea Cassatella gifted me the unpayable labour of unearthing the core intervention of this book at a time when I struggled to see it. I am so grateful! To Andrea, for the worldmaking force of our friendship.

Thank you Husam El-Qoulaq for introducing me to the work of Earl Sweatshirt all the way back in 2014. And for demonstrating solidarity as an act of love. I am indebted to you in so many ways. I honour you Reinier; thank you Mafadi, Jayson, Ibou, Bongani, Kieron, Lusanda, Zarina, Alexis, Parusha, and the shapeshifters.

Thank you to my Cape Town family, the folks at Chimurenga for holding space for my process. I want to also thank Nduduzo Makhathini from whom I learnt composing myself to return to the knowledge in this book, allowing it to write me too. Deep gratitude too to Asher Gamedze who allowed me to deepen the practice of listening and thinking through jazz. To Muntu Vilakazi, whose healers' brew sonic documentaries accompanied me for years of writing this book. To Tumi Tlhoaele, Ben V, George Mahashe, Kabelo Malatsie, Mathapelo Mofokeng, Bibi Burger, Nthupula Masipa, Matlapulana Ragoasha, Lerato Maduna, Lesedi Mogoatle – you are so damn precious to me.

In the company of Madikana Phalafala, Catriona Towriss and Smangele Mathebula I meet more and more of myself, my light is magnified. You are friends of my heart, thank you for holding and anchoring me, for mirroring me, for bearing witness and shoring me. I love you now and always.

List of Abbreviations

AAPSO	Afro-Asian People's Solidarity Organisation
AAWA	Afro-Asian Writer's Association
ANC	African National Congress
BAM	Black Power and Black Arts Movement
BCM	Black Consciousness Movements
BPM	Black Power Movement
BPP	Black Panther Party
CIA	U.S. Central Intelligence Agency
DAC	Department of Arts and Culture
FBI	Federal Bureau of Investigation
FESMAN	First World Festival of Negro Arts
FRELIMO	Frente de Libertação de Moçambique
FST	Free Southern Theatre
MDALI	Music, Drama, Arts & Literature
MPLA	Movement for the Liberation of Angola
PAC	Pan-African Congress
PLO	Palestinian Liberation Organization
SACP	South African Communist Party
SANNC	South African Native National Congress
SNCC	Student Nonviolent Coordinating Committee
USA	United States of America
VOW	Voice of Women

Introduction: Elsewhere

> African cultures and cosmologies can provide a wealth of inexhaustible resources for the project of epistemic decentring. Having exhausted technoscientific reason and confronted the civilizational consequences of its impasses, new metaphors are required for the future. We must heed the call for a renewal of the very sources of the imaginary and of a thought *coming from an elsewhere.*
>
> Felwine Sarr, *Afrotopia*
> (2019: 80, my emphasis)[1]

When South African poet and statesman Keorapetse Kgositsile (1938–2018) was instructed by senior members of his party, the African National Congress (ANC), to flee the country into exile in 1961, he packed among his meagre belongings a corpus of Tswana literary classics. To him, they enshrined a set of valuables, of knowledge systems, aesthetic practices, cosmologies, and mythologies he could marshal to counter colonial modernity's anti-Black warfare. As a revolutionary writer, he used the worlds from these classics as a basis to assert the existence of other forms of being, knowing, and belonging that were otherwise to the Eurocentric, racist, capitalist, and Christian social orders imposed by colonialism and apartheid. The Tswana literatures that accompanied him into exile were material representations of the values instilled

---

[1] Since I began thinking about other cosmologies as potentially opening otherworlds, Felwine Sarr's quotation from *Afrotopia* (2019) offered me the notion of 'elsewhere' as theoretically generative. This idea has since grown in my mind and spirit through engaging with jazz musician and scholar Nduduzo Makhathini's own use of the term in his recent jazz shows, notably at his three-day ritual performance, 'Jazz & Vines', in March 2022, where, on the last day, I was in conversation with him.

in his formative years, used as bridges to connect politics of the homeplace with those of his unfolding exile travels and writing life.

He arrived with this treasure trove in the nascent cultural and political ferment of the Black Power and Black Arts Movements (BAM) in the United States of America in 1962. He harnessed that Tswana archive – comprising dramas, novels, and an anthology of poetry – in his five collections of poetry published in the States with the intent to foster continuities between the African American struggle and the struggles of Black South Africa. Further, he understood the Black experience as connected, thereby embracing Black world politics as fundamentally opposed to the culture of Jim Crow, colonialism, and apartheid. Operating in this world of Blackness he sought to bridge geographical and linguistic chasms, to foster political solidarities through cultural relations with Black diasporans.

His literary corpus published in the States, as well as his political activities, illustrate an assertion of the existence of otherworlds within the dominant paradigm of anti-Blackness. These are the worlds to which the elsewhere in this book refers. The availability of these worlds, their active materialization in his life and work, and his intentional access to them shaped his radical imagination. Further, he produced *otherwise* grammars and registers of possibility from those elsewheres in his poetry, concepts, and terminologies that point to ecologies of knowledge and being that he in turn deployed to dislodge and destabilize colonial modernity's anti-Black social order. I borrow the 'otherwise' from Ashon Crawley, who defines it as 'a word that names plurality as its core operation, otherwise bespeaks the ongoingness of possibility, of things existing other than what is given, what is known, what is grasped' (2016: 24). This book reveals those pluralities, the multiple worlds from which he constructs and coins his poetics of possibility.

The availability and surfacing of otherwise registers by Kgositsile branded his aesthetics and politics with a particular tenor that was deeply yearned for by his African American contemporaries. The worlds he shuttled in his suitcase couched revolutionary potential to diasporans who faced the loss of those worlds due to the Middle Passage, genealogical deracination, and the passage of time. They were negotiating their shifting group and individual identities, collectively, from 'negro' to Black, and individually adopted African names to repudiate their 'slave names', reflect their heritage, and reclaim institutionally decimated ties to the continent. They intuited the potential radical dimensions of other universals, modernities, and social orderings from the African continent, and Kgositsile's work revealed and confirmed their inclinations. His work became exemplary and was emulated.

There are causal relationships between Kgositsile's decision to carry these classics across the border and pivotal lessons learnt in the domestic environment of his younger years. He grew up in rural Dithakong with his grandmother

Madikeledi, who banned the English language in her home while simultaneously expecting young Kgositsile to receive a good report, that is, to attain first-class results at his British colonial primary school. In insisting upon seemingly contradicting values, Madikeledi initiated the co-existence of two world systems in young Kgositsile's life, where the one world constituted foundational culture that embedded Tswana customs, cosmologies, and a sense of community, and the other world carried foreign value systems. Not only did the latter carry colonial culture, but it also occasioned a violent imposition of that culture onto local cultural worlds for purposes of assimilation. Madikeledi was conscious of this, and Kgositsile would later understand her stance to be political.

Madikeledi's attitude demonstrated crucial positions to young Kgositsile: she grounded his cultural and political sensibilities in Tswana culture, customs, cosmologies, and a sense of community, while also equipping him with the confidence to engage and steep himself in encountered cultures, as long as they were not coercively imposed. In this dynamic, along his life journey, he would not fall into the trap of seeking to preserve or glorify the purity or harmony of his first culture. She instilled critical comprehension of home and community cultures of Setswana as dynamics of modernity, not its antithesis. That is, she instilled a view of Tswana culture as durable, malleable, fluid, porous, and relational as opposed to rigid, fixed, and ossifying. This is crucial as it underwrites Kgositsile's assertion of continuities in his poetics between Tswana worlds and Black world politics, where the former operates in dynamic ways to shape and expand the politics of the latter. The two worlds became mutually reinforcing – with African American contexts also enriching Tswana knowledges – and cooperative in articulating a geographically unique radical tradition fashioned from a coeval elsewhere.

Madikeledi's political and cultural position crucially groomed Kgositsile's gravitation towards alignment with the mass liberation movement in South Africa, to join and participate in the public operations of the ANC and the South African Communist Party. In his understanding, her views on colonial culture and her need to anchor him in the otherworld of Setswana were coterminous with the views of the national liberation movement, an organized political expression of a cultural alternative to colonial culture. Hence Madikeledi represented the isolated sum of the organized whole, those who shaped and informed the desires and aspirations of the liberation movement. His peregrinations threw into sharp relief her struggle as tied to those of the masses.

In raising the value of home culture as first culture while not undervaluing or rejecting the English language and culture of his schooling system, Madikeledi seeded in young Kgositsile the confidence, adaptability, and dexterity to navigate two worlds and two knowledge systems from a young age. She eschewed their positioning as dichotomous and binary, thus flowering an interweaving practice that characterizes Kgositsile's oeuvre. His work gathers and conjugates home culture with Black world culture, Southern African oral/aural traditions and literary cultures with those of African America, and Southern African liberation politics with the radical traditions of the Black world. Stephen Henderson writes of him: 'Willie [Kgositsile] speaks from Black Africa to Black America; from Black America to Black Africa. He is of both worlds but not divided. There is a powerful harmony within him, a universal Blackness' (1969: 118). His work holds together these two seemingly disparate worlds, bringing them into relation without privileging one over the other. I call this bridging and interweaving practice *gathering work*, a poetic of suture which I consider to be a matrilineally inherited heirloom.

The authors of *Revolutionary Mothering*, Pauline Gumbs, China Martens, and Mai'a Williams, define radical mothering as 'the imperative to build bridges that allow us to relate across [...] very real barriers' (2016: 41). I regard this gathering work by Madikeledi as a deployment of Black motherhood towards political ends, used to impact futurity by seeding the desires for a liberated South Africa. She constructed what bell hooks (1990) calls the 'homeplace as site of resistance'. Madikeledi's radical mothering equipped Kgositsile with the tools that would later inform his rebellion, and I consider this bridge-building work a world-making enterprise. I take as foundational her home- and community-making practices, consisting of her *deliberate diffusion* and *targeted transmission* of intergenerational, ancestral, and lineage wisdoms and cosmologies, and interrogate Kgositsile's witnessing of her acts as transgressive and political. I take seriously his harnessing of that living repository of knowledge and his imbrication of homeplace politics with the mass liberation movement in South Africa and in the Black world. The actively materializing archive of his formative years becomes the oral/aural worlds that converge in Kgositsile's work, and I read Madikeledi's politics of the homeplace as world-constituting forces, radical in so far as the boundaries of the Tswana cultural universe seeded in the home reshape a larger world than the local or national community and culture.

His mother, Galekgobe, whom Kgositsile joined in Johannesburg after Madikeledi's passing, continued the teachings of the elderly matriarch, imparting another crucial lesson unto young Kgositsile. These two women are the matrilineal force to which Kgositsile attributes his political and cultural sensibilities. Asked by *Callaloo*'s Charles Rowell, in 1973, to talk about some of his early experiences that had an impact on his writing, Kgositsile responded: 'I would say that my earliest memories go back to two very strong women – my grandmother and my mother – in that order. Practically everything I write is tied up with some kind of wisdom I got from them in that hostile environment' (1978: 23).[2] When I interviewed Kgositsile in 2013, I asked him a

---

[2] Although this interview was published in 1978, it is recorded to have taken place in 1973.

similar question, to begin our dialogue with a discussion of his formative years, to trace the proverbial portrait of an artist as a young man, and he gave me the same answer. This tasked me to treat his assertion and affirmation very seriously and with great care, hearing him remain faithful, as he did, to this truth he told in 1973 and again forty years later. I began to pay closer attention to his poetry, short stories, interviews, and essays in order to read, hear, and sense where these women are mentioned, sounded, and referenced.

To illustrate my point on the gathering practice of Kgositsile's work, the bridging of Black America and Black South Africa, I resound his assertion and affirmation of matrilineal influences in his work by focusing on his involvement in the Black Arts Movement. Later in their conversation, Rowell asks Kgositsile to name fellow contemporary African American writers that influence his work, to which Kgositsile answers: Amiri Baraka. Rowell pushes, 'specifically, how did he influence you?' – both important questions as the topic of influence is central to this book. Kgositsile offers:

> [...] in terms of thinking, not style, but thinking; in terms of realizing more and more, although I did already, that writing had to be directly connected to actual life. I would say the impact of someone like Baraka made or fertilized the ground, say in my mind, to be receptive immediately to people like Malcolm, Fanon, and others. What that did, too – which *is interesting, because it might not have happened if I had not come here* – was to open up in me memories of earlier wisdom during my young years in South Africa. Weirdly enough, I recalled a lot of things I had read in Tswana and Sotho literature which, later, I think, informed the music or the rhythm in my work (1978: 30, my emphasis).

In his response, Kgositsile traces and surfaces numerous aesthetic and political influences in his work. He emphasizes that Baraka – a figurehead of the Black Arts Movement – reinforced the importance of what he was already doing: connecting his writing to real life. But the impact the years in Black America had on him in relation to South Africa, signalled in 'it might not have happened if I had not come here', is the revelation of the role the matriarchive has had in his life and work. The reinforcement by Baraka tilled the grounds of his mind to trace the sprouting political philosophies of Malcolm X and Frantz Fanon to the same seedbed as the wisdoms and teachings from his youth. Part of this golden thread that ties together the homeplace and Black world politics are the Sotho and Tswana literatures that resounded the oralities and auralities of his homeplace, modelling for him the scriptural transcription of those worlds in printed literature. There is a throughline between the matriarchal knowledge systems of his formative years, indigenous languages literatures, the Black Arts Movement, and Black world politics, not in any linear form but all interwoven and intertwined to produce his poetic and political expression. To be clear, an understanding of Kgositsile's relation with Black America is also an understanding of his relationship with his grandmother and mother in South Africa.

Keorapetse Kgositsile & the Black Arts Movement contributes to scholarship the concept of the matriarchive. The matriarchive is a living repository of sound knowledges transmitted by matrilineal members of the family. These knowledges are rooted/routed in cosmologies and mythologies of the lineages and are at once intergenerational, communal, relational, and ancestral. They enshrine indigenous languages, names, songs, prayers, and rituals practised in the homeplace and actively materialize in their progenies' lives and ongoing becoming. In his work, Kgositsile draws from the matriarchive to assert different origins and beginnings beyond the inauguration of colonial history, to proclaim alternative creators to the patriarchal Christian Holy Trinity, to assert the existence of another world whose cultural universe enables him to repudiate a Black subjectivity based on the Black Other. The matriarchive offers him a knowing of oneself fashioned not through negation and difference but ontological affirmation and belonging. The matriarchive informs his acts of disobedience to the ruling order, to speak from an elsewhere that generates other forms of being, knowing, and relating in the world. The matriarchive teaches him to be suspicious of the myth of pioneering individualism, of the singular genius, and of structures of relations shaped by domination and coercion. The matriarchive enables him to navigate his worlds of first comprehension *and* the colonial cultural universe, granting him confidence to sing to new gods and make new languages, to (inter)weave possibility out of alienation and disenchantment through philo-praxis of interrelation, collaboration, and solidarity. His work being 'connected to actual life' produces theory from collective practice: poetics of possibility.

Kgositsile speaks about Amiri Baraka, Malcolm X, and Frantz Fanon, figureheads of the Black arts, Black nationalism, and Black world philosophical tradition, in the same breath with the matriarchive. In locating the matriarchive in Black arts' discourse, Kgositsile deviates from the norm of the milieu that was characterized by Black nationalist ideology, which often valorized men and lauded male achievement, spotlighting the Black man as not only the racialized other of the white man but also his worst victim. The Black man was preoccupied with emerging from the embattled 'zone of nonbeing' (Fanon 1967) to be the natural leader of the Black liberation movement and subsequent independent Black nation. The desires of androcentric Black nationalist movements are tied to the singular achievements of the Black male, achievements that erase the diverse worlds from which their political consciousness emerges. This eclipses and silences the achievements of Blackwomen and reproduces the colonial violence of undifferentiation and homogenization inflicted on their communities. To be blunt, Black nationalism culminates in the reproduction of the founding fathers as emergent natural leaders of the Black nation. In dialoguing with and positioning the matriarchive as genealogies and framework in his life and work, however, Kgositsile fashions alternative origins outside of the founding fathers of history. He departs from the myth of linear progressive teleology by deploying ancestry and birth rituals as centrifugal to land and revolutionary politics, singing the achievements of the collective constituted by the sum of all its parts, and speaking not with the singular but with a communitarian voice.

In citing *wisdoms* from the matriarchive as foundational influences that impacted his writing, he centralizes relationality and dialogic structures of being and becoming in knowledge production. The matriarchive offers him a counterpoint to Europatriarchy's terms of order underwritten by ocularcentric machinery which organizes the world in materialist, hierarchical, dichotomous, and binary terms. This machine produces a bogus science that was also responsible for the making of race and un/making of gender. The cultures of 'Europatriarchy', to use Minna Salami's (2020) formulation, are upheld by the supremacy of the printing press, which legitimizes some knowledge while undervaluing or rejecting knowledge from oral and aural cultures. Kgositsile's interweaving practice operates at the level of coalescing oral with print cultures, and the ocular with the sonic to abolish the boundary between cultures of the matriarchive and dominant culture. He explains how this is achieved in his work:

> My aims? [...] *continuity*, not *return*. [...] My sense of aesthetics is tied up to, and with, [...] continuity. If a poem I write is ritualistic and inspired enough, its content – African worldview (philosophical orientation) and my view of the world (my thinking and understanding) – plus its music or sound patterns reflect my connectedness to the collective circle without sacrificing the realities of the present, the cycle or time I live in [...]. (1975a: 16–17, emphasis in original)

We observe that Kgositsile here once again uses the phrase 'tied up' – earlier he asserted that everything he writes is 'tied up' with the matriarchs – to emphasize the continuities that he speaks about. The aim of his poetry, then, is to sound the knowledges of his collective circle to reinforce his belonging and connectedness to the world of his ontological affirmation: his people. As it pertains to the tying up of aesthetics and politics, to cycles or times, he coins the phrase *coil of time*, which enables him to think of these continuities and antiphonic relations between rural Dithakong and Black America, sound knowledges of the matriarchive and mbaqanga, jazz, blues, and spoken word poetry, the ANC and the Black Power and Black Panther Movements, and Tswana and Sotho literature and African American and Black world literatures. The Latin etymology of 'coil' – *to gather together* – is that gesture of bridging and gathering work. He aims for ritualistic writing, because, he believes, 'poetry is at its best when it approaches ritual, aspires to song. Which means it attempts to make music out of language'.[3] The approximation of his poetry to song as the primary objective, as *the long durée of sound* and *the scale of voice* locates into a chorus the sonicities and auralities of the homeplace, the community, the national liberation movement, the Black expressive cultures of the nation, and those of the continent and its diaspora. In espousing song as modality, his poetry becomes the meeting place of individual and community, past and future in the NOW, and Black South Africa and Black America.

In light of these central features of Kgositsile's work – the matriarchive, sound knowledges, and song – I deploy the methodology of *diligent looking*, paying close attention to where the two women tied to everything he writes appear, and employing a deep listening/feeling practice to hear where they are sounded. This method functions on two levels: in his oeuvre, Kgositsile wrote one poem to his grandmother ('The Elegance of Memory', 1971) and two poems to his mother ('To Mother', 1971, and 'Requiem for my Mother', 1975). He published an excerpt of his childhood memoirs in 1973 ('I Know My Name') that centres his relationship with Madikeledi and Galekgobe. He later penned a revealing poem, 'Manboy' (1995), a neologism that deepens the understanding of the coil of time through the contraction of himself as both man and boy. These become the literal site of looking and reading about the women in his life and work, producing materials for close reading. These poems reveal Kgositsile's 'writing as riting' practice, which is writing as ritual, or writing as reciting – a gesture of allowing the self to be saturated by presence in the act of writing. These presences, the active absences, have to be sensed or *felt* in the process of reading his work. Whereas scholars of Kgositsile's work have previously attended to jazz in his poetry (see, e.g., Jaji 2009; Robolin 2015; Crawford 2007), this book is invested in *the scale of the sonic*, which traces sound knowledges of the matriarchive within the genealogies of his orientation to oral traditions, workers' songs, protest songs, political speeches, mbaqanga, blues, bebop, jazz, spoken word, and rap.

On another level, the act of *looking where the women are sounded* is a methodology that is in line with Kgositsile's own approach of sounding the matriarchive in his work: it is a practice of looking with my ears to be loyal to the oralities/auralities of his work, and hearing with my heart/skin to pay attention to what he calls 'depthoffeeling' in his work. In Southern African languages, the

---

[3] Author interview with Keorapetse Kgositsile, Pretoria, March 2013.

sensory perception of hearing – *go utlwa* – implies both to *listen* and to *feel*. To hear and to listen is a modality of relation, of feeling and sympathizing with. Therefore, 'diligent looking' harnesses the meaning and etymology of 'diligent', which as an adjective means 'having or showing care and conscientiousness', and whose etymology from Latin, *diligens*, means to 'love' or 'take delight in'. The method of diligent looking therefore involves a conscientious reading of Kgositsile's work characterized by a multisensorial approach, attended by care and love, which is also an act of pleasure. This operates on two levels: Kgositsile's practice of 'purposefully distorting' (Jaji 2009) the written word to sound his mothers is in itself a conscientious act of love and care. He shows due diligence to the matriarchive by mentioning the two women in his interviews forty years apart and resounding their knowledge alongside Black world luminaries. On another level, to *write this book* I had to *right myself* by overturning my literary training in the ocular to hear where his mothers are sounded though not always seen.

I engage Kgositsile's oeuvre in this book with a particular focus on the collections of poetry he published in the States, namely *Spirits Unchained: Paeans* (1969), *For Melba* (1970), *My Name is Afrika* (1971), *The Word is Here: Poetry from Modern Africa* (ed., 1973), *The Present is a Dangerous Place to Live* (1974), and *Places and Bloodstains* (1975), as well as essays and short stories published in magazines and journals there. I have gathered research materials from sustained interviews conducted with him in Johannesburg and Pretoria over a period of five years (2012–18). I have further interviewed his contemporaries in South Africa, the States, Botswana, and Sweden, as well as paid visits to special collections libraries across the States and Southern Africa. Thus, the methodology of this book is itself gathering work, with this researcher once disillusioned by expectations from her literary discipline to exclusively work from within the university's (colonial) library. The edict was that literary studies do not deploy the methods of field research. As such, gathering work as method underscores a praxis of suturing seemingly irreconcilable research and knowledge traditions within institutions. It is an approach underpinned by care – etymologically tied to 'diligence' and 'curatorship' – that frames my methodologies. I consider repatriating[4] an exiled writer's literary production and suturing it to the nation and continent of his birth, a praxis of *care work* that has required heart, resilience, deep listening, empathy, intuition, and reparative gestures.

The research materials gathered here demonstrate Kgositsile's dexterity in interweaving the Black sonic worlds of his formative years and those of the Black diaspora, revealing the work of a committed writer, political activist, and teacher.

---

4 When I began this research, Kgositsile's collections of poetry were not available in South Africa. At this juncture, Philippa de Villiers and myself edited the book *Keorapetse Kgositsile: Collected Poems, 1969–2018*, which was published in January 2023.

I consolidate his concepts and terminologies from elsewhere worlds and in turn develop a poetics of possibilities beyond white settler conceptions of the human, spacetimes, ecologies, gender, and kinship. This praxis of consolidation attempts to model research in the humanities as gathering work, critical curatorship, and care work. I demonstrate throughout the chapters how Kgositsile's poetics and theorizations were indispensable to African Americans in the Black art era in their embattled zone for civil rights and self-identification.

Black South Africa in Black Arts America

The exchanges between Kgositsile and African Americans are critical to studies of Black transnationalism in the twentieth century. This scholarship is troubled by the privileging of historical experiences of diaspora populations as distinctive and contributing a unique body of reflections on modernity and its discontent – a 'counterculture to modernity' whose site is exclusively in the north (Gilroy 1993). It positions 'African Americans as vanguards of Black modernity that their South African counterparts seek to emulate' (Chrisman 2000: 1). Laura Chrisman elaborates:

> Important historiography [that] highlights relations between African-Americans and Africans [...] falls upon Black Americans, their travels, their solidarity movements, their perceptions and conceptions of Africa. [...] Only very rarely does work from within this bloc feature Africans as major thinkers, influences or interlocutors. (2012: 15)

I engage this historiography to reveal productive reflections that emerge from experiences grounded in distinctly national liberation and decolonizing projects in South Africa. I demonstrate how modern South African political and cultural subjectivities are shaped and informed by a distinctive form of Black South African agency which they bring to bear upon their diasporic interlocutors.

I centre the identity and geographical scope of the watershed cultural moment in American literature, the BAM, through attentive reading of Kgositsile's crucial presence therein. The movement (1965–75) is historically told in one way, giving central stage to the figures of Amiri Baraka, Larry Neal, Jayne Cortez, Hoyt Fuller, Nikki Giovanni, Maulana Karenga, Etheridge Knight, Haki Madhubuti, Ishmael Reed, Sonia Sanchez, Ntozake Shange, and Quincy Troupe. Kgositsile's omission is founded upon the movement's African American centrism, underscored by shared traumatic racial histories overdetermined by the Middle Passage, the afterlives of slavery, and the twentieth-century problem of the colour line. Black arts proponents positioned themselves in the African American intellectual traditions of W.E.B. Du Bois, Martin Delany, and Alexander Crummell, as well as the Harlem Renaissance, legitimizing their voices by bringing together different streams of African American political and cultural expression. This shaped their Black nationalist project.

Looking to Johannesburg and Dithakong in historicizing the BAM because of Kgositsile's presence and contribution to that movement disrupts its nationalist framing and northern hemisphere positionality. Originating out of a Black American cultural struggle, BAM was deeply interested in defining Blackness and the Black aesthetic, but it often did this in relation to some conception of Africa that was dated or oversimplified. The mobilized cultural riches with which Kgositsile arrived in this milieu brought to their consciousness a coeval Africa whose geography also expanded diaspora relations with the continent, thus far often limited to West Africa or Egypt. During their cultural and political renaissance under the banner of Black arts and Black power, African Americans yearned for a 'radical reordering of the western cultural aesthetic. [The BAM] proposes a separate symbolism, mythology, critique, and iconology' (Neal 1968: 29). This poetic and aesthetic were defined by Amiri Baraka as one capable of 'creating an entirely different world organically connected to this one' (1970: 163).[5] The search for Black aesthetics was a quest for otherwise imaginaries and practices brought about by otherworld cosmologies to disorder the settler's world and unsettle its regimes of order, truth, law, power, and beauty.

Literary critic of the day Eugene Redmond surmises that Kgositsile's

> Afro-American brothers incorporated the Africanisms into their world, and Kgositsile combines his own indigenisms with a mastered fluency in Black American idioms. He assays the whole of our tumultuous times (in Africa and America), intermingling an acquired Black street language with a demanding and stringent form. One of the most able craftsmen […]. (1976: 402)

The worlds Kgositsile shuttled in his suitcase enshrined those indigenisms – cosmologies, symbolisms, mythologies, languages, proverbs, and modalities of relation – which he interwove with African American oral/aural and literary traditions. I refer to these as erotic and ritual archives to echo Kgositsile's concept of *depthoffeeling*. The erotic and ritual attend to interiority and performativity, and also draw from Audre Lorde's theorization of the erotic as 'a resource within each of us that lies in a deeply female and spiritual plane, firmly rooted in the power of our unexpressed or unrecognized feeling' (1984: 87). I am also enthused by psychotherapist Esther Perel's use of the erotic to

---

5 Amiri Baraka writes these works in his preface to *Poetry For My People* by Henry Dumas. Dumas is recognized by Kgositsile as a dreamkeeper, a practitioner of this gathering work, lauding him for a *reeding and riting*, a literacy I explicate later in this chapter, and further in Chapter 2.

understand the ways in which 'people connect to this quality of aliveness, of vibrancy, of vitality, of renewal'. As she argues, the erotic 'is way beyond the description of sexuality. And it is mystical. It is actually a spiritual, mystical experience of life. It is a transcendent experience of life, because it is an act of the imagination' (Tippett & Perel 2019). It is crucial to position the erotic within the body to recast and re-enchant the body as enshrining an inner vastscape from which to cull grammars, gestures, and registers of enlivenment and possibility, rooted in the imagination. Kgositsile's work published in the popular print culture of the BAM harnessed these erotic and ritual archives, enthusing his African American contemporaries, who understood his work as models for aesthetics, politics, and spiritualities they themselves sought to redefine, rebirth, and rename. His political essays on decolonization in Africa and the third world, and his poetry that sounded a clarion call for Black liberation, were 'understood as historically-situated cultural practices which could be rehearsed, learned, and performed for specific political ends' (Jaji 2009: 287, 291). Eugene Redmond gives the following insight:

> The atmosphere of 1960s and '70s Black American literary circles was enhanced by a number of African thinkers, artists, poets, and novelists who arrived in America to teach, lecture, perform, and travel [...]. The importance of this interaction among Blacks from various parts of the globe in America cannot be overemphasized. (1976: 306)

Throughout the chapters I reveal Kgositsile's place in the canonical anthologies of the Black Arts Movement – *Black Arts: An Anthology of Black Creation* (1969); *For Malcolm: Poems on the life and the death of Malcolm X* (1969); *Malcolm X: The Man and His Times* (1969), edited by John Henry Clarke; Addison Gayle's *The Black Aesthetic* (1971); and most notably *Black Fire: An Anthology of African American Writing* (1968), edited by Amiri Baraka and Larry Neal. The latter, in its own naming, throws light on the nationalist project at hand, whose contours and geographical limits Kgositsile's presence in the movement challenged (see Crawford 2007). His ubiquity in *Negro Digest*, which was later retitled *Black World*, spotlights the milieu's developing self-understanding beyond the nation. The role Kgositsile played in these developments cannot be overemphasized. In *The Black Arts Movement Enterprise and the Production of Poetry*, Howard Rambsy II argues: 'The appearance of Kgositsile's poem on Lumumba reveals *Negro Digest*'s commitment to addressing the struggles and injustices on the African continent. Further, the publication of Kgositsile's poem anticipates *Negro Digest*'s developing focus on "Black world" issues beyond the United States' (2013: 31). This is crucial to this book's aims and objectives: how the presence of a South African in exile committed to speaking with a unified voice from Black

Africa to Black America, and Black America to Black Africa reconstituted the identity of an ostensibly African American cultural and political movement. His work and political vision influenced many, and, in this book, I focus on: Maya Angelou's engagement with Kgositsile on her television programme *Blacks, Blues, Black!* (1968); the adoption of Kgositsile's poetics by Larry Neal, co-editor of *Black Fire*; Kgositsile's mentoring of Tom Dent to found the BAM chapter in the American south, BLKARTSOUTH in New Orleans; the adaptation of his poetics by the members of the poetry outfit The Last Poets; the impact of his work on twenty-first-century arts collective Otabenga Jones & Associates; as well as what Kgositsile would consider the rebirth of memory through his rapper son Earl Sweatshirt.

I crucially pay attention to the matriarchive Kgositsile encounters and spotlights in the Black diaspora. While lauded as a touchstone of African American culture and politics, the criticism of the Black arts era as homophobic and masculinist plagues that movement's history, tainted by its gender politics in which Black feminist creativity was routinely silenced (Dubey 1994; Clarke 2006). What could the method and practice of *diligent looking* reveal when approaching the Black Arts Movement archive? Here I listen into Kgositsile's identification of Black American women whose lives and work fostered intergenerational continuities of ancestral wisdom and Black American mythologies as sites from which to fashion poetics and wage oppositional politics. In her introduction to Kgositsile's *My Name is Afrika* (1971), Gwendolyn Brooks pens a homage to this sensibility: 'he is very busy with his looking. / … / Not, Merely, Medgar, Malcolm, Martin and Black Panthers, / but Susie. Cecil Williams. Azzie Jane' (12–13). Brooks identifies something critical in Kgositsile's approaches to community-making: she witnesses his otherwise gender relations that are incongruent with the mood of the milieu. His work destabilizes the androcentric 'nation time' that was the movement's credo, which ultimately envisioned a new and emergent nation with Black man as natural leader, as opposed to a recuperation of an existing social order which would encompass all constituencies of a multifaceted Blackness.

In her work, Michelle Wright (2004) studies the poetry of BAM women writers Audre Lorde and Carolyn Rodgers to reveal how Black nationalist ideology erases both Black female achievement and diversity in Black subjectivities; unlike the trope of the founding father, however, 'mothers point to the endless line of ancestry that precedes and overlaps with each subject: all human beings emerge from the mother, are conflated with and distinct from her – and are therefore undeniable product of the past, shaped by it without being wholly controlled' (2004: 180). This crucial point on ancestry, community, and the mother is at the heart of what became apparent to Kgositsile in exile, which, as he attests, 'might not have happened if I had not come here' (Rowell 1978: 30). Distance and alienation from his land brought upon him the recognition of just how much the matriarchive mattered in his life, producing an important line in his poem to Madikeledi: 'distances separate bodies not people' (1971: 80), to further reinforce his awakening to the entanglements of his being and becoming, to his ontological, cultural, and political sensibilities, to his mothers. This tasks us to pay attention to the immaterial worlds he ferried across the Atlantic that comprised different social ordering, familial structures, and gender dynamics, and to how those are sounded in his work.

Charting Elsewhere Terrains for Grammars of Possibilities

I introduce, surface, map, and populate otherworlds that shape Kgositsile's radical imagination. These otherworlds undergird the continuous flow, materialization, and praxis of precolonial history with and alongside colonial history, and from his imagination Kgositsile wages revolt against the dominant oppressive culture. The latter did not, and simply could not, entirely uproot or erase the former. As Kgositsile asserts, 'our ways still exist among the majority of the people; in most cases covered up or twisted around in a hostile white environment, but still there. They can be unveiled and unleashed' (1975a: 15–16). Here Kgositsile entrusts 'our ways' with the power to explode the continuous flow of hegemonic history, the 'hostile white' culture. He demonstrates the utility of those worlds through coining concepts that I call poetics of possibility, which deconstruct coloniality of power, being, and knowledge. These poetics renew sources of the imaginary from his universe to produce thought coming from elsewhere, as charged by Felwine Sarr in the epigraph to this introduction, which I in turn assemble and develop in this book for epistemic decentring.

Amilcar Cabral writes that 'African culture [...] survived the storms, by taking refuge in the villages, in the forests, and in the spirit of generations of victims of colonialism' (1973: 147). We can think of that African culture in the spirit of the colonized generations in terms of what Chakrabarti calls History 2. Chakrabati (2000) delineates two vectors of history, history 1 and history 2, where the former refers to 'histories posited by capital' and the latter to other histories that capital encountered as its antecedent, which Chakrabati refers to as 'capital's life process'. History 1 was a race-making, differentiating, gendering, and dehumanizing force that produced Black as a constructed political ontology fashioned in the cauldron of colonial encounter. History 2, however, precedes the political ontological moment and is thereby beyond the symbolic order of white hegemony.[6] The latter, encompassing the diverse life-worlds of the worker or the colonized, constantly influenced and transformed the former.

---

[6] I owe this formulation to Fred Moten (2003) in his conception of Black as political ontology and Black as paraontology.

The continuous flow of these two histories alongside, tangential to, and entwined with one another points to the failures of colonial modernity's mission to be a totalizing hegemonic force. The advent of colonialism did not annihilate local traditions, languages, cultures, and customs. Some attempts were made to stop the rhythms, sounds, and music, or change its tempo, as seen in the acculturating efforts of missionary schools and churches. But the songs and stories from diverse sound worlds of the colonized reconstituted various forms of being and belonging, knowing and becoming from elsewhere, continuously reverberating. They were nucleic to storied lives, repeated with variation, transmitted orally/aurally and intergenerationally, and sung in various gatherings geared towards family and societal cohesion. These stories, songs, and other sound knowledges are critical living histories from which resistance against western civilization and its dehumanizing taxonomy of categorical being were wielded. They are and continue to form the basis for the antithesis of social death.

Sound Knowledges of the Black Experience

sound (adj.): in good condition; not damaged, injured, or diseased.

sound (adj.) competent, reliable, or holding acceptable views

The Southern African cosmological archive offers a philosophy of the human and humans' relation to other humans and the larger non-human living world that is fundamentally different to that of the western Enlightenment. In this cosmology all matter is in a constant state of being, all pervaded by Ntu, a lifeforce or spirit, and an all-encompassing energy, vibrating at different but unified frequencies. The human is understood as a composite of three ontologies, as being constituted by the living, the living dead, and the not-yet-born, what Mogobe Ramose (2003) calls the onto-triadic conception of being. Complex rituals and ceremonies are undertaken to ground and ensure continuity between the living and their composite non-human world. These rituals function to preserve communal relations, foster historical continuities, and ground the living in the memories and desires of the living dead. They are mnemonic devices that remind the living to renunciate actual being for historical being, that remind them their lives are not limited to this one generation. This imbues their lives with historical purpose and future responsibility – the central tenets of Black radicalism from Southern Africa.

The way of knowing self, each other, and the world is organized around the principle of *go tswamaya ke go bona*, or, as Kgositsile translates this maxim, *to wander is to see*. A few critical points must be illuminated: firstly, there are philosophical underpinnings to this wandering that emerge from the nomadic milieu of hunters and gatherers. To wander is to be on the road or *tsela*, which functions doubly as the literal road, and as 'the *ways* of the people' or 'the *way* of doing things', reflecting their communal values and principles. One is taught the ways of the people through various oral and aural practices – lore, storytelling, proverbs, songs, and other generationally transmitted wisdoms. Primacy is given to naming: one's praise names or praise poetry imparts upon one the history of one's lineage, grants one ontological affirmation through the grounding of one's being in historical continuities, and affirms belonging to the larger living world through one's animal totem. The ceremonies and rituals around birth and naming articulate the aspirations of the lineage and community. Critically, these social functions were the domain of women. From the onset, the transmission of these traditions, through orality and praxis, were understood as central to one's knowledge of oneself and orientation to one's living environments, the shared value systems of the lineage and community, and its self-understanding. They are invariably invested in futurity.

Secondly, in the philosophy *to wander is to see*, seeing is not limited to the province of the eyes, nor does it refer to sight as the exclusively sensory perception of the world. When one wanders, constituted by the onto-triad, one is always accompanied by the living dead, the ancestors. Clapperton Mavhunga calls this accompaniment 'guided mobility' (2014: 23), where 'the ancestors were the sight, the eyes, of the living, without them the mortals were *mapofu* (blind people)' (24). It is only through the ancestors' eyes that one could 'see' and sense as they wander. For the Enlightenment-era wanderer, 'universal reason is an interior guide'[7] (Cervenak 2014: 5), whereas for the Southern African wanderer the living dead, the felt but not seen were the guide. These two positions are oppositional: the latter regards knowledge acquisition that arises from wandering as relational, while the former, supported by the Cartesian *cogito, ergo sum*, 'I think, therefore I am', structures knowledge acquisition as the individual pursuit of the rational subject, attained through the mind and reason. In the languages of the land, knowledge is acquired through 'seeing' and sensing – the ability to see implying the gift of vision[8] and discernment –

---

[7] Interiority here is not what Lorde would call the erotic; rather, it refers to the self-propelled and self-motivated, buoyed by reason. In *The Theological Origins of Modernity*, Michael Allen Gillespie explains: 'To be modern is to be self-liberating and self-making, and thus not merely to be in history or tradition but to make history. To be modern consequently means not merely to define one's being in terms of time but also to define time in terms of one's being […]' (2008: 2).

[8] The Zulu greeting, *sawubona*, means 'we see you', addressed to an individual person who is perceived in plural form to acknowledge those they walk with, unseen to the eyes, but considered and acknowledged as part of the onto-triadic form of the human in cosmologies of the land. The word '*bona*' refers beyond the sensory perception of the eyes towards a multisensory perception.

achieved through revelations by the ancestors, visions and dreams, epiphanies, and shrine-work.

Critically, listening is trusted as a primary mode of perception which activates both *hearing* and *feeling*, as well as knowledge acquisition. On the one hand, knowledge is referred to as *tsebo*, which is etymologically tied to *tsebe*, the ear. On the other, the Tswana word for listening is *utlwa*, which means both hearing and feeling, but which also connotes adherence to the ways of the people, to the collective path and value systems. When one veers off the path (*o tswile tseleng*), one is reprimanded for failing to *utlwa*, failing to learn from the teachings of the collective, but also failing to feel their needs. It implies a lack of sympathy to the other, which is condemned as it exposes an inability to be humane. And this is the measure of personhood in this cosmology: the ethical call to be accountable to yourself and the community. Hearing is also a critical faculty for the wanderer as the road is considered alive and agential, teeming with life, vibrations, sounds, smells, and phenomena that make it incumbent upon the wanderer to attune to its variegated multisensory transmissions and frequencies of non-human life, if they are to survive. Acoustemology, as a 'knowing-with and knowing-through the audible' (Feld 2021), is a feature of the world that Kgositsile ferries with him in his suitcase, into exile.

Sound knowledges destabilize the supremacy of seeing or the ocular (Oyěwùmí 1997) as a way of knowing the world in differentiating, hierarchical, anthropocentric, racializing, gendering, and dehumanizing models that underpin colonial modernity. Sound knowledges privilege *hearing* and *feeling* as modalities for finding relationalities, congruencies, and solidarities within the multisensorial self, where the border collapses between the head and the body, the cognitive and embodied, and the rational and sensuous. They also collapse the barrier between self and other, the living and the non-living, underwriting intersubjective relationalities with each other and the larger living community through feeling and empathy. The realm of the sonic foregrounds feelings and affectivity as legitimate sources of knowledge.

I propose that we think of *go utlwa* – to both feel and hear – as a methodology of deep hearing, intricately tied to diligent looking. Deep hearing addresses expansion into the present moment during wandering, a full presence, a dwelling in the break that invites presence of body, mind, and spirit, and deliberately listens into the onto-triad. It attunes the body to hearing/feeling and intuiting the always-already-there accompaniment of the living dead and not-yet-born, but also the frequencies and vibrations of the living environment that entangle the collective becoming of all. South African singer and healer Busi Mhlongo, whose work operates within this dynamic of accompaniment, offers: 'listening, you see, happens naturally or unnaturally, while hearing is a choice. Hearing has nothing to do with the physical, it has everything to do with the deeper state of alertness: active, open, willing and ready' (2010). Deep hearing actively, deliberately, and intentionally expands into that openness as a place, a break from the ongoingness of the known. The 'active' speaks to the potentiating encounter and engagement with the invisible that has deeper histories and materializations than what the eye can see: the entwinement of history 2, antecedent to and concomitant with history 1. This reorientates the experience of time, and Kgositsile coins various generative terminologies to attend to these experiences. Deep hearing speaks to his concept of NOW, discussed in the later section on spatio-temporality.

Knowledges of the body, or 'corpus opus' as Tendayi Sithole (2018) calls them, are vital and vitalizing since western Enlightenment teaches us to escape from the body, which is 'seen as a trap from which any rational person had to escape' (Oyěwùmí 1997: 3). Since the cerebral and rational were equated, discursively and materially, with whiteness and full humanity, those cultures of the body therefore 'metonymically enact[ed] Blackness, embodiment and subhumanity' (Weheliye 2005: 37). This directly translated into justifying the enslavement of certain bodies understood to inherently embody unreasoning cultures, primed for labour. The ensuing spectacular violation and dehumanizing of the Black body, its abjection and transformation into flesh, predicated the numbing and disassociation from those corpoliteracies.[9] This resulted in mistrust in interiority, the sensuous, erotic (Lorde 1984), and performative cultures that centred the body as site of knowledges and communication. Accessing those parts of ourselves through reclaiming sound knowledges is revolutionary in its retrieval of our humanity and aliveness from elsewhere – they amplify poetics of possibility and enlivenment.

Thirdly, wandering is an aesthetic parallel to Kgositsile's practice of improvisation. His writing process mirrors the jazz practice of taking a solo, in which the improvisatory approach enables him to wander between two worldviews and cosmologies, between multiple cognitive functions, multiple temporalities, and various modalities to acquire his poetic. He calls this a process of 'sifting and shifting' (1971: 39). As he explains to Danille Taylor-Guthrie: 'I think in images. My images aspire to be clear pictures carved out of sound' (1996: 36). Very clearly Kgositsile explains the process of writing as 'listening to images', as Tina Campt (2017) dubs it, or more appropriately, 'hearing images', in which he practices deep listening with the body, actively opening feeling and intuition, striving to see and listen into what is revealed, and depict it in sonic terms for us, the reader, in his poetry. In wandering through improvisation, a

---

[9] Bonaventure Soh Bejeng Ndikung offers corpoliteracy as 'an effort to contextualize the body as a platform, stage, site, and medium of learning, structure or organ that acquires, stores, and disseminates knowledge. This concept implies that the body, in sync with, but also independent of, the brain, has the potential to memorize and pass on/down acquired knowledge through performativity' (2020: 90).

preconditional shift and divestment from settler time and dominant paradigm to elsewhere is critical. Engaging with the multiplicities of worlds sifts and shifts between the affective and cognitive, appearance and essence, the human and animal, the one and the multiple, the sonic and written, Black South Africa and Black America, and Africa and the diaspora.

In the Black diaspora, Kgositsile asserted, 'How you sound defines who you are' (Rowell 1978: 32), meaning we shall know each other through *listening*, by deeply attuning our orientation and faculties to *feel* and *hear* one another and the world. Tina Campt offers 'listening' as a way of knowing in the Black world, challenging us to delink knowledge-making with the visual, and instead privileging sound – 'a sensory register that is critical to Black Atlantic cultural formations' (2017: 6). Then again, Tsitsi Jaji offers 'synaesthesia' as the 'intersensory concatenation of the modes of perception, particularly *vision* and *hearing*', which, on one level, 'performs a solidarity among the senses' and, on the other, 'can be read as an aesthetic parallel of the search for solidarity between Black Americans and South Africans in exile' (2014: 106). She contends that synaesthesia is 'a metaphor for pan-African Relation through embodied experience' (106). I deploy synaesthesia as a critical tool in the Black sonic arsenal, building upon its uses as metaphor for solidarities of the senses – productive of the 'phono-optic' (Weheliye 2005) – towards a convergence of two worldviews and universals, a co-existence of two cosmologies, and an interweaving of two modalities of being and knowing. Crucially, synaesthesia offers a framework to read the imbrication of epistemologies with 'acoustemologies' (Feld 1992), written epistemes with embodied knowledges, and cosmologies from the rural contexts with contexts of the city, the transnational, and the international, often reified along gender lines.

Diligently Looking for Sound Knowledges

As discussed in the previous section, the Southern African cosmological archive is substantive and generative, offering philosophies of the human fundamentally different to that of western Enlightenment. Beyond the human, these cosmologies have a profound conception of the larger non-human living world, understood to be living, agential, in a constant state of being, all pervaded by Ntu, a lifeforce or spirit. For these reasons, movement is perceived as the integral force of the universe, while spirit is the force that connects all living matter. The people were therefore concerned with not only the physical manifestation of a thing, of what they encountered, but also with its essence: its inner workings, principles, and mechanisms. The physical appearance of things was not the entirety of a thing, but also what came together to make the thing, its inner logics, genealogies, and lineage.

In the realm of human relations, it is customary to address one by one's clan name or animal totem to dislodge one from individualism into communal and relational identity, to abolish the stable self, to situate one in historical being-in-becoming, and as tributary to one's qualities and/or talents. When Kgositsile addresses his mother as 'woman dancer-of-steel', he uses her totem, *mosadi mmina-tshipi*, to challenge and come to terms with the repressive condition of enclosure that Galekgobe found herself in, working and living in the white suburbs of Yeoville, Johannesburg. The inner logics and inner mechanisms of her being, which is to say her spirit, are characterized by *go bina*, which in Setswana implies both to sing and dance, and which is prohibited by the white settler world, who see her as simply a maid. In re/citing her totem, Kgositsile sees beyond her physicality into her being, haunted by this view of her that is located in her eye, a central motif in poems written to her, and in his other works. He writes, 'your / eye, I know, is stronger than faith in / some god who never spoke our language' (1971: 28), revealing that he 'sees' his mother as god through the feminine and the mother principle. She is his creator,[10] his maker, the creator. She is the matriarchive – 'what of the act my eye demands / past any pretentious power of any word / I've known?' – so it is through her and by her that he is known and interconnected to the lineage and its purpose. The poem goes on: 'Woman dancer-of-steel, / did you ever know that the articulate silence / of your eye possessed my breath for long days?'. In her eye, articulate beyond any language, he reads the subdued spirit of that purpose, incarcerated in the maids' quarters. Her eye speaks. It haunts him, making certain demands that become gospel to him, that are a doctrine in his language, a credo and chord that tie his desires to intergenerational memory.

Galekgobe's eye speaks in 'articulate silence' and possesses him; this tells us her eye is agential, it is an active absence on his exile journey, appearing to him at times even without his deliberate remembering or conjuring of it. This does not romanticize the matriarchive, nor does it celebrate it as a positive presence: it eschews the strong Black woman archetype. In exile, his mother 'possessed my breath for long days' – a possession takes control over one's body, and the duration of long days articulates an anguish which, in the same poem, he characterizes as 'wish and want, regret too'. Her eye becomes his conscience, and this articulate eye is present in other poems beyond the poems written to Galekgobe. The method of diligent looking strives to see that eye and listen to it.

Furthermore, when Kgositsile writes in the poem dedicated to his grandmother, that 'She would talk to me … I hear her now. And I wonder / now does she know the strength of the fabric / she wove in my heart for us?'

---

[10] In the poem 'The Creator' discussed in Chapter 2, he also deems his then-wife Melba Johnson to be the creator, as he does Nina Simone. These are iterations of the matriarchive in the Black world.

(1971: 80–81), I want to hear her, too, as he sounds her acoustemology, actively, in the present, 'now'. How does he transliterate what he hears from her now in his poetry? This has implications for language in his poetry, guided by the approach to language in his formative years and expressed in his 1969 story 'The Ab/Original Mask': 'in their language, the people never spoke directly about a thing, they spoke around it so that it stood out more clearly' (1969a: 57), he tells us. Thus, their expression and the language in his poetry aims to move, sing, lunge, dance, and be malleable to be commensurate with the living ever-changing world. Speaking around things is a refusal to foreclose the phenomena of the living, an espousal of dynamism and change, which is generative for a revolutionary poet. When Madikeledi speaks from the grave, she is his accompaniment in his exile wandering, the living dead who participates in his guided mobility, present and enunciative. Diligent looking then attends to listening into places where she is speaking through and to him; it is a method that seeks to see and hear, sense and feel where Kgositsile's mothers are sounded.

His childhood memoirs published in 1973 were a revelatory find. They are titled 'I know My Name'. This assertion in the title is powerful as it proclaims a knowledge of self that is not structured on the Black Other, a knowing of self that preceded and exceeds the formation of the other for purposes of constructing hierarchy and difference by the colonizer. Kgositsile claims to know himself by another force: that of the matriarchive. Therein he performs a gesture of *go itshoka*: he symbolically sings/dances his praise names to assert and affirm who he is, not only to himself but to his African American counterparts, themselves in the battle to rename their identities and their purpose. In valorizing singing as a poetic modality, Kgositsile refutes individual and pioneer status; he destabilizes the singular individual identity for a relational communitarian belonging and continuation of what has been into the future of what will be: collective memories and desire. In singing, he joins the song of the decades and centuries, moves with the collective dance, seeking to attune to the frequencies and vibrations, the rhythms of the active presences that accompany him on this life journey – in his exile. Singing as opposed to writing opens a mode of relating with those for whom literacies and epistemes of missionary education were not an option or from which they were excluded. Singing is returning to the song that was and is always-already-there, in an elsewhere place; singing is therefore also a praxis of appeasing and petitioning presence and accompaniment. Singing is chanting, and a praxis of re-enchantment: the remediation of colonial disenchantment that sows alienation from the self, community, land, continent, oceans, and cosmos. Singing is 'writing as reciting', as speaking from and with the chorus, with the voices of the living community and living land. To rite and sing is a strategy to be legible to himself and his community. Diligent looking is thus a method that attunes to a multisensorial mode of reading to feel the saturation by and enunciations of these communal presences.

If Kgositsile rites instead of writes his poetry, then diligent looking requires me to reed instead of read his acoustemologies. He offers the literacy system of *reeding* and *riting* to attend to the dynamics of writing as ritual in his work. Deploying jazz improvisation as a writing/riting method facilitates a wandering into the break that reanimates him as an intersubjective, polyvocal, and intra-active[11] being in sympoiesis.[12] His fields of perception are enlivened, bringing into existence otherworlds from which he transcribes what is revealed through a process of *reeding*. *Reeding* is an active channelling of elsewhere knowledges activated by the saturation of presences and accompaniment. *Reeding* is akin to the wind passing through reeds, producing sound. *Riting* is the grasping or catching of what is revealed 'there', the transliteration of acoustemologies from the elsewhere to the 'here' of his page. Seeking to retain the musicality and the sound patterns of what is received there, Kgositsile strives to bring his poetry close to ritual through sonic aesthetics in a practice of 'writing as *riting*' and 'writing as reciting'. Here, recital attends to making sonic that which you have written in order to honour its oral/aural origins. *Reeding* and *riting* is a literacy system that attends to sound as the fundamental generative force, creative energy, and locus, where the presence of the felt but unseen is amplified. *Reeding* and *riting* is how the matriarchive can materialize from elsewhere to direct, instruct, or command the affairs of the 'here'. *Reeding* and *riting* hacks/hexes Europatriarchal frames of intelligibility, legibility, and transparency, undermining its barriers through poetics of porousness and permeability, frequencies and vibrations, and collaboration and relation with other presences in the entangled, agential, co-constituted, living world.

Elsewhere Space and Time

Kgositsile teaches us that 'there is no word for *citizen*' in Setswana, 'we speak of *moagi*, resident. *Go agisana/agisanya*, from *aga*, from which moagi derives, means 'in the same breath', "building together" and/or "living together in harmony or peace"' (2004: 144). I think of this as a critique of not only the Europatriarchal nation-state formation and its afterlives, but also of settler geographies, racial capitalism and its temporalities, and anthropocentrism in this human-centred modernity. I organize this critique around the word

---

[11] Physicist Karen Barad (2007) offers *intra-action* instead of interaction: when entities *interact* they each pre-exist independently from one another, and maintain that level of independence. When they *intra-act* they materialize through their co-constitutive entanglement, and the ability to act emerges from within the relationship not outside of it.

[12] A heuristic offered by Donna Haraway (2016) that means making-with, rather than auto-poiesis, or self-making.

'eco', prefix to economy, ecology, and ecosystem, and whose Greek etymology connotes 'home' or 'members of the family', implying 'kinship' and 'relations'. The principle of 'eco' is congruent with the principles of interconnectedness, interdependence, and interrelationality that underwrite cosmologies and philosophies of being from Southern Africa. Therein all life is internetworked, agential, and intra-active in its collective materialization.

At a fundamental level, capitalism fails to recognize all life; it fails as an economic system in its incongruence with 'eco', splitting and severing communities, families, and kinship. This economic system also splits bodies of land, bodies of water, and celestial bodies from human and animal phenomena. Moreover, as Kgositsile offers, it inaugurated the splitting of time, of the living past from the present and future, but also of the day into units of production and the worker into extractable units of labour. Capitalism equated time with profit: time is money! Therefore, the masculine conception of time is tied to capitalist production. Kgositsile offers a critique of racial capitalist production of the mining industrial complex in Southern Africa in temporal, mnemonic, and ecological terms: the 'rape by savages who want to control us, memory, and nature. Savages who even forge measures to try to control time' (1971: 83). For Kgositsile, the barbarism of colonial conquest violently extracts from communities their temporality ('pastpresentfuture is always now', 1974b: 5; 'time is not a succession of hours', 1971: 83), their memories (colonial alienation[13] from self, the immediate community and surroundings), and their relationality with nature (intra-action and sympoiesis with cycles and seasons of life).

Kgositsile brings the elsewhere relationalities from Southern African cosmologies and ontologies to bear upon the dominant paradigm and its linear progression of time. He reorders temporality, coining four crucial interrelated temporal formations: NOW, future memory, coil of time, and pastpresentfuture. They function within the onto-triadic conception of being, as well as frame the sifting and shifting between the two worlds. NOW enfolds all time in the expansion and deepening into the present, filling it with the presence and accompaniment of all time, of the living dead and the yet-to-be-born, in flux. It is related to coil of time in that the spatio-temporal device of the coil is utilized as an enfolding agent. The Latin etymology means 'to gather together', and here functions to gather the past, the present, and the future together in the NOW moment, transgressing and collapsing the barriers between these time frames to make the future and the past alive in the present, producing pastpresentfuture. He refers to this as 'the union of pastandfuture'. This union is gathering work, and when deployed in Kgositsile's work it is always accompanied by song, dance, drums, fire, and discourses of spirit. Sound facilitates the disordering of time,

---

[13] As theorized by Ngugi wa Thiong'o in his *Decolonizing the Mind* (1986).

important for the relationship between Africa and its diaspora discussed in the next section.

As Kgositsile explains, memory is assimilated in the union of pastandfuture. In that union, the future enfolds as opposed to unfolds. The future is grounded in the possibilities of recovering the past, operative in a relationship between memory and desire. As such the past can be 'in front of you' as you imagine the desired future, making the future mnemonic. This perception of memory is attributed to a world sense from history 2, where movement and continuity are principal forces of life, and whereby nothing ever dies but continues to exist in different realms and dimensions, at times returning in the future. In a dynamic of radicalism in which historical being is embraced to fashion resistance, continuities of the past into the future, that is, ontological totality, are the fuel for the desired future. This locates the living and materializing past in the future, opening a future memory.

In Kgositsile's writing process of taking a solo, improvisation is conditional to wandering between two worlds, two cosmologies, two geographies and knowledge systems, to hear them coevally in his process of writing. In the elsewhere, he is grasped by the enfolding world of history 2, whose quivering potentiality and possibility reveals itself and becomes knowable. His writing practice seeks to grasp or catch what is revealed there and transcribed into language. He explains this process as a way of defining future memory:

> When we say someone is visionary or prophetic, what we mean is that they can see past the imposed boundaries. What that would mean, the closest scientific way, is that they are, at a conceptual level, able to analyse a number of different things all at the same time at the speed at which it happens in a dream. Therefore, they might see *there* before others do. And when they talk about it, they would be remembering what they saw *there*.[14]

Kgositsile is keenly aware of imposed boundaries of time and speaks of his practice as visionary in his ability to access a 'there before others do'. This is the break with Europatriarchal chronological time. The accessibility of 'there', an ostensibly unfolding and not enfolding time and space, before others do is a radical remembering of the future, which can be seen as conjoining or suturing the future with the past in the present. It articulates the fact of 'coeval otherworlds that [...] require a complete break with time as we know it' (Brown 2021: 15). Kgositsile's wandering 'there' is that break with spatio-temporality, a poetics of possibility Jayna Brown dreams of as a practice of *Black Utopias*, one that 'jump[s] into the break, the cut, into an entirely different paradigm,

---

[14] Author interview with Keorapetse Kgositsile, Pretoria, April 2014.

opening up the possibility for radical temporalities: those not governed by earth time and that are intertwined with equally radical notions of spatiality' (2021: 15). It is this 'unknown' 'there' – into the spatio-temporal break – that Kgositsile wanders when taking a solo, from which he listens into and retrieves elsewhere knowledges. His writing process involves sifting and shifting to those worlds 'at the speed at which it happens in a dream', implying a multisensory experience saturated with presence, which I have called guided mobility.

With regards to rezoning space and geography, the presence and aliveness of these worlds in diaspora and their accessibility to Kgositsile produce a productive experience of space. In the chief leitmotif in his work, discussed in Chapters 2, 3, 4, and 5, the role of the wind in the union of Africa and the diaspora, the wind as coil that collapses the boundary between these two geographies, is crucial. This wind carries sonic knowledges in between the two geographies in a circuitry, non-linear manner, which he listens into, retrieves, and transcribes in his poetry. He refers to them as 'the rebirth of memory' (1971: 64) – which points to the presence of the future and the past in the present – memory which is 'timeless', adaptive to every time, which is all time.

Further, the poetics of race and space in his work reveals continuities between celestial bodies and bodies of land, articulated in the commensurate relational motif of 'the son' and 'the sun'. I coin *terrafirmament* as a heuristic to attend to his rezoning of the celestial body and the human body in his poetics, which is rooted in the cosmologies of the land. In the origin stories of Southern Africa, life began in the cosmos. The people's sacred mythologies venerate the great creator, Nonkulunkulu (the great one), Modimo (the one above), and Ramasedi (father and mother of light), all of which point to the expanse of the universe and the cosmos above. Modimo is in the *legodimo* or cosmos; below is the earth or land referred to as *lefatshe*, the one below, which also comprises subterranean worlds. The language tells us, *legodimo lefatshe* (the cosmos is on earth/land), and *lefatshe legodimo* (earth/land is in the cosmos), that the below is the subset of the above, and vice versa, in continuity. This implies that the phenomena of life above descended below and are, inversely, in a circuitry relationship. *Terrafirmament* is the understanding of the cosmos and land phenomena as continuous with one another, explored in Chapters 4 and 5, respectively, in which the *terrafirmament* dynamic makes interventions in the study of Afrofuturism and reimagining Black futurity.

Black Diaspora Family Tree

Kgositsile deploys cultural configurations of sound to address questions of identity, difference, solidarity, and relation in Black America. Scholars such as Tsitsi Jaji (2014), Mukti Lakhi Mangharam (2013), and Stéphane Robolin (2015) have written on Kgositsile and his interlocutions with Black diaspora cultural and political figures and movements. Robolin rightly points out that Kgositsile's nine volumes of poetry should be viewed through the prism of jazz (2015: 71). Jaji organizes her study of his work around the hermeneutic stereomodernism, which she describes as 'cultural practices that are both political and expressive, activated by Black music and operative within the logic of pan-African solidarity' (2014: 14). Further, Mangharam argues that 'Kgositsile's poetics allows him to emphasize lived, felt, and embodied particulars of identity. [...] He] posits a common humanity based on the shared suffering of the Black body' (2013: 89). The lived, felt, and embodied in Kgositsile's work are articulated within structures of Black music, which he understood to be 'the strongest art form that has always explained the African community, its spirit' (Rowell 1978: 32). I centralize the body and its variegated metaphors in thinking about Black music's role as a gathering agent. I think in Kgositsilean terms about the union of Africa and its diaspora.

Kgositsile conceived Africa's relationship with the diaspora through the metaphor of a tree with roots in Africa and branches in the diaspora. Further, the coevality of the two geographies' engagements, in his work, takes place in a dynamic of the tree's relationship to the wind, which produces sound between these geographies in an antiphonal manner. This metaphor is invested in the integrity of the totality of the world by unbordering the division between land masses of continents and centring the bodies of land and bodies of water in between as alive, agential, and in constant relational motion. It is a metaphor that gathers together, like a coil, the seemingly disparate into conciliation. This image in turn informs an opening of multiple approaches to Black world relationalities, through the framework of sound knowledges and Black sonics: the coil recasts the congruent image of tree rings as an aesthetic parallel. Through the tree rings, we may learn the age of the tree, the weather conditions in each year of the tree's existence, and the climate of the area where the tree is rooted. The tree rings are maps that track the living conditions of the tree. In Kgositsile's dynamic of the tree as convergence point between Africa and its diaspora, the tree rings would be able to hold a longer arc of history traversing spacetimes and finding union in the non-linear spacing of the rings that resound and hold deeper memories of history 2 in continuance with colonialism and its total climate of anti-Blackness.[15] The inner tree rings offer a profile of the tree's history and identity.

---

[15] In what she calls 'the weather', Christina Sharpe offers, 'antiBlackness is pervasive *as* climate. The weather necessitates changeability and improvisation; it is the atmospheric condition of time and place; it produces new ecologies' (2016: 106). Kgositsile's metaphor of the tree and my extension of it towards the tree rings and cochlea operate within this dynamic space of changeability and *improvisation*, producing new ecologies of relations.

The second enunciation of the coil metaphor is the inner ear, congruent shape-wise with the spiral image of the cochlea. A particular quality that literary scholar Sterling Plumpp revered in Kgositsile's poetry is 'an inner-ear sensitivity to Setswana' orality and aurality, as he called it. Plumpp asserts: 'Kgositsile is not into his South Africanness; I can say that Wole Soyinka is in his Yorubaness. Kgositsile takes off those garbs, retains the essence of it, so that his voice becomes more universal. And I think the blues and jazz makes him more universal'.[16] I draw parallels between these two 'bodies': between the tree and its inner rings, and between the human body and the cochlea, its inner ear. Both are generative in thinking about the inner workings of these two bodies – the tree and the human in relation to the land and the lineage respectively. The inner-ear sensitivity to Setswana is the orientation to the language of the lineage, which Kgositsile theorizes in sonic terms: it requires a 'collected step', the 'soildance' necessary to enliven the 'toehold of the coil / through and around / our soul and soil' (1974b: 9). The toehold[17] of the coil gathers together the soul and soil, the body and the land, through song and dance, performative and ritual gestures that bring the body back into harmony and equilibrium, as a sound cochlea does.

The inner-ear sensitivity to his language, lineage, and land realigns him to his history, identity, cosmologies, belonging, and purpose, while the inner-tree rings' sensitivity to the soil in which the tree is rooted orients the tree's becoming and growth to the land in which it is grounded. In their routes occasioned by exile and forced migration, the two 'bodies' do not have to consciously work at retaining their Tswananess or Africanness; there are no essentialisms here. The soil (*roots*) continues to nourish their growth, channelling and commanding their *being*, but contingent upon their attunement to its sonics and frequencies through devised ritual technologies such as 'soildance' and deep hearing, reeding and riting the wind, while remaining continuously open to encountered cultures in their relational *becoming* (*routes*). This is 'so that [the] voice becomes more universal'. Plumpp expounds:

> I do not believe Kgositsile consciously retains the essence of Setswana in the aesthetics of his poems as he writes. It is a subconscious act. His imagination bends his language that the autonomy of his mother tongue takes over. [...] He has an assurance of a self born out his [sic] superior knowledge of his history, culture and

---

[16] Author interview with Sterling Plumpp, Chicago, September 2014.
[17] Kgositsile metaphorically performs *go gata mabala*, the ritual of visiting ancestral land or visiting home in order to reconnect with the soil, the living dead, and the not-yet-born. This is accompanied by ritual, in which *sa koša ke lerole* – the soildance – is the rousing of *lerole* or dust through *koša* or song/dance.

family and the particular circumstance at hand. He is someone so imbued with his history and culture and language that when he writes in English some *committed inner ear* instructs the ink in his pen to preface authentic nuances of history and culture and therefore, Setswananess of his language, therefore, rhythms and tones of the English language.[18]

In Chapter 3, this instructive inner ear that possesses his pen is explored in detail. Plumpp's summation of the sonic and auditory qualities of Kgositsile's work reveals Plumpp's close study and appreciation of the elsewhere acoustemological orientation under investigation in this book. He reveals the 'subconscious act' of retaining Setswana in the aesthetic of his poems as inextricably tied to Kgositsile's self-assuredness of history, culture, family, and language, resulting in a becoming that is closely tied or tethered to a 'particular circumstance' that I have framed as the matriarchive. Plumpp's sophisticated conception of an 'inner ear sensitivity' biologically evokes the cochlea, which 'contains nerve endings essential for hearing' (Merriam-Webster n.d.). Damage to the cochlea throws into crisis the body's orientation, balance, and equilibrium, causing vertigo and nausea. I read this as a metaphor for Kgositsile's orientation in the Black world to what he calls the spirit of its people, its inner working that reveals to him their Africanness, even when the tree has grown away from the roots. It is that shared spirit which he rallies as unifying matter in his debut collection, *Spirits Unchained*, potentiating and inviting, through shared histories of struggle, a formidable kinship.

The body and the tree are brought into relation and into communality through the dynamic of *moya*, which in Southern African languages refers to air, breath, wind, and spirit. The implications thereof are pertinent: *moya* rezones, remaps and reterritorializes diaspora spacetime through liberating both body and land from their rigidly compartmentalized moulds of nation-state and separate continents, unbordering them to restore the integrity of totality. *Moya*'s radical dimension is its ability to make borders and barriers unsound through asserting interconnectivity over separation. Here, poetics of shared breath are pervasive in *moagisani* or resident as antidote to nation-state citizenship, privileging 'building together' and 'in the same breath'. This shared, interdependent, and interconnected poetics of shared breath underscores Black sociality.

The tree and wind suture Africa and its diaspora and position and ground Kgositsile in his quest to co-exist 'in the same breath', through 'building together' to produce solidarity politics and poetics in the Black world. He deploys the

---

[18] Author interview with Sterling Plumpp via email exchange, April 2015; emphasis in the original.

names-songs-places matrix to proclaim that solidarity and kinship – 'names, songs, / places we only remember / in the blood like everpresent melodies' (1969c: 22). His names-songs-places nexus is a strategy that coalesces names with lived experiences in places subject to white settler colonialism. Almost all his poetry is dedicated to named individuals or movements. Further, as Stéphane Robolin argues, his poetry is 'far less governed by physical contiguity than by experiential continuity' (2015: 89). His *Spirits Unchained* consists of 'paeans', as the subtitle of the collection suggests, praise songs in the tradition of history 2, that extol political and cultural figures from Africa and its diaspora. He names them to gather together otherwise marginalized subaltern biographies and histories, to suture them to dominant history. He draws from the function of praise poetry in Southern Africa as generative of oral/aural documents of history, asserting it to expand and transform dominant epistemologies.

In using shared structures of feelings to underwrite their collective heroic roles in history, he also draws their bodies into kinship and relation, but also the bodies of land into continuity: Harlem is Sophiatown or Soweto, Watts is Sharpeville, and the Mississippi and Limpopo Rivers converge, while Amiri Baraka is Can Themba, Nina Simone echoes his mothers, Malcolm X is with the brothers on Robben Island. If places and names are 'everpresent' in their blood like melodies, then in singing these names and places a 'rememorying' can happen, in Toni Morrison's sense of 'reassembling the members of the body, the family, the population of the past' (2019: 324). Songs and names activate the 'coil through and around our soul', while places are enlivened through dance, activating the 'toehold' of the collected step into a 'soildance' to choreograph solidarity movements in and by those with lived and shared experiences of racial oppression. This happens within the tree as metaphor for diaspora, winds passing through the branches to produce sonics, moving it into dance while firmly rooted in the soil.

Song, as detailed earlier in this introduction, is critical to politics of community and resistance. Song imbues the collective with aliveness, animating the spirit that defines their sense of self, community, and meaning in the world. In using the African American vernacular, blues, and jazz idiom in his work, Kgositsile captures their depthoffeeling, speaks to their interiority and spirit to articulate their struggles, joys, pain, disgruntlements, and triumphs. He aspires, through deploying those oral/aural poetics and Black sonics, to give that spirit a language, to imbue his poetry with the aliveness of those languages of the people, to transforms his poetry into their collective song, and to use those songs as fuel to combust revolutionary fires.

Chapter Movements

Chapter 1 is titled 'A Writing Life – A Riting Life – A Rioting Life' and comprises a literary biography that maps Kgositsile's storied life. Studying the relationship between his life and work, it focuses on his formative years in Dithakong, his move to Johannesburg to live with his mother, and his eventual immersion in the mass liberation movement. This chapter emphasizes the arc from homeplace politics to national liberation movement and Black world politics, one grounded in the orientation to Tswana customs, cultures, and cosmologies, which instilled history 2 as the first cultures of comprehending the world.

Chapter 2, 'Names: Mother, What is my Name?' introduces the names-songs-places matrix as a nexus that shapes identitarian politics located in the languages, lineage, and land, which are enshrined in individual and familial praise poetries, rituals of homemaking and placemaking that underpin belonging to land, and their translation by Kgositsile to produce poetics of possibility in liberatory politics. The translation and transformation of sound knowledges and oralities from history 2 underwrite articulations and performance of solidarity with Black sonic worlds of the diaspora. Here Kgositsile's dexterous gathering work offers Maya Angelou and the viewers of her 1968 show *Blacks, Blues, Black!* entry and meeting place, through the Setswana language, into memorial points of reference to the African continent. His poetry published in the Black arts bible, *Black Fire* (1968), produces poetics of possibility that inspire Larry Neal. They are in turn recast in his imbrication of poetics of the body with those of the land, underscored by depthoffeeling as meeting place.

Chapters 3 and 4 centralize Kgositsile's poem 'Towards a Walk in the Sun'. Four sets of relationships are studied: firstly, I amplify song as produced by the relationship between the tree and the wind; secondly, I sound the production of Black sonic cultures in the antiphonal relationship between Kgositsile and members of The Last Poets; thirdly, I study the relationship between Kgositsile and his rapper son Earl Sweatshirt; and, fourthly, I trace how the poem became inspiration for a Houston-based arts collective in the twenty-first century, which translated it into rap, visual art, and a comic. 'Towards a Walk in the Sun' is vital and vitalizing: Kgositsile mined its poetics, aesthetics, and vernaculars from Leetile Raditladi's *Motswasele II* to produce a language of resistance from elsewhere, a poetics of possibility which in turn suffused the politics of the nascent Black Lives Matter movement. Members of The Last Poets in turn inspired a whole era of rap, with Earl Sweatshirt as inheritor, while Otabenga Jones & Associates, the art collective, produce a generative Afrofuturist aesthetic that inspires a study of difference in solidarity. The art collective demonstrates the continuously generative archive of the Black Arts Movement as inspiring and productive in the unfinished struggle for Black liberation.

Chapter 5, 'Places: Black Consciousness Ecologies of Futurity', delves further into the study of difference in solidarity explored in Chapter 4. It zeroes in on the ritual archive invoked through a Tswana proverb uttered by a traditional healer in Kgositsile's essay on Malcolm X, producing a poetics of possibility. Through a comparative analysis with Robin D.G. Kelley's use of Kgositsile's Tswana proverb in another work, I demonstrate how the proverbs couch otherwise possibilities for Black diasporans even when they have no access to the language. In this chapter, I follow the accessibility of Kgositsile's aforementioned essay to South African Black Consciousness poet and visual artist Lefifi Tladi beyond the apartheid project of provincialism and censorship. As a Tswana speaker, his visual interpretation of the proverb and ritual archive into a body of visual art grants us opportunity to intervene in discourses of surrealism and Afrofuturism as they occur on the continent and its diaspora.

A Writing Life – A Riting Life – A Rioting Life   1

Kgositsile was born on 18 February 1938 in rural Dithakong, on the outskirts of Mafikeng. The town of Mafikeng as a colonial urban centre under the British protectorate is historically important. In the early nineteenth century, the capital of the Batlhaping sub-branch of the Barolong people was in Dithakong (erstwhile Dithakwaneng). Towards the mid-nineteenth century, the sub-branch of Kgositsile's lineage of the Barolong, the Molema, settled in small, clustered villages on the banks of the Molopo River, producing a flourishing urban area that the Dutch called 'the Stadt', or 'the city'. Towards the end of that century, in 1895 Mafeking was selected as a location for the British colonial administrative offices of the Bechuanaland Protectorate outside the colony of Bechuana (now Botswana). This administration leased land from the Tswana chief immediately adjacent to the village clusters.

As a British protectorate, Mafeking became the ground for territorial fighting between the Dutch and the British during the Anglo-Boer war, with both sides waging a fierce battle for that region between 1899 and 1900 in what is known as 'the Siege of Mafeking'. As a 'final frontier', Mafeking was a prime location, as it was near both the border and the railway between Bulawayo and Kimberly. The latter was a booming mining town at the time since diamonds had been discovered there in the 1860s. The 'Siege of Mafeking' also politically conscientized a young Barolong court interpreter and journalist, Solomon Plaatje, who, funded by the Tswana chief Silas Molema, founded the newspaper *Koranta ea Becoana* (Newspaper for Batswana) and later, *Tsala ea Becoana* (Friend of Batswana).

Plaatje's work through the newspaper medium addressed the Batswana directly, asking them to maintain a love for the Setswana language, cultures, and identity. He asked them to use Setswana even when the British were teaching them English language and mannerisms; he asked them to love their language, pray in it, study it, and develop it. This sensibility was crucially instilled in him by the womenfolk of his matricentric upbringing, whom Plaatje acknowledges in his various published works. In his biography on Plaatje, Brian Willan writes:

> Plaatje's mother was one of several women at Pniel who told him of family and tribal traditions, and from whom he learned Setswana, his first language. 'The best Sechuana speakers known to me', he observed later in life, 'owe their knowledge to the teachings of

> grandmother, or a mother, just as myself [...] am indebted to the teachings of my mother and two aunts'. Among these 'teachings' was a fund of fables and proverbs, highly valued as repositories of the inherited wisdom of their people and passed on from generation to generation. [...] 'Au Magritte', or 'Granny Masweamotho', Plaatje's grandmother (on his father's side), left a deep impression, and it was from her that he derived 'complete information' about the details of his own ancestry. (2018: 15–16)

When Laura Chrisman observes in her study of Solomon Plaatje's political relationship with W.E.B. Du Bois at the beginning of the twentieth century that Du Bois would have been transformed by Plaatje's radical collectivist approach to politics (2004; cf. also Olver & Meyer 2004: 8), we must understand the communitarianism and collectivism of his politics to be shaped by a matriarchival worldview. This way of being that centres on the people, their languages, customs, and culture in waging a battle against the tide of ontological, epistemological, and cosmological violence is what Chrisman identifies as 'distinctive forms of Black South African agency' (2000: 16). This resistance, born in the homeplace, is what made Plaatje's politics evolve into co-founding a national liberation movement. It is what shaped his view of the Native Land Act in 1913 as an attack on the natives' history through silencing its custodians, attempting to sever their tongues and displace them from the very land which is constitutive of the materialization and practice of their traditions, customs, and culture.

At the Second Convention of British and Afrikaners in 1909, the negotiations for a Union of South Africa were discussed. It was to be a union of four entities, the Cape and Natal provinces ruled by the British and the Oranje Vry Staat and Transvaal ruled by the Boers (Boer republics), and it came into being in 1910. This is an important era in South African history, because these two groups created a union among themselves, the minority population of the country, without considering a union with Black South Africans, who constituted the majority of the country's population. It was during these negotiations that English and Afrikaans were installed as the official languages of the country, which showed how Plaatje's advocacy for the love, usage, and development of Setswana was prophetic. In 1911, the Workers' Act was passed, which stipulated that all skilled work must be reserved for white people. The introduction of the Native Land Act in 1913 was a devastating blow to the Black majority population of South Africa as their loss of cattle, due to displacement from grazing lands and cattle theft, equated to a loss of economic, political, and social power. They were forced into a wage labour system through the introduction of poll and hut taxes that required Africans to pay 'rent' on the land on which they lived, coercing them into an exploited labour force to service the growing economic activity on the Reef, where gold had been discovered in 1886. These events greatly unsettled the Black population, leading to increasing support for the South African Native National Congress (SANNC) which had been formed in 1912.

Poet-Revolutionary as a Young Man

Kgositsile's grandmother Madikeledi, who would have been born in the late 1800s, lived through the social unrest of these historical events that would have in turn politicized her – the flourishing of the Barolong city, the annexing of Mafeking by the British, the 'Siege of Mafeking' at the turn of the century, the resistance waged by their chief who funded Plaatje's cultural endeavours, as well as the founding of the SANNC. She would have been privy to the discourse of the day around land, language, culture, and the foreign invasion and ultimate rule by the British. Madikeledi had a daughter, Galekgobe Mary Kgositsile, who, as Kgositsile details, was more like an extension of his grandmother in sensibility.[1] I refer to them in this book as his mothers when talking about them collectively, or as Madikeledi and Galekgobe to single them out. Kgositsile's father, Neo Moagi, was from Lehurutse in Zeerust, also in the region of what was then known as the Transvaal and is now called North West. While attending school in Dithakong, Moagi met and fell in love with Galekgobe Mary Kgositsile. Soon after the end of their school years, Galekgobe became pregnant. The Moagi family presented themselves to the Kgositsiles to acknowledge the pregnancy, as per custom. However, Galekgobe decided against marriage and chose instead to go in search of a better life and future away from rural Dithakong, and instead in urban Johannesburg.

She gave birth to a young boy whom the matriarchs named Keorapetse Kgositsile, after Madikeledi's younger brother. Young Keorapetse was called Boykie or Boinyana (young boy) to avoid confusion. Galekgobe reached an agreement with her mother that she would find employment in Johannesburg, and once she was settled, they might be able to bring young Kgositsile to the city to pursue his studies. So Kgositsile remained in Dithakong with his grandmother while his mother lived in Johannesburg. Kgositsile's father meanwhile became a court interpreter and was often transferred to various courts in the Transvaal region. He eventually settled in Zeerust where he married Sebueng Moagi, with whom he had three daughters: Dineo, Tshidi, and Thuli. After some time, Moagi was transferred again to Mafikeng but, for fear of uprooting his children, travelled by himself and reached out to the Kgositsile family who provided him with lodging for the duration of his Mafikeng employment. He had good

---

[1] Author interview with Keorapetse Kgositsile, Pretoria, April 2014.

relations with the Kgositsile family but was largely absent from Kgositsile's upbringing. However, Madikeledi made sure to tell young Kgositsile about his father, while Moagi also mentioned to his three daughters that they had a brother. The two families always knew of each other, and Kgositsile even named his first-born son, who was born in 1957, Moagi, after his father.

While raising Boykie, Madikeledi the matriarch instituted a few non-negotiable rules: never to speak English in her home, and to always tell the truth, for which, in return, she would always believe him. She was steadfast about the first rule: 'I don't want to hear English in my house. That language arrived here on the ships'. She rejected the English language. She knew it to be a language of violence, a tool to bludgeon and kill the cultures and languages of her people, thereby severing kinship and enforcing a colonial way of thinking: an exile. She spoke in no uncertain terms, calling the language 'very dangerous', and was quick to admonish young Boykie's transgressions:

> The worst condemnation I would feel from as early as I could remember was if I had blundered into an English phrase or word, and she just looked away from me and shook her head and said something like: '*heeee, se re ena le makgowanyana mo*' – or 'there's some junior Europeans here'. That would be worse than any kind of punishment, that is why I call it condemnation instead of punishment.[2]

Condemnation is a complete disapproval, a type of productive shaming in this case that instilled in young Kgositsile the lesson to value his mother tongue.

The image of the ships in Madikeledi's condemnation evokes a haunting of violence on board, transmogrifying humans to property and erasing histories and cultures of the people. The flag, the bible, and the rifle aboard these ships transform their point of arrival into holds, reserves in which to gather dispossessed natives using judicial and military violence. The language of violence used to concretize their dispossession – bushmen, natives, non-Europeans, bantus – hacks their own navigation systems by which they understand who they are and what they know; this completes the mission disindigenize the native and indigenize the settler, making the natives pariahs in their own land, establishing difference, ingraining white superiority, and fetishizing, dehumanizing, criminalizing, and mutilating the Black body, thereby justifying the exploitation of Black labour. Violence from the ships transmogrified inalienable natives into aliens, chattel, trespassers, and kaffirs. Madikeledi knew!

She, however, also expected Kgositsile to achieve good results at his British colonial primary school, ensuring that he had available to him a culture and

---

[2] Author interview with Keorapetse Kgositsile, Pretoria, March 2013.

world system that would be foundational to his being and becoming, from which he was able to move with self-assurance and confidence as he engaged with other cultures and the world at large. What Madikeledi was ultimately preventing by disavowing the English language in her home was the home invasion of that culture: Englishness, she was keenly aware, contained ways of being that were not in alignment or concordance with those of the Batswana. She was clear about encounters and relations with other nations and people in the past, but none of them had ever wanted the other to desert their cultures and spiritual practices to follow the incoming one. This is what she saw as dangerous. In preventing their home from being invaded by English and Englishness, she, firstly, equipped Kgositsile with another way of being, another form of humanity, and another world with which he could undermine and rupture western categories of selfhood and the human, as well as western cultural universalism. Secondly, she equipped him with the confidence to engage with Tswana customs and cultures without falling into the traps of seeking to preserve or celebrate their purity, harmony, and integrity. Hence Madikeledi's lessons and rules in her household, parsed through a set of practices, discourses, and performances, modelled subversion and radicalism for her grandson and seeded young Kgositsile's political and cultural consciousness. In instilling a love for Tswana language, customs, and literature in her grandson, Madikeledi was 'nostalgic for the future'.[3]

The matriarchive rejects the settler colonial inauguration of time – a border of time that marks the beginning of history – by revealing a world knowledge, political, and cultural system that precedes the arrival of settler colonialism. Colonialism inaugurated time by forcing a newness on the landscape of the colonized, thereby constructing a new history and a new future in which the colonialists are central actors and the natives are acted upon (Baderoon 2014: 33; Said 1978: 84). By being agents of historical continuities and acting upon the future, matriarchival sensibilities, as demonstrated by the matrilineal members of Plaatje's and Kgositsile's upbringing, recognize the desired absenting of Black people in the inauguration of colonial history as grounds for also absenting them in the future. In insisting upon and imparting local customs, culture, spiritual beliefs, and cosmologies that the colonial administration criminalized and targeted for erasure, the matriarchive illuminated entangled universalisms to their proponents in which multiple histories, modernities, and knowledges could coexist. These became infinitely generative in fostering oppositional forces against colonial alienation and assimilation that prevented, to a large extent, the capitulation to total colonial rule by the colonized. These world systems were deployed by their proponents to fashion tools with which to bludgeon

---

[3] This is Grace Musila's (2019) formulation in her paper 'Desire and Freedom in Yvonne Vera's Fiction'.

the totalizing force of colonial genres of the human, colonial geographies and temporalities, and the ghettoization of Black life, experience, knowledge, and expressive cultures.

Kgositsile recalls the reinforcement of colonial alienation in his youth: 'going to school was a threat to try to dismiss the relevance of African languages and African culture. [...] If you were anywhere on the school grounds speaking a language other than English, you would be very seriously punished' (in Salaam 1991). The school is transformed into a New World plantation where the native tongue is banned. In the battle for his mind, Madikeledi strategically guided Kgositsile away from that colonial infiltration by insisting on Setswana and encouraging young Kgositsile to read Tswana literature. This, he asserts, shaped how he 'reacted in certain ways for the collective whole, away from that other mess', and by the time he started writing in junior high school, 'because there is a very long tradition of storytelling and poetry, the oral tradition, it was not difficult. I think although most of the time I write in English, I think the way that I handled the English language was informed and shaped by the oral tradition' (ibid). His colonial education sought to destroy *continuities* between the language of his *home*, of his education, and that of his *immediate* and *wider community*. This was a grave concern for Madikeledi and famously theorized by Ngugi wa Thiong'o (1986). When Kgositsile was in exile in Black America, he finally grasped the magnitude of Madikeledi's intervention, and understood her teachings to be in line with those of Amiri Baraka, Malcolm X, and Frantz Fanon (Rowell 1978: 30).

Madikeledi was therefore vital in transforming the 'homeplace into a site of resistance' (hooks 1990). The direct seeds of her teachings sprouted in five principal moments in Kgositsile's formative years, namely, in his radical imagination, his processing of missionary education, his rejection of the church, his renouncing of formal employment, and his repudiation of Englishness. He reflects on how existing between the two worlds of his homeplace and British colonial school shaped his imagination from a young age:

> One time an English teacher gave us an assignment to write something about Christmas. I wrote my little piece in terms of the way I knew how people celebrated Christmas in the township. He got very upset because I guess it didn't mimic what some white boy of my age wrote about Christmas. That time in South Africa, where I grew up we didn't have things like Christmas trees and people singing Christmas carols. So my little piece didn't have any of those things. After he told me how bad it was, I gave it to another teacher who read the thing and told me this is a very good piece; it is 'bad' simply because he doesn't want you to reflect this reality. He wants

you to reflect another reality but didn't have the guts to say we should write like little carbon copy white boys.[4]

As a result, when he emerged as a writer, he became preoccupied with what he calls 'taming the English language'. The long tradition of storytelling, poetry, and general orality of his upbringing became central in his practice. He emerged from a Black intellectual tradition of writers whose pressing task was to record the oral traditions shared with them by their grandmothers. This is true of Tswana writers Solomon Plaatje and Leepile Raditladi, Kgositsile's predecessors who advertently sought and rejuvenated oral traditions in their work, and whom Kgositsile admired. His mothers' insistence that he read Tswana literature informed his decision to pack Tswana classics in his luggage into exile. If their lessons, oratory, and performative practices reinforced his resolve to tame the English language, then Tswana literature became a companion and archive he was able to reference in exile as a sturdy source of his flowering imagination.

He studied the cultures of the Batswana and lamented the boundaries imposed between poetry and song, which he also used as a metaphor for the imposed borders that produced nation-states. In his reckoning, colonialism is the major culprit for both. He offers a poetic meditation on how the imagination of young children is destroyed in the classroom, in the home, and in the church, so that by the time they are adults they do not trust themselves:

> Our introduction to language in relationship to lived experience in our formative years consists of more 'no' than 'yes', in terms of what we can do. The average parent, when the child is playing around, says 'no don't do that', 'no don't touch that flame', instead of letting you find out. So as you grow, when you start school, the teacher also has a series of 'no's'. If your people are religious and they take you to church, there also you hear 'no'. By the time you realise you have an imagination that wants to explore and be creative, there are all these walls you have to break.[5]

Kgositsile centralizes his grandmother and mother for his knowing, being, and becoming – their affirming 'yes', their validation of his boyhood, and their fostering of trust that supported his active resistance all form the basis of his life and work. As he confesses, 'everything I write is tied up with some kind of wisdom I got from them in that hostile environment' (Rowell 1978: 23). The absence of their affirmation of his humanity would have constituted 'a kind of deprivation that creates some holes in [my] wholeness'. Their encouragement – lack of 'no' – set him on a path of radical intellectualism and political

---

[4] Author interview with Keorapetse Kgositsile, Pretoria, March 2013.
[5] Author interview with Keorapetse Kgositsile, Pretoria, March 2013.

activity fertilized by a radical imagination that fortified him and supported his transgression of geographical, temporal, linguistic, and creative borders. He was at ease interweaving the African American vocabulary with Tswana or Zulu proverbs, transposing Sophiatown into Harlem, and sounding his grandmother and mother in a Charlie Parker riff.

The radical imagination seeded in the home shaped his attitude to school, the English language, church, and, later, his rejection of employment. He narrates his time in primary school to Kalamu ya Salaam:

> [...] in school we had this imposition on us of mainly British but some American literature. A lot of that stuff was totally irrelevant to our lives. It came from different cultures, different centuries, different social concerns and so on, than ours. In the same manner that the National Liberation Movement had to exist and work out its strategies and tactics in the interest of the collective whole, then, *even without consciously thinking so*, some of us reacted in certain ways for the collective away from that other mess. Also, because there is a very long tradition of storytelling and poetry, the oral tradition, it was not difficult. I think although most of the time I write in English, I think the way that I handled the English language was informed and shaped by the oral traditions. (1991, my emphasis)

Here Kgositsile links four pivotal and causal events in his life and work, namely, the subconscious flow of his grandmother's and mother's teachings that made him innately resistant to the Britishness and Americanness couched in the lesson of the day, which in turn made him work out strategies and tactics to overcome the colonial 'mess'. He countered the totalizing force of colonial education by using oral traditions as a shield, in the form of storytelling and poetry, that would have been accessible to him in the homeplace and immediate community. This fuelled his suspicion of the English language and shaped his approach and sensibility in handling that language. In his view, these sensibilities were akin to those of the national liberation movement that similarly formed strategies to reject western civilization and epistemology, driven by the aspirations of the people and their cultures – a Cabralian impulse. Thus, his evolution and progression from the bosom of the homestead to the African National Congress was organic, marked by the principle of continuities.

By the time he finished school, Kgositsile took a decision to 'never ever work for anyone in South Africa again'. This was due to his observation of the Bantu Education system introduced in schools, 'in which Africans were essentially trained to be subservient to whites', he tells Charles Rowell of *Callaloo*. He is sure to quickly mention that 'I was already conscious enough to resent that' (Rowell 1978: 25), indicating his developed political consciousness, unusual for one his age. This consciousness extended to his understanding of racial capitalism in Southern Africa and led to the subsequent outright rejection of conscription. His politicization that was seeded at home in Dithakong was nurtured in his prepubescent years while living in Johannesburg with his mother in the servants' quarters of the Yeoville suburb. Here, the final stroke in his total rejection of westernism occurred through renouncing its 'strongest psychological weapons': 'the Bible and Christianity' (Rowell 1978: 26). In the excerpt of his memoir, focusing on formative years, and titled 'I Know My Name' (1973), he writes of this denouncement that took place one afternoon when a kind white woman, his friend's mother, spoke of his mother as a 'girl' – commonplace in that milieu as a tool to reinforce white superiority and Black inferiority. Enraged by this incident, Kgositsile recalls later asking his mother:

> Mother, these white people, do they believe in the same god we
> pray to? Are they Christians, Mother?
> Mother would say that they were Christians but that they were the way they were because maybe God had turned his back on them. Some day God would show them the light.
> Even my young years could not trust a god like that. I stopped reciting prayers before I went to bed and before I got up in the morning. I stopped 'blessing' my food before eating it. I stopped going to church (Rowell 1978: 64).

These were the makings of his political coming of age. They come together to give us a portrait of a Black radical intellectual as a young man. These themes are central to Kgositsile's political and literary biography. I close this section by making important observations for reading his oeuvre. When Kgositsile refers to himself as 'Boykie', most of the time in relation to how his grandmother referred to him, as well as when he dubs himself 'Manboy', he signals a moment of speaking from this world of matriarchival knowledge, from the oral and oral performative world of his mothers that shaped the acoustemological orientation of his work. For example, he sounds the wise words of his grandmother in the poem 'Manboy': 'when I overheard grandma / telling a neighbour / 'Masemangmang you must stop / sending this child when he has seen / you doing nothing when the others / would not be sent by you / you will make him a stubborn monster' (1995: 19). His grandmother knew and told of a white regime that puts Black bodies to work in brutal conditions around the clock, workers who witnessed the sloth and avarice of their masters daily, turning them into 'stubborn monsters' who rose in revolt. Madikeledi was advising their neighbour against breeding a terror in her own home, about recognizing the unexpressed and unrecognizable feelings in the child that will one day surely make sense and create discord. Madikeledi was exercising empathy by addressing a disharmony in the community which would impact its future negatively. Kgositsile was acutely conscious of that.

Matrilineal Politics of Refusal

Galekgobe, Kgositsile's mother, refused to live according to any script that determined her fate. In moving to Johannesburg right at the end of the Great Depression during the seeding of a militant mood in the African population, Galekgobe joined the exodus from the fringes of rural South Africa into the Witwatersrand region. This greatly disordered the population of Johannesburg, which tripled over a few months, causing the Black population to vastly outnumber the white population and expanding the slum areas of the city. Galekgobe became part of a fugitive population exceeding the bounds of the white man's dreamed-up societal structure in which Blackwomen were on the periphery of the city, controlled by their men. Blackwomen were to be locked away in native reserves. By leaving Dithakong, Galekgobe was among those Blackwomen who struck a blow against the ruling order and asserted themselves as full political subjects and not legal minors to their husbands. She joined the chorus, 'we don't know where we are going, but we are leaving this place!'. Their rebellion and waywardness were unforeseen and radically unruly, throwing the dreamed-up 'white man's towns' into crisis. Galekgobe *refused* the terms set for her life by patriarchy and white supremacy. She took the errant path to unknown urban life, in what must be read as 'an untiring practice of trying to live when you were never meant to survive' (Hartman 2019: 228). As we shall see, this experience had a deep impact on her son.

In 1950, Kgositsile lived briefly with his Uncle Tholo, the jazz aficionado, to complete his school year. This was immediately after Madikeledi's death in 1949, a traumatic event, the grief of which followed Kgositsile well into adulthood. During this time, young Kgositsile suffered an acute attack of appendicitis and was rushed to hospital for an appendectomy. A few days after the operation, while in recovery in the hospital, a white nurse conducted a check-up of his wound, negligently pressing and squeezing the affected area in a rough manner. In pain, Kgositsile regained his composure and informed her that natives feel pain, too, to which she responded that Johannesburg kaffirs think they are white people.[6] It was the assumption of the white supremacist apparatus of 'care' that 'relative to whites, Blacks feel less pain because they have faced more hardship. [...] Because they are believed to be less sensitive to pain, Black people are forced to endure more pain' (Silverstein in Sharpe 2016: 10). Further, receiving 'care' in state hospitals extends state-sanctioned violence that misidentifies a

---

[6] 'Kaffir' is a derogatory term equivalent in its tone and severity to 'nigger'.

Black 'boy' as a 'man' since Blackness and innocence are incongruous. Young Kgositsile let the nurse's comment pass, as he was still groggy and in pain.

A few days later, the same nurse returned to remove stitches from his wound. She was ripping, pulling, and tugging vengefully, very evidently enjoying putting him through this torture. Kgositsile moved quietly to one side, balanced himself on his elbow, and with all the force he could muster, slapped her so hard that the forceps flew out her hands as she staggered back. When she regained her balance, she stormed out of the ward. The other Black people in the ward were mortified, and some commented, '*o tla re bolaisa ka makgowa*' – you will get us all in trouble or killed by these white people. The nurse returned after a few minutes with the doctor who performed the operation. Before the doctor could take any punitive measures, Kgositsile lifted his bloody pyjama top to show him where the nurse had torn his stomach just moments before. Shocked himself, the doctor led the nurse away and came back with a different nurse who stitched the torn part of his stomach.

Later that day, when his mother Galekgobe arrived from Johannesburg to check up on the patient, the doctor told her that Keorapetse was being badly brought up and should be given a good flogging as soon as his stomach was healed. His mother told the doctor that no such thing would to happen. She informed him that she had brought Kgositsile up to respect any person who respects themselves enough to show respect for other people, young or old, and that since the doctor had given her no reason to believe that Kgositsile was disrespectful without a valid reason, she very much suspected that the nurse must have been at fault. To conclude his narration Kgositsile says:

> consistency in support was there with the confidence that I did not start the nonsense. That made a very significant contribution. Now talking about the point of departure, these are points of references that have had enough of an impact on my life to shape, and, in a sense, direct it. I was fortunate to know there was some adult around me who on principle would take the necessary risks. If they had betrayed me, I might not be who I am.[7]

Those are the years that fostered conditions of total trust where a mother's love and trust remained unbroken by the son's active resistance.

Kgositsile's relationship with his mother came into maturity when he moved to Johannesburg to live with her in the kitchens of Yeoville, where she worked as a house servant, in 1951. Their exchanges are inscribed on both their bodies in the domestic and intimate space of those servants' quarters, with Galekgobe's corporeality a brooding presence in Kgositsile's poems. He witnessed her

---

7   Author interview with Keorapetse Kgositsile, Pretoria, April 2014.

'morning odor', her 'anxious breath', and her 'ready-for-work-mask' (1975a: 10), which articulate 'an iteration of the revolution of Black intimate life', producing tales of untiring acts of survival (Hartman 2019: 60). He deploys her totem *mosadi mmina-tshipi*, or 'woman dancer-of-steel', to heighten her confinement in this carceral geography of the white man's city and his designed servants' quarters – a straitjacket that constrained her. He sees her restriction in the same frame as that of the miners, the slaves, and the exploited labourers under apartheid's surveillance. The mask she puts on to get ready for work tells us she has to step into the role of domestic work, of servitude, a role that conceals her authentic power. She is *mmina*, dancer or singer, and Kgositsile invokes her totem to simultaneously lament her compromised positions in white South Africa as well as celebrate her strength as observed when living with her: a caged bird that sings. These poetics culled out of her totem simultaneously haunt his imagination and fuel his resolve and action.

He recalls that when he and his white friends from the neighbourhood, Mario, Michael, and Leon, decided to join a boxing club, he was singled out and told he could not be a member. In his stubbornness, he insisted on joining the club, citing his skill and love for boxing. He was not able to join the boxing club on account of his race. In a solidarity informed by the innocence of childhood, his friends refused to join if he could not, so they left the club. They went to Mario's house and boxed in his backyard, which 'enjoyed the cover of a thick blanket of well-groomed green grass'. When he fought Mario, Kgositsile's dexterous right hook busted Mario's left cheek, turning that grass 'redder than horse meat' and sending Mario to hospital to be stitched. Mario's father, furious and vengeful, went to Galekgobe in her servants' quarters and insisted on giving Kgositsile a whipping. To this she replied 'over my dead body' – he would have to go through her to get to her son. Mario's father, furious, stormed out and banned Kgositsile from ever setting foot in his house or playing with Mario again. Once everything had calmed down, Galekgobe sat young Kgositsile down and explained to him why they would not allow him in the boxing club.[8]

Both white men's – the state hospital doctor and Mario's father – demands to have her son punished by flogging Galekgobe unrepentantly refused. Perhaps having herself been instructed to 'not ever take any nonsense from them' by her mother (Kgositsile 1971: 81), Madikeledi, and now modelling for young Kgositsile the command in praxis, she transcended the role of servitude that her position as a domestic worker demanded. Her act of refusal against a state representative and a domestic 'master' is transgressive and might have warranted her own flogging in another context. She owns herself despite her subjection and wants to leave that legacy for her son. This defiant self-possession may be

---

[8] Author interview with Keorapetse Kgositsile, Pretoria, April 2014.

what Nadine Gordimer calls our attention to when she witnesses the subversion that characterized some domestic workers:

> Every household in the fine suburbs had several Black servants – trusted cooks who were allowed to invite their grandchildren to spend their holidays in the backyard, faithful gardeners from whom the family watch-dog was inseparable, a shifting population of pretty young housemaids whose long red nails and pertness not only asserted the indignity of being undiscovered or out-of-work fashion models but kept hoisted a cocky guerrilla pride against servitude to whites: there are many forms of resistance not recognized in orthodox revolutionary strategy. (1984: 143)

This statement plays on the double-agent identity of both gardener as watchdog and housemaid as a feral cat, portraying a courageous panther, pert with long, sharp nails. The 'cocky guerrilla pride' evokes a deadly sin in the Black world where uppity Blacks would be lynched for daring to express their humanity. And, indeed, Galekgobe could have faced grave consequences for standing up to the two white men, the masters, as a slave. But for her, obedience was not a disposition that occurred as an option. *O tla re bolaisa ka makgowa* is laughable to her given the overwhelming Black majority that will surely rise against the white oligarchy. She performs these acts in full view of her son; standing combatant and undisciplined, audaciously wielding a metaphorical axe that asserts freedom and self-ownership against white and patriarchal legislation, constitute a practice and politics of refusal. The sociologist W.E.B Du Bois (1898: 18) wrote that children learn more from what you are than what you teach. That is, children do as you do rather than as you say. Galekgobe modelled refusal for young Kgositsile.

Johannesburg Years

Kgositsile would reflect on the moment when tragedy befell the family, in 1949, with Madikeledi's passing, in a rare experimentation with form in exile in his short story 'Grandma's Favourite Son', published in the Black periodical *Black World* in November 1972. The timing of this short story is synchronous with him finding out about his mother's passing in 1968, five years after the fact. Both occasions launched Kgositsile into inconsolable alienation that consequently marked the chief transformations in his life and work. It is the first passing that I will focus on, which resulted in young Kgositsile relocating to Lomanyaneng in Mafikeng, to live with his Uncle Tholo, a teacher at Tshidi Barolong Secondary School, where Kgositsile enrolled. Bra Tholo's house was known as a place where the latest jazz records could be heard blaring on the weekend, hosting a distinguished calibre of jazz-loving friends. In the late 1940s, and after the Second World War, Bra Tholo discovered bebop through Sam Tshabanga – a township jazz trumpeter and friend who came into contact with American jazz pianist Horace Silver while playing for the legendary mbaqanga group African Jazz Pioneers. Silver would send Tshabanga new records from Blue Notes upon release. Living in a house filled with jazz would shape Kgositsile's relationship with the art form, and, today, his work cannot be read outside the frame of Black music. He would later understand its development in Black America, and its development in South Africa from marabi, to be the most advanced cultural or artistic affirmation of Black people's determination to live in spite of the conditions they were faced with. The Setswana language and jazz worked in tandem as political building blocks to counter colonial and other alienations.

Kgositsile moved to Johannesburg in 1952, into the cauldron of deep cultural, political, and economical tectonic shifts, to continue his high school studies in then-Western Native Township's Madibane High School. The move was preceded by a short stint at the Ohlange Institute in Durban. Ohlange was the brainchild of ANC co-founder John Langalibalele Dube, who modelled it on Booker T. Washington's Tuskegee Normal and Industrial Institute, in Alabama, where Dube had completed his studies in 1899. Ohlange ploughed Kgositsile's mind into fertile ground for political activity and prepared him for the pace of urban socio-political life. He was expelled from Ohlange due to his involvement in explosive student politics during the height of mass students strikes against the newly formed apartheid regime. At Madibane High, his love for Setswana was deepened by Daniel Philip Semakaleng Monyaise, a renowned Tswana author, who taught language and literatures there. If Madikeledi had sowed the oral component of the Tswana language seed in Kgositsile, then Monyaise, this colossus of the Tswana novel, now tended to that seedling by making it possible for Kgositsile to start thinking about the written component of that language. Until his death, Kgositsile nourished a deep desire, borne out of a sense of gratitude, to translate Monyaise's work into English.

Even before completing high school in 1954, Kgositsile was privy to currents of a Black literary renaissance that were underway in the '50s – the fabulous decade of *Drum* magazine in Sophiatown – so that by the time he finished his studies he was resolute in his decision to be a writer. He vowed to never work for a white man in his life and, more importantly, to never sound or write like one. He started interacting with writers like Can Themba, Casey Motsisi, and Stan Motjuwadi, who, in his reckoning, did not express themselves like carbon-copy English writers. Themba was most appealing to Kgositsile, and the former's writing made the latter realize that his poetic references were, in spite of the language he was using, not English, which inspired Kgositsile's life mission to make English native to South Africa. The supreme intellectual *tsotsi* among them all, as Lewis Nkosi deems Themba, fought against apartheid's attempts to retribalize the natives, fashioning an urban literature that was deemed unacceptable. Themba's rejection of the countryside and its indigenous languages and his writing in a new lingo of the townships became an act of protesting against apartheid's retribalizing project. Nourished by the Setswana matriarchive, Kgositsile also rejected the countryside and its tribalism, but committed himself to a unique project of finding continuity between the cultural imperative, his emerging urban identity, and later diasporic identity. This commitment is key to his appraisal as a bridge between Black South Africa and Black America.

In 1955, Kgositsile pursued and found tutelage with then-Cape-Town-based journalist Alex la Guma, whose work in the communist weekly paper *New Age* deeply moved him. Soon after, in 1956, Kgositsile established himself as a writer through the medium of journalism. His work appeared for the first time in print in the *New Age*, known as *The Guardian*, just before the Treason Trial, under the editorship of Ruth First. All of the editors of *The Guardian/ New Age* – Ruth First in Johannesburg, Brian Bunting in Cape Town, Govan Mbeki in the Eastern Cape, M.P. Naicker in Durban – stood accused in the 1956 Treason Trial. They were not just journalists but also political activists. It was in this cultural and political matrix that Kgositsile joined the ANC. His life mirrors that of Sol Plaatje, not only as grandchild of the Barolong and as proponent of the matriarchive, but as being crucial in reconstituting the ANC as an organized political expression of a cultural alternative to the culture of colonialism and apartheid. This is of paramount importance. When Kgositsile became disillusioned with the leadership of the ANC for not taking the role of culture in the liberatory project seriously, he lambasted the party for being 'criminally backwards about culture', citing Plaatje in his cause:

> This backwardness becomes even more perplexing, at times very infuriating, when you consider that Sol Plaatje, the first Secretary General of the ANC, was a leading writer, translator, publicist, editor, capable singer, and so forth; in short, not only was he an outstanding figure in the top leadership of the ANC, he was also a leading artist and cultural worker with a keen sense of social responsibility. (1992: 48)

Kgositsile's argument is a timely one: the 'birth of a new nation' is happening without culture, cultural workers, or an ethos of social responsibility being married to politics. It is only politics that is involved in this birth. This is highly ominous and prescient. Elsewhere, in his essay 'Culture and Liberation in South Africa', he defined culture as 'the sum total of what is produced by man's creative genius; this creativity is collective', and wrote that 'all cultures have a social and political base' (1978: 10). The triad of culture, society, and politics, interconnected, interdependent, and interrelated, is enfolded in the culture of resistance and should also come to define the culture of liberation. The splintering of politics from culture is a splintering of politics from society, which can only lead to calamity, particularly for a mass national movement formed in the name of the people. He is acutely aware of the substantive and rich intellectual, cultural, and political archive of 'the people', the political currency of their cosmologies and mythologies couched in their wealthy languages and other oratory practices.

In the late 1950s, Kgositsile was entrusted with the responsibility as messenger between the ANC leadership and some of its detained members, most importantly, Alfred Nzo, ANC chairperson of the Alexandra branch who was detained at the Modderbee Prison for not carrying a resident permit. As he recalls, he always outsmarted the prison guards, who were certainly not the brightest and who believed all natives looked alike. This put Kgositsile on the radar of the ANC leadership; he rose fast through the ranks in the liberation movement during its most illustrious years.

Politically, things reached fever pitch: in 1959, the Africanists who were against multiracialism broke away from the ANC to form the Pan-African Congress (PAC), demanding government of the Africans, by the Africans, for the Africans, and promising military action to achieve it. They announced a campaign of mass protest against the hated pass law system, and on 21 March 1960 in Sharpeville, the recently formed radical PAC led by Robert Sobukwe held an anti-pass protest. They were met by police who opened unrestrained fire on protesters, indiscriminately killing sixty-nine and wounding 186. The Sharpeville massacre became a symbol of the brutality of the apartheid system. Hendrik Verwoerd, the second president of apartheid South Africa, ordered a massive crackdown. Using emergency powers, the government banned the ANC and the PAC and detained thousands of anti-apartheid dissidents. The ANC responded by ordering some of its members, including Kgositsile, to leave the country. In a meeting with Walter Sisulu, Duma Nokwe, and Joe Slovo, Kgositsile was instructed to leave with a Tanganyikan journalist to Dar es Salaam.

In 1961, at the age of twenty-three, overwhelmed by the turn of events, but heeding the instructions of the ANC leadership, Kgositsile went home to pack a few of his meagre belongings. He could not tell his mother the truth of his impending political exile, so upon his farewell he told her he 'was going to do an assignment in Lesotho so that if the special branch came to harass her she would lead them, if she broke down, to the opposite direction'.[9] In his last hours, standing face to face with the reality that he might never come back to South

---

9   Author interview with Keorapetse Kgositsile, Pretoria, April 2014.

Africa, Kgositsile packed his Setswana books into his luggage. He recalls: 'by then already I considered them part of my most valuable movable property, so to speak. They were practically like friends, very close friends that I spent a lot of time with. At the time I would not have been able to explain the attachment.'[10] And so Kgositsile would depart the next day, his Setswana literary classics in tow, comprising the first published books in the Setswana language, including: L.D. Raditladi's dramas *Motswasele II* and *Dintshontsho tsa Lorato*, his poetry collection *Sefalana sa Menate*, and an anthology of poetry featuring his work, *Boswa jwa Puo*; D.P. Moloto's *Motimedi*; P. Leseyane's *Moremogolo wa Motho*; and D.P.S. Monyaise's novels. He understood them to be 'nourishment'.[11] They became his muse and archive of Tswana literary heritage.

With no clearly articulated mandate for the young would-be poet, Kgositsile and his companion left South Africa after midnight, headed for Tanganyika via Botswana through the Ramatlabana border. What followed was a harrowing passage into exile. In the 1974 edition of the New Orleans-based magazine *Nkombo*, which he co-edited, he writes about travelling with Spearing, the journalist, to the border, where Kgositsile had to disembark from the car and cross on foot, in the thickets, in order to hide from border officials. He had to find his way in the dead of night, on foot, riddled with paranoia as he, like a fugitive, trespassed across boundaries of white settler farmers' lands in the country of his birth. When he reached the Limpopo River, whose threshold promised a new beginning in exile, he shuddered at the thought of the crocodiles that dwelt therein, a terror that moved him to pause and write a letter to his mother, 'to tell her that I might never reach the other side of the river'. The reality of being nowhere near a mailbox or person to deliver the letter hit him with tacit force. He crossed the river, 'almost in a trance', resigned to the fact that he might never reach the other side. Kgositsile recalls this moment of estrangement:

> Trouble started when I did reach the other side very much alive and my mind, all of a sudden, racing like some wild animal disturbed by an unseen, though felt, agent of probable doom. [...] I have not ever been able to articulate what I felt, what I experienced, then. There are sacred bonds, I believe, between you and your land, the land that mothered and fathered your people's authentic spirit. I ask in Setswana, *Motho yo ke mokae*? (This person, he is of where?) It is about nationality, the beginnings of you and yours, physical and spiritual, past the battered lips whose silence testifies to the loss of the *where* consciousness. The land is older than and will outlive, your flesh to mother and father more of you. [...] You

---

[10] Ibid.
[11] Author interview with Keorapetse Kgositsile, Pretoria, March 2013.

> are of the land. Thus it is, for instance, that individual origin, like where the individual person was born, which at best might tell us where the family has travelled, is not as important as the collective roots (1974b: 43).

In the moment when he finally made the crossing he was confronted with his new status as an animal vulnerable to predators; he speaks to the sanctity of the land and its connection to authenticity, immediately invoking Setswana wisdom to make sense of his new position as an exile. This *where consciousness* is the primary concern of this book as it is directly linked to the matriarchive and what I call the 'names-songs-places matrix', where the reclamation of land is the reclamation of spirituality, communal bonds, collective purpose, and meaning. Reflecting, in 1931, on the twenty-first anniversary of the Union of South Africa, Plaatje lamented, 'in *the widest spiritual sense* South Africa stands divided, nay, even torn asunder to a degree that the dreamers of the union would have argued as sheerly impossible' (in Molema 2012: 96, my emphasis). The formation of the Union and the passing of the Land Act of 1913 all come to bear upon Kgositsile's 'pariah' status that rendered him a trespasser on the land that mothered and fathered him. This dispossession of land is the gravest wounding, the original sin which, *in the widest spiritual sense*, severed those sacred bonds between Black people's material and spiritual lives, their knowledge systems informed by their relationship with the living land and the cosmos, between man and woman, the ancestors with the living and the yet to come, and between the past and the future.

Kgositsile arrived in Tanganyika at the end of 1961, on the eve of its independence. In Dar es Salaam, Kgositsile settled in the ANC camps and wrote for the communist journal *Spearhead*, edited and published by ANC member and lawyer Frene Ginwala. She assisted many exiled members of the ANC and helped establish the ANC in exile. *Spearhead*, a monthly journal, was conceived as a tool to bring continental attention to the atrocities of the apartheid government, to put pressure on that regime. The title is a reference to the ANC's armed wing uMkhonto we Sizwe, or 'the spear of the nation', which was already sprouting underground. Also finding root in neighbouring Uganda was a new crop of African authors writing in English, gathering in June 1962 at the Makerere conference on 'African Literature in the English Language'. Kgositsile's *Spearhead* colleague, journalist Joe Louw, attended and returned with new novels out of West and East Africa. As an aspiring writer with a project to tame the English language, this treasure box of African contemporaries cemented Kgositsile's ethos. His field of writers that influenced him grew. It was in Dar es Salaam that he started toying with the idea of writing fiction. During this time, the ANC offices, through diplomatic relations, received scholarship offers to African students on a programme administered by the

Africa-America Institute, funded by the U.S. government. This scholarship offer sent African students to Lincoln University, a historically Black institution. Kgositsile received that scholarship and left Tanzania for the United States. He arrived in New York in December 1962.

United States of America: 1962–75

Kgositsile arrived in New York City to the ferment of the nascent civil rights uprisings. His strong sense of community readily transitioned him into solidarity with the African American struggle. Coming from the South African liberation movement, he fought alongside his African American counterparts against white supremacy and saw their struggle as a different site of his people's struggle, with an internationalist perspective. Isolated in rural Pennsylvania, at Lincoln University, he spent most of his time in the library, imbibing African American literature and finding striking parallels between the two geographical loci. The cultural convergence of experiences as witnessed in African American texts and jazz provided him with emotional placement. He soon after penned his first poem and published it in the university's newspaper, *The Lincolnian*. He had finally found his medium, and his poetry was sought after by Black magazines, newspapers, and journals such as *The Liberator*, *Negro Digest*, *Black Dialogue*, and *Soulbook*.

Kgositsile spent his time between Lincoln University and New York City, where he stayed with South African exiles Hugh Masekela and Jonas Gwangwa, who shared an apartment. The apartment building was in Harlem – a predominantly Black political and cultural hub of the civil rights movement which was often under the 'eyes' of the government's Federal Bureau of Investigation (FBI). Kgositsile's name made it onto their list shortly after his arrival in America. It would seem the scholarship which enabled him and the likes of Joe Louw, Peter Davidson, and Harold Head (Bessie Head's then-husband) to reside in the States advertently gave the FBI a list of insurgent PAC and ANC students to watch. It was a plan concocted by the Central Intelligence Agency (CIA) to bring young political students from Southern Africa closely under their watch, and to, in effect, tame them into noble savages through American education. There was a crude flaw in their plan: this congregation of anti-colonial and anti-apartheid Southern African activists in a historically Black university robustly engaged with their African American counterparts, resulting in mounting resistance which gained attention from influential civil rights leaders such as Malcolm X, Stokely Carmichael (president of the Student Nonviolent Coordinating Committee, or SNCC, and later Miriam Makeba's husband), Ahmed Mohammad Babu (one of the leaders of the 1964 Zanzibar Revolution), and Abdullah Abdur-Razzaq (Malcolm X's right hand), who all visited Lincoln University to mobilize. The grounds of Lincoln swelled with political activity, attracting even the eyes of the Ku Klux Klan. Kgositsile soon absconded from Lincoln to join the SNCC. The SNCC, founded in 1960, was a political student organization that started direct-action protests in the form of sit-ins through mobilizing local communities, particularly in the south. Kgositsile was soon travelling to, notably, Mississippi, as part of the Freedom Summer campaign, to incite the struggle of the southern civil rights movement.

In New York, Kgositsile had already established a base. He, Amiri Baraka, and Larry Neal were inseparable, and, alongside writers David Henderson, Ishmael Reed, Askia Toure, Jayne Cortez, and Quincy Troupe, became the cultural mouthpiece of the Black Power Movement, known in retrospect as the Black Arts Movement. Kgositsile's thrust was cultural and political by this time, and the pan-African articulations in his work soon injected the Black Power and Black Arts Movements with a consciousness of Africa and its diaspora. The scope of the African American struggle now extended to alliances with anti-colonial movements on the African continent, in Latin America, and the Caribbean. With an identity they deemed fraught by doubleness and hyphenated by blood, African Americans began gravitating en masse towards Africa in defining themselves. Le Roi Jones became Amiri Baraka, Ronald Snelling became Askia Toure, Stokely Carmichael became Kwame Toure, Don Lee became Haki Madhubuti, Paulette Williams became Ntozakhe Shange, and Gloria House became Aneb Kgositsile. Africa became a prime metaphor through which African Americans sought to define themselves, and Kgositsile at the time represented the materiality of the continent. His astute decolonial politics inspired the Black Power and Black Arts eras, and he was embraced and celebrated by Black publishers, jazz musicians, writers, politicians, and painters alike.

I cannot cover here all the influences Kgositsile had in the Black diaspora, but I shall provide examples of those I consider most significant. His artistic relationship with tenor saxophonist Pharoah Sanders resulted in Kgositsile writing liner notes for Sanders' 1971 album *Thembi*. Kgositsile's decolonial vision and sense of community, as eloquently expressed in the poem 'Towards a Walk in the Sun', inspired revolutionary poetry outfit and purported grandfathers of rap The Last Poets. They responded to Kgositsile's call for the end of poetry and the beginning of armed struggle, by declaring 'therefore we are the last poets of the world' (Oyewole 2014: xx). As I discuss in a later chapter, Kgositsile's poetry also shaped the content of their 1971 eponymous album. I argue that Setswana language and literature, which by now instructed Kgositsile's pen, moulded 'Towards a Walk in the Sun's keen sense of collective action, its powerful poetics, rhythms, and overtures, and in turn made the poem stand out for the group that would become The Last Poets. The effects of Tswana language and customs across the Atlantic is to be taken seriously. Writer-Activist Tom Dent writes of Kgositsile in his preface to *Magnolia Street*:

> Kgositsile is a powerful poet whose voice contains an innate, almost divine authority, as if he is participant in a privileged conversation about the nature of life. Always struggling in his life and work to come to terms with a home he was and is exiled from, he encouraged me to better understand mine. (1976: n.p.)

This is the collectivist virtue and ethos that has come to define Kgositsile. Giving himself without losing himself is why he was a powerful geopolitical bridge, and I truly believe these qualities have strong ties with his matriarchal upbringing and the generative and transformative matriarchive it imparted.

Kgositsile had already widely published and had won the Conrad Kent Rivers Memorial Award by the time he released his 1969 debut collection *Spirits Unchained*. This collection earned him the Harlem Cultural Council Poetry Award and the National Endowment for the Arts Poetry Award. His second collection *For Melba* (1970) is a homage to his first wife, Melba, and their daughter, Ipeleng Aneb Kgositsile. This monumental collection's sensitivities complicate the braggadocios and rampant masculinity that are often a problematic part of the Black Power and Black Arts legacy. In the introduction to this collection, he laments the disrespect for women and elders in his immediate community and renounces it as alien from where he comes from. Kgositsile's third collection *My Name is Afrika* (1971), his *magnum opus*, was initially submitted to Columbia University as part of the requirements for the fulfilment of a Masters' degree in Arts. He had by then completed his unfinished Lincoln degree at the New School in New York. In 1972, Kgositsile put a call out to African writers to submit poems for the publication of *The Word is Here* (1973), which he edited. *The Present is a Dangerous Place to Live*, his fourth full-length collection of 1974 symbolically marked his imminent departure from the U.S. and expressed his deep depression post finding out about his mother's death five years after the fact. *Places and Bloodstains*, his fifth offering, demonstrates a shift in consciousness from the other four which were largely dedicated to diasporic political figures and movements. Introduced by Chinua Achebe, it is dedicated to Southern African political movements and figures. By now a towering figure in the worlds of politics, culture, and academia, Kgositsile's official ruminations on art were solicited by Gwendolyn Brooks and Haki Madhubuti (founder of Third World Press, which published *The Present is a Dangerous Place to Live*), and he collaborated with them on the publication *A Capsule Course in Black Poetry Writing*, published in 1975.

Return to Source: 1975

The circumstances surrounding Kgositsile's decision to leave the States had to do with his frustrations of being away from his site of struggle, despite his internationalist outlook, and notwithstanding his new family, Melba and Ipeleng Kgositsile. He travelled to London to meet with Oliver Tambo, discussing conditions in which and ways to return to the continent. In London he also reunited with Duma Nokwe, recently appointed deputy secretary-general of the ANC, and director of international affairs. Kgositsile's time with Nokwe in London, albeit less than a month, was one of learning and being inducted in the more complex politics of internationalism. Nokwe, who had travelled with Moses Kotane and Oliver Tambo to the Soviet Union and China on ANC missions, soon evolved into a mentor and the main catalyst for Kgositsile's alignment with the South African Communist Party (SACP). So magnanimous and such a firebrand was Nokwe that Kgositsile would soon name his son after him. Nokwe gifted Kgositsile with Kotane's biography *Moses Kotane: South African Revolutionary*, as well as pamphlets from previous key conferences in the Soviet Union, China, and Cuba. He also appeased Kgositsile's desires by buying him a ticket to Tanzania, to be stationed at the ANC camps in Morogoro, 169 kilometres west of Dar es Salaam. Upon his return on the continent, Kgositsile allegedly sent one-way tickets for his wife and seven-year-old daughter to join him, but they decided against a move to Tanzania. He filed for divorce from Melba in 1976.

In Tanzania, Kgositsile was appointed by the University of Dar es Salaam, where, in 1975, he invited SACP-aligned Cuban-based Alex La Guma to become writer-in-residence. La Guma was the Deputy Secretary-General of the Afro-Asian Writer's Association (AAWA) that year, a cultural wing of the Afro-Asian People's Solidarity Organisation (AAPSO). In 1976, Kgositsile became the Assistant Editor for *Lotus: Afro-Asian Writing*. Through these networks, he started carving his cultural and political pathways in the Soviet Union, as a member of both the SACP and AAWA. His work and commitments coalesced Black Consciousness with third world consciousness. His poetry started articulating an uncompromising leftist and socialist stance, alignment with the Soviet Union, and aspirations of the proletariat masses' march towards the inevitable D-day. These poems appeared in a 1981 poetry anthology titled *Somehow We Survive*, edited by Sterling Plumpp, introduced by Kgositsile, and illustrated by South African abstract expressionist Dumile Feni. In this set of poems, we witness principal shifts in Kgositsile's development as a writer. He decisively identifies himself as the poet of the revolution, and this anticipates his inauguration as democratic South Africa's National Poet Laureate. He aligns his work with other poets of the revolution: Jorge Rebelo of Mozambique's Frente de Libertação de Moçambique (FRELIMO), Agostinho Neto of Angola's Popular Movement for the Liberation of Angola (MPLA), Mahmoud Darwish of the Palestinian Liberation Organization (PLO), and Ho Chi Minh of Vietnam. These were poet-revolutionaries that Kgositsile held in high esteem because they symbolized the necessary conjugation of culture and politics.

In 1978, Kgositsile met and married exiled South African Baleka Mbete. Mbete was running a fundraising campaign for *Voice of Women* (VOW), a quarterly magazine of the ANC Women's Section. Kgositsile was immediately taken by the brilliant comrade whose incendiary sentiments in support of the struggle were symbolized in the firearm she carried. At the time, Kgositsile was resolute that armed struggle was the only feasible way to overthrow the apartheid government. Mbete became instrumental in relaying the struggles of women in the liberation movement to Kgositsile. She grounded Kgositsile's revolutionary sensibilities. His 1980 poetry collection *Heartprints*, his sixth, combines old and new poems, all dedicated to women, with all proceeds going towards saving VOW. It is 'dedicated to our grandmothers, mothers, aunts, sisters, wives, daughters and cousins in our struggle for national liberation and especially to the Women's Section of the African National Congress' (1980: 6). The poems appear in both English and German, and the collection was published in East Germany, with illustrations by Dumile Feni. This is Kgositsile's lesser-known collection, and one that demonstrates his relationship with the Soviet Union.

In 1980, the ANC adopted tactical principles aimed at developing insurrectionary potential in the townships of South Africa from neighbouring Botswana. This was the 'all-out people's war' mandated by the ANC's declaration of 1979, the Year of the Spear. There, in Gaborone, a troupe of artists with ANC affiliations had formed an art collective called Medu Arts Ensemble. Among the members were ANC-trained members Wally Serote, Thami Mnyele, and Mandla Langa, who tasked themselves with providing propaganda to send to South African townships to ignite popular revolt. As links between the ANC in Botswana and progressive organizations at home were developing, the ANC sent Kgositsile and his then-wife and singer, Baleka Kgositsile. They arrived in Botswana in 1982, after having lived in Lusaka, Zambia, between 1980 and 1982. That year, from 5 to 9 July, the 'Culture and Resistance' conference organized by Medu was held at the University of Botswana with the aim of examining and proposing suggestions for the role of art in the pursuit of democratic South Africa. Kgositsile delivered the keynote address and his passionately partisan speech set the politicized tone for the rest of the festival. He proposed the title 'cultural worker' as opposed to the more elitist term 'artist', the former highlighting that the workers who serve culture also have a struggle with its own needs. This way, Kgositsile elevated the position of the cultural worker to that of any other worker in the struggle.

Out of these developments, the role of culture in the struggle for national liberation became a mainstream agenda for the ANC in exile. By this time Kgositsile was outspoken about the 'backwardness' of the ANC when it came to culture. He wrote in *Staffrider* magazine of 1992, that 'within the movement [...] there is an annoying, criminal backwardness about culture, generally, and its role in society at any given time' (48). He laments that 'it took the ANC until 1982, a period of seventy years, to establish the Department of Arts and Culture (DAC); and that was after the unarguable success of the historic Culture and Resistance festival earlier that year'. Medu's 'Culture and Resistance' conference of 1982 stands as a watershed moment which led to the establishment of the DAC in exile and the launching of in-house cultural journals, *Sechaba* and *Rixaka*. The ANC started taking the role of culture in revolution very seriously and, through the newly-founded DAC, began garnering international anti-apartheid support via the 'Amandla!' cultural ensemble.

The political and cultural work of the ANC had now started receiving international recognition and response. In 1987, Kgositsile joined Amandla! on its international tour to the United States. The main objective of this tour was to pressurize companies doing business with South Africa to divest. Whilst in Illinois, Chicago mayor Harold Washington conferred the key to the city of Chicago to Kgositsile. Washington died later that year, and Kgositsile wrote and read a tribute from the ANC at Washington's funeral. *When the Clouds Clear*, Kgositsile's seventh collection, was the first to be published within South Africa (by the Congress of South African Writers or COSAW) in 1990. COSAW also organized a homecoming for him, where he toured the country reading from his newly printed collection. On that tour he performed the poem 'Red Song', and his melodious rendering struck Vusi Mahlasela's musical sensibilities, leading to Mahlasela recording it as a classic blues song on his 1992 album *When You Come Back*. Another poem in the collection, 'Luthuli Detachment', laments as a form of 'ambush' the ideological conflicts within the ANC, between capitalism and socialism in the period leading to the release of political prisoners from Robben Island. The dream of a socialist post-apartheid South Africa had collapsed with the Berlin Wall and the dissolution of the Soviet Union. It soon turned into a long and drawn-out nightmare during the negotiation period between 1991 and 1993, and Kgositsile responded to the stillborn revolution with his eighth collection *To the Bitter End*. The 1995 title carries his resolve on its inner sleeve: 'COME THUNDER! CONFLAGRATION! [...] I will tell you right here and now that, like Castro, no force on this planet can move me from my conviction about the principles of socialism. To the bitter end. Socialism or death. *Daar's kak in die land*' (There is shit in the land).

Baleka and Kgositsile had three children – Duma (after Nokwe), Ipuseng, and Neo. As active members of the liberation movement, Kgositsile and Baleka travelled so much that their youngest daughter at the time, Ipuseng, when asked where her father was and she could not find him in the room, would answer, 'he is at the airport'. Kgositsile disclosed in our discussion that because of revolutionary commitments, they did not enjoy much of a family life.[12] Their interactions were mostly conducted by letter, or through encounters in transit. All three poems written for Baleka during that time lament a distance between them 'like mountains'. They cherished the ideals of a revolutionary love, 'as I miss you now / without complaint or despair / my heart defies every inch of air / between Dar es Salaam and Mayakovsky Square'(Kgositsile 1990: 54). It was around 1992 when their marriage was officially annulled.

After his South African book launch of *When the Clouds Clear*, Kgositsile returned to Chicago in 1990, where he taught at Wayne State University in Michigan. He took his son Duma with him. In 1993, he married Chicago-based law scholar Cheryl Harris, described by fellow academic and friend Sterling Plumpp as a brilliant scholar whose knowledge of jazz and Black politics was unsurpassed. The newlyweds celebrated the birth a son, Neruda Thebe Kgositsile, in 1994, named after revolutionary Chilean poet Pablo Neruda, whom Kgositsile considered 'the foremost poet of the twentieth century'.[13] They moved to California, where Kgositsile taught at Los Angeles University. Thebe drank from the gourd of poetry handed to him by his father, and his rise to fame as rapper Earl Sweatshirt would eventually catapult him to the world stage.

In California, Kgositsile missed an opportunity to reunite with poet-comrade and South Africa's first National Poet Laureate, Mazisi Kunene, who had left UCLA in July 1993 after having made his academic home there since 1975. Kgositsile spent the next six years following a pattern of spending six months in Los Angeles, where he taught one semester a year, and another six months at Fort Hare University in South Africa, where he taught the other semester. This arrangement, in combination with other personal matters, did not work for his marriage to Cheryl Harris, and they finalized their divorce in 2001.

A notable development in Kgositsile's trajectory as a writer was his change of heart regarding the question of language. Upon returning from exile, Kgositsile published a critical piece in the *Southern African Review of Books* in 1993, in which he crucially revises and changes his tune concerning the use of language. As he details in the article, he did not consider the issue of writing in African languages, raised by Ngugi wa Thiong'o and Wole Soyinka, as important for or relevant to South Africa since, because, he writes, 'most African literatures in South Africa were in African languages anyway' (Kgositsile 1993: n.p.). Moreover, the ANC community in exile conducted their affairs in English and, except for Mazisi Kunene and Joe Bulane, English was also used to create literature. Moreover, at the crucial and historic 'Culture and Resistance' conference of 1982 in Botswana, 'the language question was not even part of the agenda', indicating how this issue was furthest from their minds. However,

---

[12] Author interview with Keorapetse Kgositsile, Pretoria, September 2015.
[13] Ibid.

Kgositsile now understood that 'the defence and promotion of English, or any other language, at the expense of my language, or any other language, [is] an act of aggression, a declaration of war'. For years in exile Kgositsile had defended his use of the English language, proclaiming his ability to 'tame' it, to make it carry and sing his world and experiences.

At this crucial juncture of a looming democratic South Africa, of a dying long twentieth century, and of the end of exile as it were, Kgositsile gracefully conceded that the use of the English language in any way would inadvertently be in 'support of English cultural imperialism'. He writes: 'every language embodies and projects, propagates, the cultural values of its users; that the distribution and uses of English are dialectically related to the uses and abuses of power, economic, military, political' (1993: n.p.). As he brings the question of a democratic South Africa of 'majority rule' to 'cut through all that excess verbiage', he asserts, 'FACT: the majority of South Africans do not speak English. Are they doomed to remain this side of the twenty-first century?' Finally, he ends his article with this concession:

> Ngugi and I pursued this discussion for a while [...] He maintained that no matter how much I could 'tame English into my language', as I used to argue I would, I would finally be enriching English and not Setswana. How could I possibly argue against that level of clarity? As the blues singer says: hit me in the eye! Maybe then, maybe then I'll see better.
>
> [Yevgeny] Yevtushenko used to ask me with intense concern, almost childlike, how I could settle for writing in a backward language like English when I had a rich poetic language. I now find the ready answers I used to have embarrassingly arrogant and ignorant. (1993: n.p.)

There is an admirable quality in elders who change their hearts about beliefs they steadfastly held, a lesson there that can be applied to our own milieu of cancel culture. Kgositsile returned to finally settle in South Africa in 2001. He published a selection of poems from previous publications in his collections *If I could Sing* (2002) and *This Way I Salute You* (2004). He served as Special Adviser to Ministers of Arts and Culture Pallo Jordan and Paul Mashatile. In 2006, Kgositsile was inaugurated as the second National Poet Laureate of South Africa. In his speech, Jordan praised Kgositsile for being not only a truly engaged poet but also a political activist of long standing, 'who like Mao Zedong and Pablo Neruda had mastered the art of producing politically inspired poetry that did not compromise poetics to make a political statement' (2006). He was honoured with the degree of Doctor of Literature and Philosophy (DLitt et Phil) by the University of South Africa in 2012. He spent his time as a national ambassador of culture, outspoken critic of the 'new' ANC, and a fervent cultural worker committed to mentoring a new generation of young South African writers.

On 3 January 2018, in the year that would have marked his eightieth birthday, Kgositsile departed for the land of his ancestors. His life story and corpus of literature is a testament to what he calls 'future memory': desires for the future-shaped memories of the past. This book delves into his body of work that enshrines elsewhere concepts and theories of the human, temporality, literacies, gender, Black geography, ecologies, and mythologies. His concepts and theories are crucial for intervening in the coloniality of being and knowledge, and I develop them to produce decolonial hermeneutics fashioned from those otherworlds, their histories, and cosmologies.

His tombstone carries words from the poem 'Requiem for my Mother' – 'the roads to you / lead from any place / I am' – and I find this apt for discussing his point of departure as his point of return, spiritually and otherwise, very much promulgating the notion that one goes away but never leaves, that the sacred bonds with the land, indigenous language, and collective memories keep one 'here' as a living ancestor, entwined with the living in their continuous journey in the enfolding moment of the NOW, quivering with the triad of the living, the living dead, and the not-yet-born. May you experience wonder as you wander with this book.

Names: Mother, What is My Name?   2

Kgositsile's work demonstrates how monopolized colonial geographies and politics of knowledge can be reconfigured through poetics of the body. In his poetry, his body is mobilized as a body of knowledge that enshrines principles of interconnectivity, interrelationality, and interdependence with other living bodies, human and non-human. His political commitment to Black liberation and solidarity in the Black world is fortified by gestures of intimacy, interiority, depthoffeeling, 'breathing together', and belonging. At the foundation of this sensibility is the bedrock of the matriarchive that attuned him to his feelings as a legitimate place from which to fashion a political identity as poet of the revolution. The matriarchive underlines his erotic registers and poetics that are productive in asserting and affirming his purposeful action: to his mother, he writes of the 'slow sadness of your smile' and 'the slow sadness in your eye / remains fixed and talks' (1975a: 9). Her unwavering eye, fixed and articulate, is 'stronger than faith in some god who never spoke our language' (1971: 28). Galekgobe's enunciating eye transmits knowledge in his mother tongue that he receives as gospel: her sadness commands a course of action to overturn the conditions that would have her live in so-called maids' quarters in white suburbs of the white man's city, in the country of her birth. Her eye becomes his faith, the clear conscience and compass that orients his purpose in exile – 'the determined desire / past the impotence of militant rhetoric' (1971: 28). While the matriarchive entangles his political sensibilities with poetics of the body, it also demands – beyond the poetry – political action.

The matriarchive is his navigation system in exile, an internal guide with coordinates in a rich and substantive repository of mother tongue, Tswana oral/aural cultures, Southern African cosmologies, and philosophies of being. Kgositsile grounds his felt sense of self and orientation to the world in a creative grammar of geopoetics. In his poem to Madikeledi, 'sadness' appears thrice, which he writes of as 'more solid' than any system that 'tried to break our back', and which 'strength[ens] the fabric of his heart, for us' (1971: 80–1). He entangles her sadness with the body of land to which he must 'return behind whatever useful weapon […] and fight for my land, the space, spiritual and physical, on and in which to create and strengthen the sons and daughters of the soil we must reclaim and be a part of' (1974a: 43–4). On the other hand, his mother's eye makes demands for his reclamation of the land. The bodies of the mothers are the bodies of land, spiritually and physically, through symbolic interrelations between birth and death rituals, and the collective corporeal burials at the beginning and end of physical life: the burial of umbilical cords in the land after birth; and the burial of the body at the end of life. In reclaiming the land Kgositsile simultaneously reclaims his mothers and himself.

A leitmotif running through his poetry is his self-reference as 'the son', and this interconnects him with two bodies: bodies of water and celestial bodies. The bodies of water are charted as waters of life: amniotic fluids, which recentre the feminine principle in creation, creativity, regeneration, and intergenerational continuity. In his revolutionary poetry, that feminine principle is central to the poetics of rebirth. Referencing self as 'the son' also interrelates his body to celestial bodies through the wordplay, 'the sun', locating his body in a larger Black geography that ruptures white settler geography. His body in this configuration remains connected with the bodies of the mother, bodies of land, and celestial bodies, further rearticulated with bodies of water as a reparative gesture towards healing Black alienation and attaining wholeness. This reparative gesture reanimates and re-enchants geopolitics with geopoetics from the vantage point of ecosomatics: Kgositsile recentres women and the more-than-human world in the living web of his life, work, and politics.

Ecosomatics is deployed here to attend to ways in which the human body is tied to the 'eco', with a Greek etymology that underscores 'home' or 'household', which also implies the familial and intimate. In its reference to the 'home', the 'eco' is invested in kinship, reciprocity, responsibility for one another, and *boagisani*: 'building together' and 'in the same breath'. The etymology of 'eco' attends to wounds of separation caused by colonial Manicheanism. Ecosomatics returns, recovers, and recuperates the human body as interdependent and in relation to other bodies of the living environs. Recovery and recuperation are grammars of healing which also link healing to retrieval. This grammar is resonant in the naming practices of Southern Africa whose totems and praise poetry locate the individual in a larger belonging not only to the family and clan – the living, the living dead, and the not-yet-born – but the living land at large. The 'eco' is commensurate with the 'whole', central to the Germanic etymology for 'healing', *heilen*, which means 'making whole again'. In this book, ecosomatics is therefore a grammar of Blackness that recentres healing as return to the whole, repairing the wound of nonbeing, ontological negation and melancholy wrought by colonialism and anti-Blackness. For Kgositsile, this return is not only to the whole, but also a metaphorical return from exile.

Healing his body is simultaneously healing the lineage and the land, where the severing and splintering of the earth and the planetary by colonial New Worlding forces undermines that integrity of the whole that structured Southern African forms of being and relating. Kgositsile's creative articulation of ecosomatics-geopoetics is a poetic of suture that seeks to recuperate alienated bodies and gather them into communality, reciprocity, intimacy, and solidarity.

Ecosomatics engenders a sensuous, open, relational and ongoing kinship in and with his body, the bodies of his mothers, and the greater living body of earth to whom he belongs. In the Black diaspora, this sensuous openness becomes a model for fostering conviviality and solidarities. This sense and sensibility are serviced by and in the service of the matriarchive.

Kgositsile's grandmother and mother attuned him to the repository of his people's wisdom, philosophies, and mythologies as foundational knowledge that could vitalize his political commitment. I utilize the concept of the matriarchive to attend to the historical fact that women were by law mandated to reside in rural areas and native reserves of the Union of South Africa. As such, they were the group that largely continued the practice of those non-modern philosophies and cosmologies of being and knowing. In addition, Blackwomen such as Kgositsile's mothers were not passive observers of this momentous force that fractured their families and communities. They were observing, thinking, and strategizing actively about their ascribed roles of rural production and as agents of reproductive labour that would inevitably be absorbed by racial capitalism. Through a critical comprehension of the status quo, they devised or buckled down on already existing sets of kinships and relationalities and deployed them in the highly politicized space of oppositional ideological formations.[1] In Kgositsile's case, his mothers wielded culture as a weapon, reinforcing the existence and vitality of elsewhere cosmologies consisting of the diverse and substantive life-worlds of the Batswana.

The matriarchive taught Kgositsile alternative forms relating to self as full subject with flourishing inner worlds and living ancestors to whom his existence is deeply tied, as opposed to as an object useful only for capitalist extraction and profit. It taught him forms of relating to other beings and lifeforms outside of structures of domination, to live with the land in a relationship of stewardship and custodianship as opposed to proprietorship, and to consciously consider the wellbeing of the living land as inextricably tied to his and the collective wellbeing. This corpus of being, knowing, and becoming from elsewhere transformed his relation to communal, national, and anti-colonial politics of resistance. The foundational tenets of cultures from the matriarchive were understood by him as antithetical to colonial cultures of domination and were deployed by the national liberation movement and revolutionary fighters as a counterculture to apartheid and colonialism. They crystallized the terms of their collective humanity.

Those born of, socialized in, and entangled with cosmologies comprehended at the hands of matrilineal members of the family have access to elsewheres that shape their desires for another world. Cultures of the matriarchive continuously

---

[1] I think with Jennifer Morgan, whose scholarship in *Reckoning With Slavery* (2021) sharpened certain aspects of my theorization of the matriarchive.

charged Kgositsile's poetics with a living memory tied to his ongoing desires for decolonization and the demise of apartheid. Therein the ecosomatics-geopoetics of suture generated conceptions of land, death, the body, and gender that disrupt linear time, rezone spatiality, and fundamentally disorder the terms of order prescribed by the Christian, capitalist, patriarchal settler cultures of history 1. I focus on the ostensibly 'heretic' (Bogues 2016) and 'demonic' (Wynter in McKittrick 2006) nature of these histories in Black radicalism, fuelled by 'occult visions of other worlds' (Hartman 2019: 288), engaging with ways in which these worlds were influential and inspiring to Black America.

Regarding the Matriarchive

In an interview conducted for the 1973 of edition of *Callaloo*, Charles Rowell asks Kgositsile to talk about his earliest memories that are relevant to his writing life. Kgositsile offers: 'my earliest memories go back to two very strong women – my grandmother and my mother – in that order. Practically everything I write is tied up with some kind of wisdom I got from them in that hostile environment' (Rowell 1978: 23). I have looked diligently for these two women in his work, paying close attention to where they appear and employing a deep listening/feeling practice where they are sounded. It becomes clear that he writes of them in sonic terms: in his only poem to Madikeledi ('The Elegance of Memory', 1971), he writes 'I hear her now', implying an active and coeval materializing of her voice in his life. And as I have shown above, his mother Galekgobe is referred to on numerous occasions in his poetry as 'woman-dancer-of-steel', which is a direct translation of her totem *mosadi-mmina-tshipi*. *Bina*, from which *mmina* derives, connotes both to dance and to sing in Setswana.

These are harnessed by Kgositsile to tap into the world*sense*, orientation, logics, and sound knowledges of the matriarchive, an elsewhere from which he fashions his poetics and politics that is otherwise to the Europatriarchal ordering of the world. He deploys her totem to recast embodied phenomenology as a critical opening into the body as an intimate contact zone, as a portal and passageway to another value system. In ascribing song and dance to his mother, he shifts the modality of his engagement from the exclusively ocular, to open otherwise possibilities of encounter, relation, and exchange that are enabled by the phonic, sonic, and embodied. In addressing Galekgobe using her totem, he harnesses song and dance as the meeting places where she can be sounded within the larger gathering of resistance, the wider community of resistance song and dance.

In his poem titled 'Manboy', to signal the presence of the boychild or his boyhood in his life as a man and to emphasize the active materialization of the homeplace of his formative years in his latter years, he writes:

> Sometimes the childhood possesses
> And with ease carries heavy files of memory
> Which open without a creak
> Frightening me with knowledge I must now
>   reclaim (1995: 20)

The image of a childhood that carries heavy files of memory, and that appears or reveals itself to him without his particular invitation, making claims upon him, is what set me on the path of investigating the matriarchive. When I write of his co-constitutive materialization with his mothers, I refer to this agency, which, he seems to suggest, they exercise even from beyond the grave. There is a haunting by the childhood that frightens him, a spectre that shapes and is tied to his ontology, that points to a present absence in his life. It presents itself in unspecified or unceremonious moments. There is joy and empowerment in the matriarchive, in witnessing and benefiting therefrom. But there is sorrow and mourning, too, a disenchantment that lies between 'spirit and spectre, [and] between ontology and hauntology', in Jacques Derrida's words (quoted in Laclau 1995: 110). That is, the matriarchive is fortifying and ontologically affirming, but also orientated towards a future through demanding reclamation of a living past, its synthesis and execution into decolonial futures. And this is 'frightening', as expressed in his title 'The Present is a Dangerous Place to Live' (1974); the past will not let him be, but makes demands on/for the future in the present. The onto-triadic conception and experience of being in Kgositsile's work is enriched by this refusal of *return*, choosing rather to embrace *continuities*. This is how Kgositsile thinks of his mothers as alive and does not hark back to ancestors as ossified in a prehistorical time. He smashes the frames and barriers of the dominant paradigm, its overrepresentation of the white male as human par excellence, to retrieve other forms of being that offer him otherwise possibilities for thinking, for producing, and for existing.

This is informed by a cosmological system that couches different conceptions of death and which, in turn, bears implications on temporality. The materialization of the matriarchive tasks Kgositsile to rezone space and reconfigure time in his poetics. He puts to practice gathering work, interweaving the two worlds and cosmologies as dynamics of each other, in which the past has not passed but is living and breathing, with the future grounded in the possibilities of recovering that agential past. In his work, the past can be 'in front of you', as witnessed in the childhood memory that possessed him in his exile years in the States, making the future mnemonic. The practice of gathering in his work tasks Kgositsile to coin different understandings of the concept of memory:

> I would say memory sometimes in my usage might be misunderstood. In English, memory is something static. It is something you remember in terms of looking back at another period. In my usage, memory is more an assimilated aspect of your every day living and thinking. In that sense, memory can be, or it is, all time – i.e., it is past, it is present, it is future, too (1978: 31).

In this definition, he points to the existence of two worlds and two cosmologies: in the one world, memory is static – it is the dominant culture of colonial modernity invested in an inert chain of events unfolding in linear time. In the otherworld, memory is 'living and thinking' in everyday life, is agential and materializes with the 'host' as an enfolding – as opposed to unfolding – agent throughout their becoming. I have conceptualized the matriarchive as a living and thinking repository of elsewhere modes of being, relating, and knowing that are simultaneously antecedent to and concomitant with its alternative archive: the western patrilineal archive of being/power/truth/freedom (Wynter 2003). As witnessed in Kgositsile's work, accessing the matriarchive is not contingent upon the living – it 'opens without a creak' by itself, surfacing in his consciousness knowledge that he might or might not have been aware of prior to this, and making demands upon him to reclaim and transcribe it 'for us'. The matriarchive as such, at this cosmological level, continues unabated by the limitations and boundaries of Europatriarchal frames of intelligibility and legibility. It is a fugitive force that exists despite the dominant paradigm's insistence upon transparency, beyond its secularism and material fundamentalism. If Kgositsile can 'hear her now', then the registers of sound knowledges exceed the totalizing thrust of the hegemonic order.

In addition to reconfiguring temporality, the matriarchive has implications for how spatiality is understood. Kgositsile also radically positions his own body as a doorway to the matriarchive, through the intimate connection of mother to 'manchild', forever connected by the umbilical cord. He writes of reaching into 'my navel / into the soil that buries my mother' (1975a: 22), offering alternative conceptions of land from his otherworld of history 2, which are infinitely generative. He presents philosophical underpinnings of burying the afterbirth in the birth rituals of the land, where those rituals are concerned with placemaking and homemaking. Land on its own, materializing for millennia, is not necessarily a 'place' or a human geography; it exists independent of the human. It is its inhabitants that make it home through ritual. The ritual of placemaking is one concerned with connecting humans to the land through the afterbirth and thereby investing in the land as home. It is a grounding ritual that enfolds one's beginnings and belonging to the immediate and larger ecologies and ecosystems of an internetworked living world. The binding factor is spirit, which pervades all matter and with which we seek to be in sympoeisis and interdependence. These rituals confer custodianship of the land to the newly born and ascribe a relationship of stewardship that is marked by what Kgositsile calls '*where consciousness*' (1974a: 43) which becomes the complex matter that moulds revolutionary politics.

These rituals are also a birth of the symbolic being, one that converges with the biological being 'born of the womb' to produce the Wynterian hybrid being: the symbolic is born through 'the shared storytelling origin out of which we are initiatedly reborn. In this case we are no longer, as individual biological subjects, primarily born of the womb; rather, we are both initiated and reborn' (McKittrick & Wynter 2015: 34). These rituals reorientate Kgositsile's understanding of his reconstituted material and spiritual connection to the mother and the land, which equips him with what he calls a '*where consciousness*', derived from Setswana:

> There are sacred bonds, I believe, between you and your land, the land that mothered and fathered your people's authentic spirit. I ask in Setswana, *Motho yo ke mokae*? (This person, he is of where?) […] It is about nationality, the beginnings of you and yours, physical and spiritual […]. The land is older than and will outlive your flesh to mother and father more of you. […] You are of the land. Thus it is, for instance, that individual origin, like where the individual person was born, which at best might tell us where the family has travelled, is not as important as the collective roots (1974a: 43).

The fight for land is waged from a matriarchal positionality informed by the feminine principle, and without which no continuity, birth, rebirth, or regeneration is possible. Birth rituals place matrilineal energies at the centre of processes of territorialization in significant ways that differ fundamentally to Europatriarchal territory-making: in matrilineal conceptions of land, territory is living and agential; the people's connection to the land is not bound with ownership of the land but with the intergenerational responsibility of custodianship and stewardship. Their connection to land emerges out of the entanglements of the land with their buried afterbirths as sacred sites of where the lineage has been. These sites gather collective roots to give one a *where consciousness*. These landmarks are recorded in praise songs of the clan or family, sung by elderly women who constitute the birthing community during the birth of newborns. When Kgositsile asks, 'Mother, what is my name?' (1973a: 65), he reaches into the 'sonic substance' – mother (woman-dancer-of-steel), soil, navel, naming ritual, praise songs – to activate and be activated by historical being. The buried umbilical cord signifies the archive of the lineage stored in the land, a matriarchive that binds mother and child, that reminds one of one's names and purpose, and that opens a temporal arc of the living dead and the living. This is what Kgositsile reaches for in his navel: a propulsive force that fuels his political imaginary through depthoffeeling.

In this sophisticated manner Kgositsile offers a gendered conception of land that is productive for our understanding of anti-apartheid and anti-colonial struggle against white settler invasion. Three moments emphatically locate naming rituals as central to his political imaginary: the line 'Mother, what is my name' from his childhood memoirs titled 'I Know My Name' (1973), which I delve deeper into in the next section, and the title of his third collection of poetry *My Name is Afrika* (1971), which is his longest offering and which I consider his magnum opus. The naming complex locates his political struggle not only in the genesis of its conception, not only as 'a simple dialectical negation' of western civilization (Robinson 2000: 73), but also as preoccupied with the preservation of his and his people's 'ontological totality' (Robinson 2000: 168). This totality refers not only to interpersonal relationality but totality, too, with the land and the living environment.

These characteristics of the matriarchive inform his poetic line 'distances separate bodies not people', which is tied to another formulation Kgositsile uses to assert belonging to this land, upon return from exile. In the essay 'Crossing Borders without Leaving', he writes, 'I went away [...] but I never left. Even if I had wanted to "leave" my *language* would not have allowed it; my *memories* and our *collective memory* would not have allowed it; my concerns, my *daily preoccupations*, would not have allowed it' (1991: 8, emphasis in original). This proclaims a possession by the mother tongue (its storied sonic substances such as song, praise poetry, ritual, dance) and the memories – the heavy files of memories – that would not let him go, that possessed him and informed his daily preoccupations. These informed what he called 'purposeful action', couching the memories and desires of his homeplace, of his immediate South(ern) African community, and of his wider community of the Black world in continuity. This is an assault on Europatriarchal modernity's failed attempt to destroy – through its variegated borders –the continuities between the language of his home, his education, and his political expression.

This section has shown that, for Kgositsile, names and naming rituals are sonic substances tied to indigenous languages. The names matrix also enfolds place or the *where consciousness*, tying being to the land to produce a potent political imaginary not exclusively based on the dialectic of resistance, but invested in the ontological totality of the internetworked all. In his 'I Am Music People', Kgositsile concludes this naming complex thus: 'names, songs, / places we only remember / in the blood like everpresent melodies' (1971: 22). That is how names and places constitute and are constituted by sonic, phonic, and sound knowledges, which explored in depth in the next section.

Names-Songs-Places Matrix

I return to 'The Elegance of Memory' in which Kgositsile tells us 'I hear her now', 'Her voice clearer now than then', instructing him, 'Don't ever take any nonsense from them, you hear!' (1971: 81), which impacts Kgositsile with the whole spectrum of Madikeledi's command – her strength and vulnerability and her resolute desire shaping the future as her voice gets clearer and clearer on his exile journey. This entanglement of matriarchival knowledge with the prevailing social reality of Europatriarchal modernity compels Kgositsile to fashion technologies of attuning himself to and hearing the matriarchive, of shifting between dominant and elsewhere orders, and of bridging these two worlds to produce his poetics. He calls this process 'sifting and shifting', and we understand this process through the framework of wandering, of 'guided mobility' (Mavhunga 2014), and through the gathering power of jazz improvisation as method. Wandering as departing from the known, as taking a solo, ventures into and out of worlds, bringing them in relation to produce an otherwise poetics. In an excerpt from his childhood memoirs, *I Know My Name*, Kgositsile 'sifts and shifts' in between the matriarchive and dominant paradigm to fashion radical political imagination:

> So now sift and shift I must from here and always. The son must move on to set like the sun and lie buried in the young song, now rudely unleashed and though without clear voice or eye, must trample to dust those parasitic monsters. Yesterday's modicum of laughter turns to unpalatable slime then choking dust past shapes turned into shadows of wish and want; regret too. Even so thinned, I'm under the fire of pure furor [sic]. Past the rhythm of a blue day, the son must move on to set like the sun and lie buried in the west, or rise again to burn in this place with newborn fire. Mother, what is my name? Here, as any time or any place, a slave will know no dance or laughter except in memory or desire past any saying of it. My home is not my home. What then is my name! Boykie, don't ever take any nonsense from them, you hear! (1973a: 64–5)

In this excerpt, we understand the interrelationship between ecosomatics and geopoetics through the deployment of the names-songs-places matrix, which perforates borders – within and between self and geography, the bodies of the cosmos and bodies of the mothers, and between nature's and his body's temporal cycles. Sifting and shifting is a suturing methodology, taking place 'from here and always', from a past that has not passed but enfolds his growing consciousness to shape his enfolding/unfolding future. Referring to himself as 'the son' ties the body of the son to that of the mother and grandmother, as well as to ancestors, lineage, and the collective that puts him 'under the fire of pure furor [*sic*]' through their demand. They equip or imbue him with that fire. This fire is essential as a force that transforms the boy 'without clear voice or eye' into one who 'rise[s] again to burn in this place with newborn fire'. The relationship between the living, the living dead, and the newborn is here signalled. The newborn is granted fire by the living dead to burn in his time.

The fire burns, throwing light on the 'modicum of laughter' that evolved into 'unpalatable slime then choking dust', turning those childhood memories into 'shadows of wish and want' and regret, underwriting the suffering and subjection of his mothers under a white regime. The 'wish and want' becomes desire entangled with memory; this invokes the words 'mother turned shadow' (1971: 28), the line from the poem 'For Mother', where that wish and want casts a shadow on his desire for a decolonized South Africa. These images incite and light his political fires built in the furnace of exile where he lies buried in the west to rise again with new determination. The impetus is powered by the matriarchive that reminds him of his name, his purpose, his lineage, and of communitarian and intergenerational values. He invokes the mother to remind him of his name, and the grandmother to get clear instructions towards his purpose: 'don't ever take any nonsense from them […]!'. The title of his childhood memories then – 'I Know My Name' – is therefore tied to the matriarchive, the source of clarity for his political vision, his spiritual fortification, and his purposeful action.

The line 'my home is not my home' denunciates practices of place- or homemaking by white settler colonialism and affirms indigenous placemaking, opposing invasion and ownership with custodianship and stewardship. This informs his assertion in the title of his second collection, *My Name is Afrika*: the son is severed from his home, uprooted from the home he claims as his own, and therefore severed from the land upon which he can enact his name, song, and purpose – a sense of natal alienation, hence the invocation of a slave – 'a slave will know no dance or laughter except in memory or desire' – in *I Know My Name*. But this is a variation of natal alienation in which 'the dance of laughter' is accessible 'in memory or desire', which is reclaimed and reclaimable through re-membering (hyphenated to point to the binding of the one dismembered member to the whole) his name. In another poem, 'For Hughie', Kgositsile affirms that 'home is where the music is' (1974b: 34); given that we only remember names, songs, places 'in the blood like everpresent melodies' (1969c: 22), he suggests that it is possible to attune to the 'bloodsong', the lineage, kinship, and gatherings as forms of withdrawal from the dominant paradigm that unhomes and dispossesses, to home selves through poetics of communalism, commensurability, assembly, and congregation. The principal leitmotifs of song, dance, drum, ritual, and ceremony are vital and vitalizing in his poetics of homing and relation, as song is connective tissue in the Black world. He notes:

African societies all over, maybe because I'm influenced by tradition and custom, there is nothing of significance that takes place in the community without song. Whether it is celebrating childbirth, or burying somebody, mobilising, rites of passage, at rallies; everything of significance. We have not lost that. I don't think we will ever lose it, on both sides of the Atlantic. Everything![2]

The lament 'my home is not my home, what then is my name' is this practice of rehoming, a practice he achieves through the destructing and creating powers of fire that bind place – 'my home' – and 'my name'. This dynamic is put to use in the poem 'For Montshiwa & Phetoe' from his fifth collection *Places and Bloodstains* (1975), which follows the same layout as his debut collection, commencing and closing with poems that venerate the matriarchive. Important to note here is that this collection follows the news of his mother's death, which reached him five years after the fact. The collection is a turning point in his career as an author in the States, and is dedicated to South Africans, opening with a moving requiem for his mother and closing with an attempt at an epic for his daughter Ipeleng. It is an elegy for the homeland, for the motherland as it were, using fire and song to bind him to his mother. He writes:

> And when I reach into my navel
> into the soil that buries my mother
> …
> and when fire binds us
> …
> out of my navel my song. (1975a: 22–3)

Kgositsile's poetic here marshals song as 'influenced by tradition and custom' to ritualize his reformation of the body into a passageway of spirit, anchoring self in a consciousness that articulates its relational identity, asserts its being-in-becoming, and draws its sustenance from elsewhere worlds: the matriarchive. In a dynamic dance of ecosomatics with geopoetics, the body of the mother is bonded to the body of the son, and both are tied to the body of land. We heard an extension of that assertion, 'distances separate bodies not people', where the bodies of his mothers are transformed from mute and passive flesh to actively materializing bodies, as informed by the conception of death in the cosmologies of Southern Africa. Their bodies are brought into the 'internal structuring logic of matter' where they are pervaded by vibration and lifeforce, by spirit, transforming them into bodies that sing and participate in choreographic

---

[2] Author interview with Keorapetse Kgositsile, Pretoria, March 2013.

encounters with the living world.³ Through the navel, through the afterbirth buried in the land, the responsibility of custodianship and stewardship possesses and instructs him in exile to bind 'my name' and 'my home' with the umbilical cord central to rituals of placemaking and homemaking. Hence the refrain, 'Mother, what is my name'.

As M. Jacqui Alexander argues, 'the purpose of the body is to act not simply […] as an encasement of the Soul, but also as a medium of Spirit, the repository of a consciousness that derives from a source residing elsewhere, another ceremonial ritual marking' (2005: 325). For Kgositsile the navel is symbolic of the ritual marking that transposes his body and navel as sites of his habitation to the spiritual, which, as Alexander asserts, 'implies that requirements are transposed onto the body. One of these requirements is to remember their source and purpose' (ibid). For Kgositsile, the act of reaching into his navel is that act of re-membering his being, his names, and his purpose through the matriarchive. He re-members to be fully constituted by the triad; he petitions presence and accompaniment to connect with his mother, with the land that mothered him, and, finally, to move through his deep sense of grief, alienation, and heartbreak.

This crucially undergirds the terms of his radicalism with a cultural and political integrity that is inward-looking and placed outside of Europatriarchy's overdetermined universality. That radicalism is culled from elsewhere worlds that offer otherwise possibilities for existing and shaping liberatory praxis. These excerpts emerge out of and function within the names-songs-places matrix that is matrilineal in character.

Kgositsile's practice of embodiment through expanding into the navel refigures/disfigures the 'terms of order' as determined by the ruling class. It reforms his body into one vital sum interconnected to the functioning of the whole, or as Alexander defines embodiment, 'a pathway to knowledge, a talking book, whose intelligibility relies on the social – the spiritual expertise of a community to decode Sacred knowledge' (ibid). The body is (ritually) marked in the birth and naming rituals with sonic substance, inscribed by sound knowledges, into a body that vibrates and sings in relationality and continued dialogue with the body of the land. As Kgositsile states, in exile he was working towards returning to 'the land that sings who I am'.⁴ He attunes his body, those of his mothers, and the land with celestial bodies through the poetics of the 'son' and 'sun'. In so doing he seeks to bring his English language

---

3   Ashon Crawley writes: 'Everything living and dead, everything animate and immobile, vibrates. Vibration is the internal structuring logic of matter. Because everything vibrates, nothing escapes participating in choreographic encounters with the rest of the living world' (2000: 29).
4   Author interview with Keorapetse Kgositsile, Pretoria, April 2014.

poetry into chorus with the community as a whole, through resounding the vibrational frequencies of Setswana and other indigenous languages of the land in his poetics. He strives to bring the language and idiom of his poetry as close as possible to the sound knowledges of the people that are conceived and materialize through their interrelation with the land and cosmos. I refer to this as an ecosomatics-geopoetics matrix.

These sound knowledges must necessarily be understood to sift and shift between epistemology and acoustemology, as well as between the cognitive and affective, the brain and the body, in which acoustemologies and the body can be both independent of and in sync with epistemologies and the brain. We must understand the childhood memories that possess Kgositsile, frightening him with knowledge he must reclaim, to operate within the dynamic of the body passing on/down acquired knowledge without the mind necessarily instructing it to do so. In his poem 'Requiem for my Mother', Kgositsile weaves his elegy with the refrain, 'The roads to you / lead from anyplace / I am' (1975: 9), which, when read alongside the line to his grandmother, 'distances separate bodies not people', establishes firstly the body as not just flesh or just the body alone, but as housing the triad of the living, the living dead, and the not-yet-born. As Alexander argues, 'embodiment provides the moorings for a subjectivity that knits together these very elements' (2006: 325–6). By 'these elements', Alexander refers to the triad of the mind, body, and spirit, and I adapt it to operate with the onto-triadic conception of being. That is, the experience and gathering of the onto-triad is not in the domain of the mind and reason alone; it is active in the body – the blood, the song (which, in Setswana, one would *bina*, connoting both sing and dance) – and activated through performativity.

Secondly, the declaration that all roads to his mother lead from anyplace is an awakening to the possibility that he embodies those points of departure, that they tie and bind him to the land that he can access through his navel, that those origins are simultaneously in Dithakong and Johannesburg but also unmoored and embodied by his flesh-turned-body that is unimpeded by distances from that homeland or by death. The posthumous title of his selected works *Homesoil in my Blood* (2018) attempts to capture this dynamic. Thirdly, it is an assertion ('I Know My Name') that his body speaks the language of its first home, his mother, that his body is a 'talking book' his mothers can 'reed'. This is crucial and generative in our politics of community-making without which community organizing and mass movements would be impossible: the reeding of one another's bodies in the grammars of our collective experience, not eschewing difference but reaching across it, is critical for Black sociality. It requires reaching out beyond the assumed encasement of the body and relating beyond individual embodiment.

For Kgositsile this was achieved through the names-songs-places dynamic, which opened into the literacies and grammars of reeding and riting, where it was incumbent upon him to ritualize his writing to proximate *riting*, a practice contingent upon him hearing the community, the onto-triad that pries his bones open. He accessed this world through jazz improvisation as a metaphor for wandering elsewhere from which he channelled the sound knowledges 'there' – reeding them as they actively materialize – and transliterating them into his poetry through riting (writing as ritual). It transforms that process into 'riting as reciting', as a dreamkeeper's praxis of sounding the intergenerational song. The earlier jazz solo, 'the son must move on to set like the sun and lie buried in the young song' (Kgositsile 1973a: 64) deploys imageries fashioned to attend to a dynamic that happens 'there': the setting sun is the buried son, proclaiming the inevitability of rising again in rebirth. And because Kgositsile is operating in between the two worlds and two cosmologies, he knows that no birth or rebirth can take place without a womb: he is buried in the young song, the song of his rebirth, the song of his names, his purpose, his directive. These worlds and dynamics present themselves to him in the reeding, reciting, and riting process.

In his writing, he often signals the process of being possessed, commanded, and instructed by communal and intergenerational wisdom not only through 'sift and shift', but also through prefacing it with 'the ancients say' – not 'said', but in the present tense in the same way he signals communication with his grandmother through 'I hear her now'. When sifting and shifting occurs, and where 'the ancients' speak to him, like a cane or reed, he channels the sound knowledges and images of living, materializing memories transmitted. This is the process of *reeding*, in which he receives or hears the 'birth of memory', carried by the wind or *moya*/spirit; thus his formulation 'spirits unchained'. In the diaspora, the wind's relationship to trees produces this sonic substance, the sound knowledges, and messaging.

He reeds what is revealed or sounded to him. In an interrelated practice of *riting*, he transcribes what is sounded and revealed, listening to images and finding language that comes as close to ritual as possible, to be expressive of the living, materializing knowledge that tasks him to notate it. This is supported by the already cherished principle of the living word in Southern African languages, which are onomatopoeic, filled with sibilance, rhythm, and poetics to meet the poesies of the living world. As he writes in 'The Ab/Original Mask', 'in their language, the people never spoke directly about a thing, they spoke around it so that it stood out more clearly' (1969a: 57). Thus 'writing as riting' is writing as approximating, as appeasing, and petitioning conviviality, collaboration, and corroboration; it is an open field of influence by all presences; it is writing as ritual, writing as incantation, writing as recitation: writing as *riting*. The principal leitmotifs of songs, fire, dance, blood, and drums in Kgositsile's oeuvre are deployed, too, for this ritual of reeding.

Reeding and riting is a trans* (Sharpe 2016) mal/practice: *trans*gressing colonial frames of intelligibility, legibility, and its requirement of *trans*parency is a preconditional to wandering elsewhere. Subsequently, *trans*cribing through reeding is necessary to re/birth through riting. *Trans*lating the images and sound knowledges of future memory is necessary to notate his oeuvre in a manner that expresses *trans*atlantic conviviality as well as *trans*species sympoesies, as defined by Donna Haraway (2016). Traversing the bordered body is imperative for *trans*forming feelings into thought and thought into words rendered in a tamed English. For Kgositsile, travelling across, or trans*, always potentiates a rebirth characterized by continuities. This rebirth is impossible without wombs, an image that populates his work: wombs, like song, are operative within the names-songs-places matrix. The birth and naming rituals only take place after pregnancy and gestation, a feminine principle that underscores the mother archetype. This presence is in flux in his process of reeding and riting.

Bloodsongs[5] of Racial Capitalism

The names-songs-places matrix entangles the corpoliteracies of the whole – bodies of mothers, sons, land, cosmos, and bodies of water (water to be discussed in a later section) – to politics of the land, the violence of extraction, and colonial domination through racial capitalism tied to the 'mineral revolution' in Southern Africa. Part of Kgositsile's childhood memories that shape his political coming of age spring from these realities. He remembers his primary school years with fondness. Those were the years spent at the bosom of Madikeledi, doted on by his grandmother. Reflecting on these years, what stands out for him is her peripatetic nature:

> In primary school my grandmother was, I think, essentially a gypsy. We travelled outside of Mafikeng visiting relatives. Almost every year on the road. I don't even remember for instance formally when I started school. We would travel around, mission accomplished, and come back to my grandmother's base in Dithakong. I don't remember being in sub-standards. If I looked out the window and saw my grandmother talking to the principal, I packed my books; I knew we were on the road. I have, for those years, more memories of travelling around than sitting in class. But I was always reading. You'd never catch me without a book.[6]

This image of the travelling Blackwoman in the 1940s clearly demonstrates Madikeledi's refusal of the Europatriarchal script, her rejection of an enclosed

---

[5] 'Bloodsong' is Kgositsile's formulation in 'When Brown is Black (For Rap Brown)' (1969).
[6] Author interview with Keorapetse Kgositsile, Pretoria, April 2014.

geography of rural living and production, and of the desired travelling body. We get a clear sense of who modelled this refusal that Saidiya Hartman (2019) would call waywardness for Galekgobe – refusal that Tina Campt theorizes as 'a generative and creative source of disorderly power to embrace the possibility of living otherwise' (2019: 83). We understand Kgositsile's mothers too in turn have modelled for young Kgositsile radically self-fashioned terms of order that potentiate otherwise possibilities. The results of these travels were that, until Kgositsile returned from exile, he always cited Johannesburg as his place of birth. This was not an error of his making; his mothers had informed him and sustained that narrative so that when he was in Johannesburg and stopped by police, he would not cite Dithakong and risk banishment from the city. It was a cunning calculation to contravene the white man's laws.

On one occasion, grandmother and grandson travelled to Kimberly to visit family relatives. On their departure, their hosts gave Madikeledi a beautiful vase, a precious parting gift she loved, and a gesture by which she was clearly moved. This did not escape the notice of young Kgositsile. When they got to Kimberly train station, he explains,

> because the site where Africans left the station had this steep metal stairwell with openings in between the pieces of metal rung, very steep, I can remember that at some point just before she reached ground level, she missed a step and fell. The vase broke, and it was so painful, because I could tell she was much more pained by the broken vase than by her battered knees.[7]

He is quick to add that the 'European' entrance to the train station was well constructed with a ramp and an even staircase. Witnessing his beloved grandmother fall and connecting it to the reckless government architecture of the station that (under)served the so-called natives was a fundamental moment in Kgositsile's political awakening. This reminds us that public services constructed by the state ultimately served the state – to get labourers into the diamond mines for the exploitation of their labour – and not the people. This landmark fall in his childhood memory marks the rise of his social consciousness: national politics infiltrated the domicile, ending his innocent years by revealing rot in the national body.

The mining industrial complex, the foundation of South Africa's modernity had catastrophic ramifications for Black life and reconfigured categories of labour, gender, racial hierarchies, and, ultimately, radicalism. That Madikeledi had family in Kimberley, the city founded through the discovery of diamonds in the 1870s, gives us a clue that she was also marked by the hold of the mine.

---

7 Ibid.

As I argue in this book, Blackwomen such as Madikeledi and Galekgobe in the rural areas were not passive observers of the momentous force of mining's profound reconfiguration of families and societies; they were actively observing, thinking, and strategizing about the status quo, devising or buckling down on already existing sets of kinships and relationalities and deploying them in the highly politicized space of oppositional ideological formations. Kgositsile's relationship to the matriarchive is a clear demonstration of this.

His 'Point of Departure: Fire Dance Fire Song' (1971) is a four-movement suite that illustrates direct causality between politics learned in the homeplace and Black radical traditions. The first part chronicles his 'point of departure': the essence of his being and becoming, the 'first elements of consciousness and comprehension' (Robinson 2000: 122), placing his grandmother, who modelled and opened otherwise modalities of being, knowing, and doing, in the centre. She is that foundation in his life, and as this four-part suite tracks his 'broadening consciousness and conscience', it implicates solidarity with the African miner, Patrice Lumumba, and Max Stanford of the Revolutionary Action Movement during the Black Power era. It is a clear gathering together of the geopolitics of the home (Madikeledi), Southern Africa (the African miner), Africa (Lumumba), and the Black world (Stanford) into continuity. This broadening consciousness enfolds and locates his political consciousness in a coiled, rezoned temporality and spatiality by tying home and Black diaspora together through a poetics of names, songs, and places.

The four-part suite is prefaced by a narrative that uses a strategy of geopolitical relation. In that prologue he reports on a 'wise old man' in Alabama who believes in nonviolence, while also intending to 'keep a gun an' use it' (1971: 80). This man in the American south echoes the words of 'another wise old man' who told Kgositsile the same thing 'four years earlier' near Pietersburg in South Africa. This latter man uttered 'his words of wisdom in Sepedi'. This anecdote leads into the first part of the four-part suite, 'The Elegance of Memory', dedicated to Madikeledi. It primes us to receive the unfolding events in the four-part poem as structured around this: that what happens in the Black world is continuous with and perhaps reverberates with his experience in South Africa, sounded in the latter in indigenous languages and the wisdom of cosmologies they bring with them. He attunes us to the sonic and oratory rendering of Black politics, to *hear* the voices of the wise old men as they resolve the seemingly contradictory ethical position against white supremacist violence. Their wisdom echoes Madikeledi's position on speaking only Setswana at home but also expecting him to excel at the British colonial school: both face the call to preserve ontological integrity while also living the historical imperative. They also echo the politics of the ANC which, in the early 1960s, formed an armed military wing while at the core still espousing nonviolence.

These positions of Madikeledi, of the leaders of the national liberation movement, of the wise man in Pietersburg, and of the man in Alabama, are brought into *congregation*, are gathered in the conceptual coil, into multiple iterations of gathering in which the chorus of the masses is sounded. Kgositsile also gathers available resources from elsewheres – the songs, turns of phrases, vocabularies, dance, idioms, performances, and spiritual practices of the people – into an ensemble to translate the community's structures of feelings into a meeting place. In insisting upon homeplace politics and home languages, Kgositsile shapes a political imaginary in the cultures of the masses, in the Cabralian sense. Those cultures carry affective, erotic, sensuous, and performative cultures that vibrate with potential to rupture the enclosures of quotidian catastrophes visited upon Black life by the ruling order and to escape into the zone of relation, joy, pleasure, and kinship. As he demonstrates, those are the cultures of the matriarchive.

The body becomes the most intimate contact zone, porous and communal. In Kgositsile's poetry the body of Madikeledi, 'big spirited as she was big-legged' (1971: 80), meets Galekgobe's body enclosed in the servant's quarters in Yeoville, 'the morning odor / of your anxious breath / ... / your armpit odor / before the ready-for-work-mask' (1975a: 10); and they meet the bodies of the miners, 'the African miner, his body / clattering to the ground with mine phthisis' (1971: 83); of the protesters, of the leaders, and of the masses to whom he penned paeans, praise songs in his 1969 debut collection *Spirits Unchained*. They practise a refusal of silence and inertia in their bodies, always sounding out, passing on/down, reaching outward towards relation with song and the everpresent melodies in their blood. Madikeledi instructs him: 'don't ever take any nonsense from them, you hear!' (1973a: 65); Galekgobe's eye 'is stronger than faith in / some god who never spoke our language', 'the articulate silence / of [her] eye possessed my breath for long days?' (1971: 28); and the African miners 'do the dance of fire' (1971: 82). In Kgositsile's reckoning, they all constitute sonic substances of struggle and resistance, and his acute identification with their phonic matter is finely tuned by the matriarchive, the meeting place, the point of departure and return.

The strategy of the matriarchive as point of departure and return informs form in his collections: his debut collection *Spirits Unchained*, which opens with the poem 'To Gloria' (Gloria House, who when everyone else changed their names changed hers to Aneb Kgositsile), and closes with the poem 'Origins (For Melba)'. They are the matriarchive. In between the two poems are paeans, praise songs for political and cultural figures in the Black world: LeRoi Jones (Amiri Baraka), Rap Brown, Malcolm X, Nelson Mandela, David Diop, Nina Simone, Patrice Lumumba, Frantz Fanon, Aimé Césaire, A.B. Spellman, Lindsay Barrett, and Nqabeni Mthimkhulu. The opening poem invites the presence of his grandmother through the elegance of that memory of travelling with her in

Kimberly, establishing grounds for his sense of kinship with Gloria House, his comrade and sister with whom, through the Student Nonviolence Coordinating Committee, he organized Black voters in the south. He is 'reclaiming the childhood' as a frame and lens through which to feel (hear and understand) Gloria's – and by extension African American – pain, sadness, and desire, to know her/them with depthoffeeling as meeting place, which can be accessed through 'the melody of the memory' from childhood:

> … the melody of memory
> Lingered strained by bloodstained
> Diamond, whiplash
> And mother turned shadow (1969c: 7)

The melody is the orientation towards his point of departure and the collective, operating outside the frames of linear progression of time. As he offers in the primer, the 'music or sound patterns reflect connectedness to the collective circle without sacrificing the realities of the present, the cycle or time [he] lives in' (1975a: 17). The 'melody of memory' moves in and out in antiphonic cyclic motions of the coil, gathering homeplace political consciousness into sonic matter that vibrates at the same frequency as his growing consciousness of Black world politics. Shifting a mode of signification and meaning-making to hearing – of feeling, and of the affective – brings into sharp focus the image of 'mother turned shadow', of Madikeledi's sadness but also of the Black mothers everywhere who have been turned to shadow through the decimation of their families by regimes of racial capitalist expansion.

Witnessing the vulnerability of his grandmother and mother, and in turn Gloria's and other Black mothers, puts a spotlight not only on their strength and power as 'institutions of knowledge', but recasts their humanity and their lives as complex and political. He acknowledges them not only in celebratory terms but also as deeply pained by the misogynistic, anti-Black political order. This crucial intervention in the strong Black woman stereotype refocuses and acknowledges Blackwomen's suffering, alienation, and abandonment – their full humanity. Indeed, the conciliation of matriarchival largesse with sadness and grief in his work is fomented by listening and feeling, by prying his heart open to the strong fabric Madikeledi wove there, for us, by Galekgobe's eye that is stronger than any faith in some god. They are his internal compass – 'my consciousness and conscience' (1968b: 42) – moving him so he may move us with his words into revolutionary action.

Point of Departure, Point of Return

In 1968, Kgositsile appeared on a television show produced and presented by Maya Angelou, titled *Blacks, Blues, Black!* This was a critical era in Black American culture: Martin Luther King had just been assassinated on 4 April 1968, fuelling the mounting unrest that was already taking place across the country, from the Watts uprisings in 1965 to the so-called long, hot summer of 1967 riots in Newark and Detroit. A complete, total rejection of white American culture and identification was at its height, mobilized under the banner of the Black Arts and Black Power movements. Black Americans were denouncing their slave names for more African names, looking to Africa to proclaim their identity as 'Africans': LeRoi Jones, Don Lee, Rolland Snellings, and Paulette Williams changed their names to Amiri Baraka, Haki Madibhuti, Askia Toure, and Ntozake Shange, respectively. Western clothing was abandoned for African textiles such as headwraps and dashikis, afros took over as the popular hairstyles that proclaimed 'Black is beautiful', and African dance was being studied and adapted for use by theatre and dance troupes.

Proponents of the Black Arts Movement (BAM) found in 'Africa' a 'unified body image that seemed to heal the traumatized legacy of kinship haunting the post-slavery landscape' (Crawford 2007: 112). Within their midst was Kgositsile, who evidently represented that Africa they sought, and the practice of naming that was unfolding in this milieu heightened his own sense of reaffirmation through naming himself. Margo Crawford writes:

> Entitling one of his poetry volumes *My Name is Afrika*, he claimed the name of the entire continent itself, at the same time as other Black Arts poets sought bold names that would cancel out their 'slave names' from among the fragments of their knowledge of African languages. (2007: 113)

Kgositsile's assertion of his identity in this cauldron of social change was an assured stance that grounded his growing consciousness of Black world politics in relation to where he came from: the developing Black consciousness in Black America was not new to him but echoed homeplace and national liberation politics in Southern Africa. As such, he pushed his poetics to continuously sift and shift between these geographies, intellectual channels, and political traditions through the practice of gathering.

Presumably, Kgositsile was asked to submit poetry for the episode of *Blacks, Blues, Black!* in which he would appear, and his choice of poems is noteworthy. He submitted two poems, the first dedicated to his grandmother, titled 'The Elegance of Memory' (1971), and the second titled 'For Melba' (1970), dedicated to his African American then-wife Melba Johnson. The latter poem is written in Setswana and English, and Kgositsile was asked by

Angelou to read it in Setswana first, then render it in English. As Angelou imaginatively traversed the continent to Southern Africa with and for her viewership, she was visibly vitalized by hearing Kgositsile read in Setswana, which did much to populate the image of Africa in the collective imagination of her viewers with contemporary events.

Counterpublics offer a space to image alternatives forms of citizenship. The show itself represents the counterpublic by injecting 'critical Black perspectives into an overwhelmingly white televisual context, creating a Black public sphere in an unlikely space' (Heitner 2013: 2). In this instance, Kgositsile's appearance and reading of poetry in Setswana emphasizes the counter in counterpublic by offering the show's viewership a radical opening of Black as a multifaceted identity beyond America in a time when Black Americans were abandoning the nomenclature 'Afro-American' for a more global 'Black'. Further, the role of song in fashioning these intersectional Black identities is noteworthy, as acknowledged by Shana Redmond: 'Black diasporic publics grew in response to their radical exclusion from an imagined Great Society and communicated with one another through music in order to form and mobilize its alternative: the locally driven "Black counterpublics [...]"' (2014: 9).

The show opened with a dancing duo that might or might not have been interpreting Kgositsile's poem 'The Elegance of Memory', accompanied by a topless percussionist playing conga drums on stage, while the poem was read as a voice-over by Angelou. This opening poem was not immediately credited to Kgositsile – we only get to see him in the thirty-fifth minute of the show – but the poem set the mood of conviviality emphasized by Angelou as she repeated his words: 'the elegance of memories, no distances'. But it also created a container for settling into the African history and folktales narrated by Angelou throughout the episode. In the show, a conceptually revealing interpretation of and use for the poem is demonstrated, which expands the multiplicity of meanings in the words 'distances separate bodies not people' by offering a meeting place between Kgositsile himself and African Americans who are moved by this practice. In the poem, Kgositsile deploys a poetics and politics of the body and land as mediation of and meditation upon familial and diaspora kinship, of geographical continuities between South Africa and Black America, and the roles of song in the process of invocation – invocation as a practice of recollection, but also as a form of incantation and petitioning of presence.

In the poem Kgositsile brings into a relation of continuity three land features that interconnect the two continents through structures of feeling. He presents us with the 'subterranean' worlds of his grandmother's grave, the geological 'rocks with which those sinister / thieves tried to break our back' (1971: 81), and the bottom of the ocean. The first, the grave, invests land with spiritual meaning, the ancestral lands that bury the bones of his grandmother, from where she continues to talk to him, instructing him, 'don't ever take any nonsense from them, you hear!' – making these demands on him that fuel his revolutionary project. The second is a comment on racial capitalism in Southern Africa and the diaspora, in the latter represented by the mining industrial complex, symbolized by the 'rocks'. Further, racial capitalism is the unifying factor, the gathering agent between the Southern African experience and the Black world experience, with 'the cold enemy machine that breaks / the back'. Racial capitalism, overseen by overlords – thieves and operators of the cold enemy machine – is a gathering force, a shared experience in the Black world, as is the Middle Passage, the experience that connects, cartographically, the continent and its diaspora.

The 'places between us deeper than the ocean' (1971: 81) holds the double meaning of the enslaved, who were thrown overboard, at the bottom of the ocean, as well as the second meaning at which the poem also functions: at the level of using depthoffeeling, interiority, erotic power, and song for invocation. This way, the distance that separates bodies can do so physically, but the spirit of the people cannot be divided as their shared centuries-old sadness, grief, and pain unite them in solidarity, attesting to the elegance of memory. This memory and these demands bring into his ear and feeling his grandmother's instruction to not take any nonsense from the overlords of the colonial, oppressive enemy machine, doing so as a sonic command that is also affective. Her voice is both 'frightening' in its demands, but also buoying: 'does she know the strength of the fabric / she wove in my heart for us?' (1971: 81). Stéphane Robolin interprets Madikeledi's 'emboldening advice' as imbuing the speaker with 'her spirit of self-possession', generative as elements of the spiritual powers from the matriarchive (2015: 90). Here is Kgositsile on national television, offering the tapestries of that strong fabric as a love politics and missive of solidarity to Black America.

Kgositsile moves between 'sadness and joy', emphasizing the co-existence of these emotional ranges in the Black experience. He freights song with connective and unifying powers, for he believed, alongside proponents of the Black Arts Movement, that 'the strongest art form that has always explained the African community, its spirit, has been Black music' (Rowell 1978: 32). Song is 'everpresent' 'in the blood' like 'melodies', regardless of distances or the passage of time. Hence the poem taps into 'areas of feeling' – bone, colour, smell, sadness, grief, heart, love, and memory – that expand and deepen the points of conviviality and intimacy, 'stronger' than oppression. Song is deployed to overcome geographical and temporal chasms, as well as linguistic differences where depthoffeeling is foregrounded as grounds for relation: 'the music in the memory pried / open to the bone of feeling, no distances' (1971: 81). This is the expression of kinship Kgositsile extended to that milieu.

The line 'the bone of feeling' is '*pried* open' by song gives us another sense of how the matriarchive 'possesses' him: how his mother tongue and the memories of childhood would 'not allow' him to go away but only leave, while in exile. The matriarchive is agential. These are the characteristics of the homeplace and the matriarchive that he sees with his ears, seeing 'the fragile voice breaking through the walls of our exiles' (2002: 101) through the unearthing of 'my anchored memory' (ibid). His ability to break barriers and borders between self, land/geography, temporality, and difference is granted to him by the fabric woven in his heart by his grandmother, 'for us', for the return from 'our exiles'.

The poem 'The Elegance of Memory' was circulated in two critical counterpublic materials: on the television screens of America, invaded by what Devorah Heitner calls *Black Power TV* (2013), and in the African American periodical *Negro Digest*, where Kgositsile had published the four-part poem in its entirety in July 1968. It is crucial to read the appearance of Kgositsile's work in these media as disrupting what we understand as Black Power, 'negro', and, indeed, the Black Arts Movement and its geographical scope. His work, as Margo Crawford asserts, 'complicates the packaging of the core identity of the 1960s and 70s Black Arts Movement as African-American' (2007: 119). Furthermore, his regular contribution to *Negro Digest* and the focus of his essays therein on decolonization in the larger Black world – reflected, too, in his second poem in the four-part suite dedicated to Patrice Lumumba – likely contributed to the magazine's renaming as *Black World* in 1970. Kgositsile's rigorous engagement with political developments in Africa, Asia, and Latin America pushed editor Hoyt Fuller to consider the magazine's name change (Rambsy 2013: 31). What ultimately makes the four-part suite unique in its appearance on American television in 1968 and in *Negro Digest* is the recentring of love, empathy, affect, care, and kinship in an era of militancy, pointing to Black humanity, and not to hate or simply a negation of whiteness, as the roots and origins of the fury and fire on both sides of the Atlantic.

Dreamkeepers: Poets-Lovers-Warriors

The matriarchive teaches Kgositsile the value of dreamkeeping, of being engaged in compiling and consolidating intergenerational wisdom and knowledge, preserving sacred rituals and ceremonial knowledges of the lineage. In essence, he learns how to safekeep material and immaterial elements that unify pastpresentfuture. In Kgositsile's life, women were the most adept at this, a practice mandated by custom and rendered urgent by historical processes of misogynistic and anti-Black socio-political regimes. The women in his life, in the immediate and wider community, are presented in his work as wise seers and soothsayers, as possessing the powers to hack through any barriers of limitations imposed by external forces. They wield a courage whose force is not violence but something more radical: revolutionary love, care, and radical empathy as life-giving forces to survive and live through the loveless dominant culture of white supremacy. Musicians who function in this realm are lauded in his work for their sensibility and practice of healing the fragmented sense of self and community, recasting community as a locus of remedying predatory capitalism's commodification of the body, sense of isolation, lone wolf behaviour, and misguided individualism.

Music in Kgositsile's work thus aspires towards a re/creation of elsewhere outside the frames of the white supremacist, capitalist, patriarchal social order – worlds of pleasure, community, kinship, joy, congregation, and communion. The meeting place of assembly and congregation in his life has been governed by the theory of 'everything is everything', which, as he explained, was informed by the notion, in his community and later in the national liberation movement, that everyone and everything matters equally: that the cleaner and the leader, the children and the adults, all constitute a site of and for struggle.[8] He explicates that this theory is also operative in a jazz ensemble, where everyone and every instrument matters in its contribution to the ensuing area of feeling. This theory can be deployed to think through the hearth in the homeplace as a critical site where children first encounter communing around storytelling and other forms of sonic substances that emphasize kinship. These sound knowledges are foundational to the insistence of Black life on sociality, movement, sharing, and 'building together' 'in the same breath' (in Kgositsile's definition of *moagisani*).

I employ what Tsitsi Jaji identifies as 'synesthesia' and 'purposeful distortion' in Kgositsile's work: the 'intersensory concatenation of the modes of perception, particularly *vision* and *hearing*', which on one level 'performs a solidarity among the senses' and on the other 'can be read as an aesthetic parallel of the search for solidarity between Black Americans and South Africans in exile' (Jaji 2014: 106, my emphasis). I advance Jaji's generative heuristic to unearth the convergence of two worldviews and universals, a co-existence of two cosmologies, and an interweaving of two modalities of being and knowing. I reveal how music is crucial to achieving these goals, but Kgositsile taps into what I call the *long durée of the sonic* – not just the modern elements but also those found in the indigenous musical practices sounded in rituals, ceremonies, praise songs, folklores, and stories of his roots. Any discourses on Black music in the diaspora must consider this *long durée* to disrupt its exclusively northern hemisphere positioning.

Kgositsile's poems blur not only the sensory fields of perception but also of form. He creatively adapts the praise poet tradition and functions as historian, replete with the symbolisms, rhythms, imageries, and cosmologies of Southern African orational practices. He harnesses them to sing the praises of female musicians, whom he sees/hears as griots and dreamkeepers. In the praise songs he dedicates to musicians such as Betty Carter, Billie Holiday, Nina Simone, Cassandra Wilson, and Gloria Bosman, matriarchal sensibilities are channelled to locate these women as more than just musicians. He reroutes their musical energies into the names-songs-places matrix, not merely celebrating them but installing them into the

---

[8] Author interview with Keorapetse Kgositsile, Pretoria, March 2013.

pantheon of community leaders, healers, and revolutionaries. In our interview, renowned music journalist Gwen Ansell observed this dynamic in his poetry, 'if you look at his praise poems to female musicians, it is very clear that he sees them as more than *just* musicians. They are not even just griots. They are actual shapers of culture, handers down of culture, prophets, and all of those things'.[9] Kgositsile reveres these female musicians as dreamkeepers, as archives of the future and repositories of future memory in the tradition of the first-born daughter, or the grandmother, whose responsibilities in the larger family and community were as keeper of the clan names, the family lineage, and their praise songs.

It is not only that, when they sing, their voices amplify prayer emerging from them as intercessors between the living dead, the living, and the not-yet-born. In the dedication to *The World is Here* (1973), Kgositsile writes of Zora Neal Hurston as a 'dreamkeeper'; Alice Walker describes Hurston and Billie Holiday, both highly esteemed by Kgositsile, in the following terms:

> In my mind, Zora Neale Hurston, Billie Holiday, and Bessie Smith form a sort of unholy trinity. Zora belongs in the tradition of Black women singers, rather than among 'the literati'. [...] Like Billie and Bessie she followed her own road, believed in her own gods, pursued her own dreams, and refused to separate herself from 'common' people. (Walker 1983: 1)

Walker reminds us of the acoustemological tradition from which Hurston's writing had sprung, as well as these artists'/singers' 'heretical' practices of 'believe[ing] in their own gods' – grounds on which dreamkeepers' works are woven with the people, lived, living, and yet-to-live. Kgositsile aspires to their wandering 'on "their" own road', on terrains outside the Enlightenment's recognized 'governing system of meaning', just like the women who raised him, and all the others mentioned above. He extols their waywardness as exemplary and seeks their physical and poetic 'unholy' proximity. They embody the revolutionary impulse that animates his elsewhere politics and poetics of possibility.

Reading the poem written for Nina Simone ('Ivory Masks in Orbit') side by side with that written for Melba Johnson ('The Creator'), his first wife, we observe these dynamics harnessed from sacred mythologies of Southern Africa, from the names-songs-places matrix, rich in imageries of heavenly bodies and cosmic phenomena. Operating within what I call *terrafirmament*, the phenomena that attend to the imbrication of the cosmos and earth are the images, 'the sun / rise at the midnight hour' in the poem to Simone (1969c: 15), and 'the sun shining / even at the midnight hour' in the poem to Melba (1970:

---

[9] Author interview with Gwen Ansell, Johannesburg, April 2018.

11). Both images proclaim the miraculous interjection of darkness by Melba and Simone, proffering a temporary suspension of darkness in which something else rises – an edifying joy and pleasure, spiritual fortification, and love for 'the son'. The images invoke endings and beginnings, they evoke archetypal legends of primordial darkness interrupted by light of beginnings, marking the end of an era and the beginning of a more unitary life of commensurate kinship. This is the function of fire and light in Kgositsile's work: they mark endings through the destructive force of fire, but also beginnings, birth, and rebirth. He deploys those energies to will the end/death/burial of white supremacy and the beginning/birth/rebirth of a more just, equal, and liberated world.

It is crucial to read these two poems side by side as they reveal the worldview from which Kgositsile fashions his philosophical and aesthetic underpinnings that frame his vocation as a poet. Creativity, that middle ground between feeling and action that delicately shapes thought and expression, is inevitably tied to feeling like a springboard, and that feeling is shaped by a historical context that defines integrity and humanity. In his 'A Poet's Credo' he declares: 'I believe in the supremacy of spirit' (1968b: 43). This historical context adds wisdom and courage to the passion and conviction of his poetry. In the two poems, he ties creativity and creation to the 'mother principle': manifestation of life is only possibly through the transformation of feeling into thought and expression, of spirit into physical flesh, and this physical manifestation can only take place in the womb. He places mother in the centre as creator and underscores creation and creativity, recreation and regeneration as feminine forces. He implores his wife, 'give me / your cosmic embrace … eternal / like the sky's horizon', meanwhile Simone's finger moves over '300 sounds [that] burn on the ivory' (1969c: 15) – a reference to the white of the ivory, three hundred years of slavery, and whiteness as an ideology, now burning. The fire that destroys also creates a 'new kind of air', Simone's song 'Mississippi Goddam' signalling both endings and beginnings, 'the sun smiles of new /dawn'.

The image of a 'new dawn mating with this burning moment' (1969c: 15) is a potent rising of a new era out of the ashes of the old one. But, in Kgositsile's view, the new is not entirely new but is future memory: the 'ebony lady', through her eighty-eight ivory keys, now 'swims in this / cloud like the crocodile / in the limpopo midnight hour' (1969c: 15). In 'The Creator', the waters of Melba's eternal spring 'drown today's debris / preparing for a naked / future' (1970: 11). The fire and water as elementary forces are cyclic, orbiting pastpresentfuture alike in which 'desire becomes memory', that is, desire of that future is informed by memory. Simone heralds the 'new', like the sun in the cloud, and like the crocodile in the river; the binding of the heavens and earth occurs in the waters of the Mississippi and the Limpopo Rivers, confluencing in this moment to give birth to a new dawn, with the waters of creation (and destruction/drowning) embodied by and symbolic of the matriarchive. The Limpopo midnight hour convokes the sun shining in the midnight hour, the burning of white dominant orders mating with the new dawn in both South Africa and America, in Africa and the rest of the Black world. The bodies of water here are interlinked with the celestial bodies of the 'sun', the bodies of the 'son', and the bodies of land on both sides of the Atlantic.

Kgositsile works with and through the conception of relations between women and water in Southern African mythologies, as bodies of creation and creativity, recreation and regeneration. Tsitsi Jaji aptly observes this in her reading of 'Ivory Masks in Orbit': 'throughout Southern Africa, folklore centring on hybrid women with reptilian limbs abounds, and Kgositsile may be drawing upon seSotho traditions of *mamolapo* or *mamogashoa* (mother of the river / deep) snake' (2009: 229). Waters, just like human bodies, are bodies of knowledge in their capacity to hold memory. Water spirits are guardians of that memory and are known to 'abduct' the living at times, when they disappear for years and come back initiated as healers or return wiser and holding future memory for the continuity of the family, community, or society.

If we follow this logic, we understand Kgositsile to be saying something more than praising Simone for transporting him, for carrying the message of revolution evinced in the title of the poem's 'polysemic nod to Frantz Fanon, transforming (*Black Skin*) *White Masks* into "Ivory Masks"' as Jaji (2009: 297) offers. Kgositsile is fashioning new grounds for a different kind of wandering in which two geographies and knowledge systems are brought into relation, disburdening him from the shackles of the social order, to collaborate with and be corroborated by the wisdom of the matriarchive, which gift him with otherwise possibilities of thinking, being, and creating.

The refrain in the Simone poem 'do you love me!' is an assertion of affective and embodied feelings of relation, as opposed to a question, claiming from Simone a form of 'cosmic embrace' he associated with Melba. His formulation of love is beyond romantic love, espousing that cosmic primordial and organizing principle of the universe which informs his belief in the 'supremacy of spirit' – 'the white world's denial of the supremacy of Spirit [is] the white world's denial of love' (Kgositsile 1968b: 42–3). In 'Ivory Masks in Orbit' and 'The Creator', therefore, we see an example of how Kgositsile attributes this cosmic love to the feminine energies, to the matriarchive and its principle of continuity as griot, shaper and hander down of cultures, and prophet, but also to something else, that additional crucial capacity for love and creation, not of the reproduction or procreation type, but of the cosmic type which I draw from Anna Malaika Tubbs, who writes: 'Black women are the ultimate practitioners of this ability to turn tragedy into opportunity, face fear and persecution with faith and unmatched perseverance, and create something out of nothing, because it has been required of us' (2021: 28–9). It is the cosmic force of continuity that imbues women with 'love armed with future / memory', where they are able to transform and transmute tragedy into possibility: the 'new dawn mating with this / burning moment' (1969c: 15). Blackwomen, throughout colonial and postcolonial history, have been master improvisers, communing with the spirit of creation on behalf of the people – a paramount expression of love that Kgositsile is now beneficiary to in this 'Nina Simone moment'.

Matriarchive as 'Heretic'

'Future memory' is a temporality Kgositsile coined out of necessity to signal the actively materializing matriarchive in his life and work. In 1968, a set of three poems written by Kgositsile were anthologized in the seminal text of the BAM, *Black Fire: An Anthology of Afro-American Writing* (1968), edited by Amiri Baraka and Larry Neal. Two of these poems, 'Ivory Masks in Orbit' and 'Towards a Walk in the Sun', are pivotal in understanding Kgositsile's impact on the era. The latter poem is discussed in the following chapters. Enthused by the concept of future memory, one of the figureheads of the movement, Larry Neal, deployed the term to hold together his manifesto on the Black Arts era in his foundational essay published in *Ebony Magazine* in 1969.

Neal's use of 'future memory' in his essay exposes the differences or disarticulations in politics of solidarity based on various characteristics including the linguistic chasm, difference based on lived experience, and crucially, accessibility and entanglement with elsewhere cosmologies. Neal's inability to grasp the full scope of 'future memory' is exemplary of Brent Edwards's assertion, that 'the cultures of Black internationalism can be seen only in *translation*' (2003: 7, emphasis in the original): in this case, it was lost in translation. In the article titled 'Any Day Now: Black Art and Black Liberation', Neal's manifesto narrates the relationship between Black liberation and Black arts, but at that early stage squarely falls short in explicating those relations, instead leaning on essentialism: 'Black people you are Black Art. You are the poem, as Ameer [sic] Baraka teaches us. You are Dahomey smile. You are slave ship and field holler. You are Blues and Gospel and Be-Bop and New Music. [...] You are both memory and flesh' (Neal 1969: 62). Neal invokes Kgositsile's concept:

> A future society without the implied force and memory of Bessie Smith, Charlie Parker, Sun Ra, Cecil Taylor, Pharoah Sanders, and Charlie Mingus is almost inconceivable. The artists carry the past and the future memory of the race, of the Nation. They represent our various identities. They link us to the deepest, most profound aspects of our ancestry (1969: 56).

In his use of the term 'future memory', Neal is still talking about a vision of a liberated future operative in a linear time model. He cannot conceive of future memory as operating in the NOW, expanding this moment to sound the presence and force of memory, not ossifying in the past and available to us when we choose to remember, but rather memory as living, thinking, and agential. This memory at time grasps, apprehends, and possesses one, revealing a future possibility that can be remembered, brought about, and claimed. When Neal mentions Africa, it is the Africa of a 'glorious past', of Dahomey and 'Chaka' Zulu, and of ancient civilizations, a discourse that Kgositsile speaks against, rather embracing 'continuity, not return' (1975a: 57). Neal uses 'future memory' thrice in his piece, twice in his conclusion:

> The Blues God spoke to me. [...] This is the death of the white lie that our ancestors prophesised. This is the death of the double-consciousness. Listen: under the songs and the moaning night, they plotted their deaths and worked juju on the Beasts; [...] they plotted his death under the spirituals and the blues; they invoked the Future Memory which is us, and it is to that Memory that we dance and fight and sing. They invoked the Future Memory while baring their behinds to cracker whips and jack boots. They were visionaries and warriors. (1969: 62).

While the concept of 'Future Memory' clearly invigorated Neal, his application of it tends to mean a dream or vision of better days, in an unfolding future. It is an example of something that Cedric Robinson notes, where he writes that the African's epistemology of revolt 'granted supremacy to metaphysics not the material', while the New World diasporic subject's focus 'was on the structures of the mind' (2000: 169). For Neal, 'future memory' became an intellectual project. For Kgositsile, the future is not unfolding but enfolded as pastpresentfuture. He disordered diaspora time to attend to this transmission of the matriarchive. He was engaging a different experiential and accessible living archive elusive to Neal.

In conclusion, there are otherworlds conjured and asserted in Kgositsile's life and work, and they are presented as agential, with the capacity to possess and make claims upon him in exile. They shape the terms of Kgositsile's radicalism, concerned with the preservation of ontological totality, of continuity between memory and desire, of being dreamkeeper for the living dead and the yet-to-be-born. His poetics and politics have at their centre sonic substances that imbue the Black body with aliveness, with humanity, care, radical empathy, love, and affection, with depthoffeeling, names, songs, and places as meeting place. These are entangled, in his life and work, with the matriarchive – at once manifesting itself as lived experience, a present absence, and a 'shadow' that is nonetheless articulate, instructing and shaping futurity. His poetics and politics inscribe the erotic as ecosomatics-geopoetics phenomena, interlinking his interiority with a wider network of the living dead, living land, living waters, and living celestial bodies. This recasts interiority as a worldmaking force, which I discuss further in the next chapter.

In harnessing knowledges and forms of being and doing, Kgositsile fashions a radical political imagination and action from '"demonic" grounds engendered by wandering terrains outside the recognized Enlightenment's "governing system of meaning"' (Wynter in McKittrick 2006: 17). As such, he exercises errantry and fashions critical interventions through breaking out of the status quo. The otherwise possibilities offered by the matriarchive are grounded in refusal. Anthony Bogues deems these demonic grounds of Black radical intellectual traditions 'heretic[al]' in their 'unthinkable' and unimaginable rupturing of epistemic limits established by the western intellectual tradition (2003: 13). For Bogues, 'heresy' means becoming human by overturning white/European normativity. Saidiya Hartman offers a similar conceptualization of 'occult' in her reading of 'wayward women', who wander beyond legibility and transparency as a 'practice of possibility at a time when all roads, except the ones created by *smashing out*, are foreclosed' (2019: 228, emphasis in the original). This wandering, as she offers, 'traffics in occult visions of other worlds and dreams of a different kind of life' (ibid). The occult is the 'demonic' and is the 'heretic', all practices of transgressive wandering which Kgositsile achieves through thinking of his writing practice within the framework of the phonic and sonic.

In Laura Grillo's *An Intimate Rebuke* (2018), the concept of the 'matri-archive' is advanced to argue for a ritual archive in West Africa in which the female genital power has played a fundamental role as 'founding knowledge' and 'matrifocal morality' across African civilizations. I have demonstrated the work of the matriarchive as it pervades Kgositsile's consciousness and poetics, his use of ecosomatics as a gateway to critiquing geopolitics, and how these reform his cultural and spiritual capacities to ground his subjectivity in service of a radicalism that is centred in what Grillo calls 'matrifocal morality', concerned with the totality of the people. He retrieves this consciousness from his navel, which symbolizes a source residing elsewhere, from his mother, and from his lineage that enshrine his names and purpose.

The navel recasts his mothers' bodies, pointing to the womb, female genital power, and the birth canal as founding and foundational knowledge. These, too, have been demonized by Christian Europatriarchy, desecrated to sow an enduring natal alienation from the Black mother. When we recentre the names-songs-places matrix, we remember our first gathering to suckle foundational knowledge around grandmother, around the matriarchal hearth, where intergenerational knowledges were transmitted orally/aurally. Kgositsile treats them as mobilized riches. To him 'distances separate bodies not people', so he informs his mother 'the roads to you / lead from anyplace / I am', reclaiming those 'heretical', embodied founding knowledges as political and spiritual building blocks for liberatory mal/practices. These dynamics underlie his entreaty to the matriarchive, 'Mother, what is my name'?

Song: Native Sons Dancing Like Crazy 3

The previous chapter saw Kgositsile mobilize the names-songs-places dynamic to anchor his work in the bedrock of his beginnings, the homeplace of his formative years, in a poetics that centralizes the body as the most intimate of contact zones from which to foster revolutionary poetry and political solidarities. The matriarchive informed, shaped, and held together the zone of relationality and Black radical sociality through the internetworked bodies of the mothers, bodies of land, bodies of water, bodies of knowledge, and celestial bodies. In setting up this chapter's concerns as being continuous with the previous one, here I offer a recap of my findings from chapter 2. Kgositsile settled on the umbilical cord as a connective tissue between his mother and himself, the son, while birth rituals generated a poetics of relation between the mother, the land in which it is buried, and the son. Further, in his shifting and sifting, he linked the bodies of his mothers and bodies of land with celestial bodies: 'the son must move on to set like the sun and lie buried in the west, or rise again to burn in this place with newborn fire' (1973a: 64). Here the son is exiled from the land and enlists imageries from cosmological phenomena to transubstantiate himself from the son to the sun, setting in the west, and returning with 'newborn fire'. The choice of 'newborn' sets his meditation up in a dialogue with the matriarchive that makes it possible for the new-to-be-born, 'rising again', a (re)birth – 'Mother, what is my name?' – to undergird his liberatory purpose that must always be tied to the collective.

The bodies of water, central and fundamental to these relational poetics grounded in the matriarchive, are the principle of creation and creativity, recreation and regeneration that make it possible for Kgositsile to fashion poetics of death and rebirth, destruction and recreation, and flowering creativity and creation in the desolation of exile. The bodies of water in the previous chapter located the matriarchive of his formative years in continuity and locution with those encountered in exile. These were understood as held together, or, to harness the uses of the coil, *gathered together* by forces of the Limpopo and Mississippi Rivers, which confluence in the Atlantic and other oceans. In centralizing these bodies – of mothers, waters, land, and the cosmos – Kgositsile sutures their separation and bifurcation in a dynamic of re-pair, re-pairing, thereby working against the undermined integrity of the whole by colonial worldmaking.

In this chapter, we follow this logic through examining his enfolding of the politics and cultures of the homeplace of his mothers – his Setswana upbringing and its bodies of knowledges – with his growing political knowledge and cultural consciousness in Johannesburg, within the national liberation movement and in Black America. Whereas the previous chapter investigated and demonstrated the relationship between ecosomatics and geopoetics, this chapter is invested in exploring interiority as a worldmaking force. The poem 'Towards a Walk in the Sun' (1971) is central in Kgositsile's oeuvre as it holds together the dynamic between ecosomatics and geopoetics, deploying the wind as key element that ties together the collective bodies – of mothers, land, waters, and cosmic bodies. This sets the stage for inter-elemental relations, for the wind to *gather together* these collective bodies with sound knowledges from the matriarchive, the mass liberation movement, and the African continent to sound and resound in the Black diaspora. Kgositsile achieves this by tapping into the multiple meanings of *moya* in Setswana and most Southern African languages, which connotes wind, breath, and spirit. Spirit is the breath of life, the lifeforce that translates to breath which courses through the bodies of the living; spirit continues to live through the living dead, and wind is the force that moves rivers to confluence with oceans, which gather the land with the cosmos. The wind carries sounds and echoes beyond geographical and temporal borders. *Moya* is the internal structuring logic of the ecosomatics–geopoetics matrix.

Kgositsile deploys the image of the tree as metaphor for the African continent's relationship with its diaspora. In 'The Long Reach' he asks, 'how old is the tree / whose roots have defied death!' (1971: 71). Operating within the dynamic of Africa as roots, Kgositsile asks a rhetorical question, asserting that the roots of this tree in Africa have defied death at the hand of centuries of colonial domination. He affirms in this poem that the people on the move are still interwoven with the land through the birth rites of burying the afterbirth in the same way the roots of this tree continue to defy death. The connection to the land, to those buried on the land, defies physical death. The people are moved to defy death themselves by the transgenerational song of their names, 'in the blood like everpresent melodies', and connecting them to place. This invokes his poetic manifesto, 'distances separate bodies not people', an erotic elaboration that asserts his entanglement with actively materializing roots on his exile routes in other continents, where *moya*/breath/spirit links his being with the roots of both land, the living dead, and the mothers. The song of his name is the sonic substance produced by the tree's relationship with the wind, to which he is attuned as enshrining the *long durée* of sound. He parallels the distance between the bodies – the distance between his body and the bodies of his mothers and land – to the distance between diasporans and the African continent, to foster political solidarity.

He situates this politics in the heart; in the same poem he writes, 'touch he heart / and move' (1971: 71). Dissociating from geopolitics towards geopoetics in his exile peregrinations, he touches the heart, which generates other forms of knowledge that decouple from colonial epistemes. Through the heart, he edges closer to the hearth of the matriarchive: 'does she know the strength of the fabric / she wove in my heart for us?', he asks about Madikeledi (1971: 81). Thus the matriarchive holds erotics of relations that inform his political project of situating the body as the most intimate zone of relationality from which he fosters solidarities in the Black diaspora grounded in depthoffeeling, community-making, and radical kinship. In this chapter, I refer to Kgositsile's geopoetics of erotics as politics of Love and Care.

Kgositsile continues in the same poem to speak of the old spirit 'whose roots are heart in the depths / of Afrika', and whose branches clasp tricontinental skies 'where the eye blazes / like spears of gods!' (1971: 71). The primacy of the eye here references the poem to his mother, in which her eye 'is stronger than faith in some god who never spoke our language' (1971: 28). His mother's eye is the weapon, the spears of gods, that operates from beyond the grave moving into other continents to grant him purpose and incite him to action. Her eye blazes, and the element of fire is critical in burning the dominant order, transgressing and contravening its terms of order, and unmaking its world through destruction and creation to rebirth new worlds. He accesses this fire when he 'reach[es] into [his] navel / into the soil that buries [his] mother / [...] / to put fire in our hands' (1975a: 22). Therein, his mother is 'turned shadow and companion to nightmare' (1971: 28) – she is both empowering and terrifying, articulating the demand of the day. The fire which blazes in her eye could burn Kgositsile if he does not transform it to revolutionary action. It is the fire of responsibility. He writes that her eye reaches for wind to put fire in our hands. Wind is the element that moves the fire of demand to his hands like a baton, calling for action.

Kgositsile's work demonstrates how interiority is worldmaking. The roots 'in the depth of Afrika' (1971: 71), the land and the ancestors, linked with the mother's eye and the strong fabric woven by Madikeledi in his heart, are *for us*, Africa's children on the continent and its diaspora: they come together to sing an intergeneration song. These are the geopoetics of erotics that move Kgositsile's politics of Love and Care, moved by love to converge his exilic routes with roots, and Black America with Africa. It is love that moves him into fostering radical kinship and community-making, that moves him to orchestrate and choreograph the people into song and dance. This spirit is a politics of aliveness, one that insists upon love against the loveless paradigm of abiding Black death. Kevin Quashie writes of this politics: 'antiblackness is part of blackness but not all of how or what blackness is' (2021: 5), which I elaborate here through Christina Sharpe's assertion that 'we are constituted through and by continued vulnerability to this overwhelming force, *we are not only known to ourselves and to each other by that force*' (2016: 16, my emphasis). This love works against alienation and Black melancholy, enlivening both Kgositsile and Black Americans, blazing their paths, and making them incendiary 'like spear of gods' (1971: 71). Their revolt, Black revolt, should be understood as driven by a deep love and respect for self and the community. This love, as Kgositsile constantly shows, is learnt in the homeplace. With Galekgobe's eye as shadow and companion, and with the strong fabric in his heart that Madikeledi wove *for us*, he demonstrates how his mothers had an impact on futurity.

In 'Towards a Walk in the Sun', he subsequently deploys those spears and their fire for revolutionary ends, as a responsible son would. A key movement of influence and collaboration is revealed in this chapter as it pertains to this poem: the adaptation of a name from this poem in 1968 by the Black Arts era poetry outfit The Last Poets. Central to this is Kgositsile's conceptualization of the diaspora as branches of a tree with roots in Africa; and the relationship between the wind and that tree, which produces song and sound knowledges that Kgositsile dubs 'the birth of memory' (1971: 64). The aesthetics and poetic sensibilities of the poem 'Towards a Walk in the Sun' are drawn and refashioned from L.D. Raditladi's *Motswasele II* (1945), a Tswana drama based on real-life events, which Kgositsile carried with him to America. Kgositsile refashions the saga of a tyrannical king's downfall brought about by the people into the context of diaspora to inspire Black revolt against white supremacy. In the drama, the protagonist arms himself with spears to ensure the oppressive king meets his demise. Kgositsile seeks to arm himself and his Black American compatriots with those spears of the literary and real-life ancestors. As he rallies them into a solidarity dance, we understand Kgositsile to be arming them with spears as an invocation of the 'spear of the nation' or uMkhonto we Sizwe, a gesture of expressing shared experience of racial struggle and collective resistance through politically aligning the African National Congress with the African American civil rights and Black Power Movements.

Further, the language and narrative pace from the Tswana drama form and inform dramatic tension in the poem. The dialogues from the drama are strategically harnessed to imbue the poem with its rhythms, imageries, and symbolisms, but also to underscore communitarian values in the poem, crucial to the eventual release of that collective tension. To ensure its trenchancy in the Black world, Kgositsile expertly interweaves the Tswana literary classic *Motswasele II* with an African American literary classic – Richard Wright's *Native Son* (1940) – as well as African American vernaculars with Tswana sound worlds, to issue a call to action, a war cry. The war cry calls upon the end of 'art talk' and poetry, to which four young poets therefore respond as being the Last Poets. These four budding poets, living in New York amidst a flourishing artistic and literary landscape that flowered in the most tumultuous period of

African American politics, found Kgositsile's poem in the anthology *Black Fire: An Anthology of Afro-American Writing* (1968), published amidst poetry by other luminaries of the time, and were excited and incited to brand themselves after that poem.

Modern-day Moruakgomo Fashioning Spears of the Nation

Leetile Raditladi (1910–72) wrote *Motswasele II* in response to his personal experience of mutiny, betrayal, and exile by Tshekedi Kgama. Born into royalty and as the nephew to Kgama III, Raditladi was in the line of succession to the bogosi (kingship). When Kgama III died, the rightful heir to the throne, four-year-old Seretse Kgama, was too young to succeed, so his uncle Tshekedi Kgama became the regent, or custodian of law and order. This new position granted him a taste of power, rendering him hungry and unscrupulous in his ambitions to retain it. He saw Raditladi as a threat to his reign and concocted a plan to banish him from the Bakwena community. It was these events that led Raditladi to write the drama *Motswasele II*, originally titled *Serukutlhi* (rebel), in which Tshekedi is represented as King Motswasele II, a ferocious dictator and a totalitarian, self-serving autocrat. Discord is sown by that new king in this otherwise peaceful community, leading to the people's decision to topple him. The community rallies behind the drama's protagonist, Moruakgomo, who represents Raditladi, to usurp Motswasele II's throne and take over as the rightful king. Moruakgomo is much loved by his constituents, and the language he uses to gain their support in his decision to kill the king is very important here. Of course, the parallels between Moruakgomo, exiled by an unjust governance, and Kgositsile, are what draws Kgositsile to this text.

Both Raditladi and Kgositsile became fugitives in their own land, and both used literature to fight back. Tshekedi personally made sure Raditladi's text did not get published, sabotaging it for ten years, until it was finally published in the Bantu Treasury Series in 1945. This is not unlike how Kgositsile's work was banned in his country of birth under apartheid. Kgositsile draws inspiration from this literary ancestor to fashion a revolutionary poetics. Moruakgomo's measured and poetic language throughout the drama harnesses the rhythms and sounds of Tswana orality and capitalizes on alliterations and internal rhyming inherent in the language, lending it a musical register. Compared to king Motswasele's commandeering, rigid, and cold speech befitting an autocratic leader, Moruakgomo's well-thought, deeply felt, and passionately rendered monologues and public addresses set him apart from the king as a leader with heart. He exhorts the community into action against the king through using parables, folklore, and references to historical events, never using the 'I' pronoun but always speaking through the collective voice of the Bakwena. He renounces his individualism for the whole, deploying the language of the sun, moon, stars, and skies, to articulate sympoeisis between his peoples' grievances and the broader natural phenomena. This way, he casts light on the disharmony affecting the natural working totality of the larger whole, thereby ensuring his words and decisions are welcomed by his audience as a natural course of action.

Inspired by the dexterity with which the words are woven with heart and political action, Kgositsile fashions himself into a modern Moruakgomo, using Raditladi's salient dialogues as model. The dialogues represent what Kgositsile wrote in his short story 'Ab/original Mask', set in a fictional place on the African continent called 'Sun Valley' where 'in their language, the people never spoke directly about a thing, they spoke around it so that it stood out more clearly' (1969a: 57). This is the language we see in *Motswasele II*, a constant cajoling, negotiation, collaboration, and dance with language, reflecting the awareness and commensurate relation with a living and constantly moving universe. Here is Moruakgomo's opening soliloquy in which the theme of toppling the king is communicated:

> Rra, tsatsi jaanong le wela ka kgala
> Bosigo bo tla bo suma bo tswa kgakala,
> Bo ikala le boatlhamo jwa lefatshe
> Jaaka mosadi a ala phate fatshe.
> Jaanong ke nako ya dinaledi go rena
> Pele ga mohumagadi, ngwedi, a rena.
> Bakwena ba re Motswasele ga se kgosi, modipa,
> O tlhoka o ka mo phunyang ka lerumo dimpa;
> Ba batla ke dira, ke ba direla serena (Raditladi 1945: 3, my emphasis).

He speaks well, appeasing the people with poetic language which, rendered through my own translations, reads:

> Rra, the sun is sinking below
> darkness is descending upon us from afar
> covering the expansive breadth of our land
> like a woman's loincloth blanketing the ground.
> It is now time for the stars to alight
> and accompany our great matriarch the moon.
> The Bakwenas lament that Motswasele is not an honourable king
> they need someone to spear his stomach
> they chose me for the deed, to restore their godliness.

Moruakgomo leads with emotive language: there is darkness in the land – 'the sun is sinking below' – and we, the stars, must take action, otherwise we will lose our *serena*, our god-status. *Serena* is a disposition that points to the Southern

African sense of totality with the onto-triad and the living cosmos, in which the living are governed by responsibility for one another, the living dead, and the not-yet-born. The living are responsible for the past and the future, and here Moruakgomo alerts and affirms that there is a danger that threatens this harmony. An understanding of '*ke ba direla serena*', or 'to restore their godliness', is two-fold: first it is tied to restoring the totality/wholeness of the community whose whole is made up of the sum of its parts, understood as gods only insofar as they retain a godly status. It lends itself to Tswana/Sotho/Pedi men addressing one another as *morena*, or god. The second reading of '*ke ba direla serena*' connotes restoring their dignity, as *serena* also means dignity. Revolutionary action is taken for purposes of restoring that totality, fuelled by a historical demand to preserve their social order that never allowed for structures of relation based on domination. To borrow from Cedric Robinson, the impetus to preserve this 'ontological totality [is] granted by a metaphysical system that had never allowed for property in either the physical, philosophical, temporal, legal, social, or psychic senses' (2000: 168). Therefore, the dishonourable and self-serving forces of Tshekedi or the apartheid regime have to be uncompromisingly repudiated. This will become important for Kgositsile in his dramatic address to the African American community in 'Towards a Walk in the Sun'.

In the closing scene of *Motswasele II*, Moruakgomo shows the king that those who threaten the dignity and totality of their land and people must necessarily meet their fate at the point of a spear. Even when Moruakgomo is facing Motswasele one-on-one in the final scene, he is possessed by the collective desire of his people, embodying their charge and decision. The final blow by the spear to the king in the stomach symbolizes the politics of the mouth, stomach, phallus, and buttocks in African literature that address and lampoon self-serving, avaricious, and lecherous tendencies of postcolonial leaders (Mbembe 1992). The spear used to end the darkness of Motswasele II's reign is also the spear the ANC intended to use to end the dark reign of apartheid rule: uMkhonto we Sizwe, or 'the spear of the nation', redirecting the past for heroic purposes to intervene in the present. The spear of the nation is the spear of gods.

This is the politics of Love and Care, resounding the community's depthoffeeling, and rooted in the people's active history. During the second Chimurenga in Rhodesia, the leaders of the liberation army sang the song 'Mbuya Nehanda': 'Grandmother Nehanda / you prophesied, / Nehanda's bones resurrected, / ZANU's spear caught their fire / which was transformed into ZANU's gun, / the gun which liberated our land' (in Keller 2005: 145). These regional articulations of revolutionary politics are critical for understanding solidarity politics: like the 'grandchildren of Nehanda' in neighbouring Zimbabwe, Kgositsile touches his heart and moves, reminded of his purpose, of the historical demand encapsulated in his grandmother's instruction – 'don't ever take any nonsense from them, you hear!' – which instructs him to transform spears into revolutionary guns, just like the ZANU revolutionaries. Through song, he ritualizes this moment to signal not only destruction but also creation, heralding the birth of a new dawn. The opening of 'Towards a Walk in the Sun' seeks to approximate that heartfelt address by Moruakgomo, in which Kgositsile utilizes erotics of relationality and interiority:

> THE WIND IS CARESSING
> THE EVE OF A NEW DAWN
> A DREAM: THE BIRTH OF
> MEMORY (1971: 64)

The birth of memory signals the past as messianic, but not the past that is relegated to the realm of dated primordial times in colonial terms; this memory that will be rebirthed in the new dawn is defined by Kgositsile as simultaneously the past, present, and future. He writes: 'when what you do to make your life meaningful is upset by outside forces, your life takes on a certain immediacy, so that your present, past, and future are simultaneous; they are all NOW' (cited in Snyder 1995). The birth of memory is the embarkation upon the future through reclaiming and asserting the past in the present. In couching his message in natural terms, he situates the new dawn as imminent and inevitable. This is tied to the last stanza, itself capitalized to signal a return to the above opening stanza, in which 'THIS WIND YOU HEAR IS THE BIRTH OF MEMORY' (1971: 64): the transition from 'the wind' to 'this wind' tells us the time has arrived! The time to transforms spears into guns is upon the people.

Kgositsile rallies 'native sons' in Black America towards revolutionary action, opening a poetics of relation by granting them a political home in the liberation army. This was heard and taken to heart through the evolution of this poem by The Last Poets, who adopted a new identity from it, one whose genealogies are not the Middle Passage, one whose history brings to the fore the type of war that Kgositsile proposes, one that is about more than just slitting the enemy's throat, one that seeks to restore dignity and godly status (*serena*) to disgruntled native sons. Their new name maps different historical trajectories and geographical landmarks, specific traditions, and modus operandi.

Roots of the Old Tree Defy Death: The Last Poets

On 19 May 1968, a commemorative festival was held at Harlem's Marcus Garvey Park, in New York City's Brooklyn borough, to mark the third anniversary of Malcolm X's death. A group of young performers had just enjoyed a positive reception at that festival and decided to form a poetry outfit. As member Abiodun Oyewole (self-defined 'student-poet' at the time) reports in the *New York Amsterdam News* of 24 October 1981, David Nelson 'knew that history had been made on this 19th day of May 1968', but the group did not have a name. Nelson, considered by Gylan Kain ('the preacher') as 'the true poet of the group', went in search of a name in the revolutionary 'bible' of the Black Power Movement – an anthology of the Black Arts Movement that served as a manifesto of the time, *Black Fire: An anthology of Afro-American Writing*. At 680 pages, *Black Fire*, edited by Amiri Baraka and Larry Neal, collected together some of the most ground-breaking poetry, short stories, essays, and plays produced by the milieu, written by capable writers who would go on to become voices of their generation, from Amiri Baraka, Sonia Sanchez, and Stokely Carmichael, to Sun Ra, Harold Cruse, Ed Bullin, and Henry Dumas.

Nelson navigated the writings of great luminaries in the galaxy of poetic stars, encountering on his quest an offering by Kgositsile, a call to arms, a command to collective action, a prophecy of a new dawn about to break – a poem whose language 'lunges, strains its muscles' but also 'barks or howls [...] or screams', as characterized by Gwendolyn Brooks in her introduction to *My Name is Afrika* (1971: 1). Drawing from the great orators of his land, exemplified by Moruakgomo, the language and charge of 'Towards a Walk in the Sun' implicates the reader in an unfolding historical saga and the enfolding future demands that are heaving in the present moment. Upon reading this poem, the erudite Nelson had accomplished his mission, arrested in the moment by the force of its poetics culled from elsewhere, vibrating with possibility.

The poem sets its dramatic dirge, tension, confrontation, and eventual release in its capitalization of the opening and closing stanza. The opening stanza leads into the theme of the first part of the poem, rendered much like the way *Motswasele II* is structured, with the first half concerned with the community in dialogue with itself, in the grips of its own embattled existence. Kgositsile asks: 'who are we? Who / were we?' (1971: 64), preparing for a sustained self-examination of the community's consciousness, the extent of its self-awareness, its malaise and complicity in its own violation. Donning the robes and role of the poet in a traditional society, to use his own formulation, Kgositsile understands his responsibility to be 'the distilled voice of the community', 'a kind of receptacle of the feelings and the spirit of the community', 'partly historian, partly philosopher, partly the consciousness of the community, and partly a singer and entertainer' (1978: 37). The full spectrum of these roles is observed in 'Towards a Walk in the Sun'. He sings:

> Where, oh where are
> The men to matches
> The fuse to burn the
> Snow that freezes some
> Wouldbe skyward desire (1971: 64)

In adopting the tenor and register of song at the beginning of the poem, he strives to speak from the chorus, to imbue himself with the spirit of the community, to announce allegiance and intimacy with the community before launching his critique. In appropriating the dirge or funeral song, 'where, oh where', he invokes a hymnic scale, prayer in the tenor of African American spirituals, exploiting the capaciousness of that sound which historically contained deep sorrow, joy, rapture, ecstasy, and registers of repair. He interweaves himself with his poetic historical traditions as part historian and part philosopher, speaking to the collective feelings of the community. The sonic substance of spirituals speaks to the hearts and inner worlds of the people, their conscience, opening them up to be receptive of his message.

As a poet of the revolution, a poet who strives to be the consciousness of the community, Kgositsile owes the community some truth about itself, a self-inquiry, and self-examination. He addresses them: 'you who swallowed your balls for a piece / of gold' (1971: 64). His agenda is to put fire in their hands, to congregate 'men to matches / the fuse to burn' the regime of white power they are subjected to, but the men are trapped in a consumerist culture and have sold their manhoods for a piece of gold. 'Gold' here is historically and politically loaded, as discussed in detail in the previous chapter. Foregrounding racial capitalism is a pivotal move for Kgositsile as he straddles these vast geographical contexts; he speaks to the mining industrial complex that is foundational to Southern African modernity, which he routes over here to co-exist alongside the foundations of American modernity and capitalism: slavery. Speaking from America to Africa and from Africa to America, it is essential that he be a receptacle of the people's feelings underscored by their exploitation and thingification in the making of colonial modernity. In the first half of the poem, he speaks of the gold as 'beautiful from afar but far from / beautiful' (1971: 64),[1] hiding the realities of its histories of violence and Black obliteration, obfuscating 'the pus from your brother's callouses'. He warns of the trappings of modernity, which are corrupt and corrupting and always marked by the historical stain of Black death.

Inspired by the events of history and demands of the future, as well as stylistic innovations by Moruakgomo in *Motswasele II*, Kgositsile initiates a process of conscientizing those who do not have eyes in this moment to see the reality of their times. The eyes reference their conscience, and their 'sight is colored with snow', those who might be deluded by the sophisticated workings of the system, the assimilated who believe in the status quo as the only possibility for them: the hoodwinked and bamboozled. They have 'swallowed [their] conscience', as he writes in the poem. He holds a mirror up to reflect the horrors of their

---

[1] This saying could very well be from the tsotsitaal, *'mooi van ver maar ver van mooi'*, which is in line with the saying 'all that glitters is not gold'.

existence, with 'soul numbed', declaring to see them even if they 'creep' and 'hide', exploit their own brothers, sell their own sisters, or poison their own mothers. Kgositsile underlines the imperative to be responsible for one another. In many ways his attack is waged from a place of Love and Care, responsibility and respect for self and community shaped by communitarian values: in seeing them he recognizes them and acknowledges their lived realities, loving them at their worst, and believing in love's transformative and redemptive power. As self-appointed poet of the revolution, it is crucial for him to speak from the community not as an outsider but as its member, dealing with the entirety of its troubles, not just the 'glorious' parts. He seeks to raise their collective consciousness.

The figure of Bigger Thomas from Richard Wright's classic *Native Son* (1940) comes up as an immediate example and symbol of this depraved person being addressed in the opening of 'Towards a Walk in the Sun' and is referenced in its closing stanza. In many ways, he represents a cautionary tale against what Kgositsile calls 'revolutionary soloism' (1986: 31), the socio-political malaise that, in his view, plagued Bigger to act in blind rebellion without the collective, without discipline or purpose, turning his activity into criminality as it is driven by neither Love nor Care, but instead individualism. He agonizes over Bigger's misdirected anger which would have been transformed into a productive force of collective action if Bigger had been acting in and on behalf of the community. In an interview with Danill Taylot-Guthrie, he muses: 'if we understand a Bigger Thomas in Chicago, we are equipped to grasp their South African counterpart. Bigger Thomas did not belong to a movement. What happens to Bigger Thomas when he is part of Umkhonto we Sizwe, the ANC's liberation army, and has learned a sense of accountability?' (Taylor-Guthrie 1996: 37). Bigger becomes for Kgositsile an example of why no revolutionary can act on his own. Even when Moruakgomo faced the tyrannical Motswasele to spear him to death, it had been in conference with the community, and he had been charged by that community to act. That is accountability. He thus stands before the African American community in this moment, calling them to unite towards the necessary action. He deploys the images of spears to invoke both Moruakgomo's action as well as uMkhonto we Sizwe, the ANC's liberation army to which he now seeks to enlist African Americans.

As Kgositsile states above, 'if we understand a Bigger Thomas in Chicago, we are equipped to grasp their South African counterpart'. In South Africa around the same time, the Black Consciousness Movement (BCM) was burgeoning, also warring to save the minds and consciousness of would-be self-destructive individuals. The lamentation in 'Towards a Walk in the Sun' would be echoed in Stephen Biko's words, written in 1969 but published in 1978:

> The type of Black man we have today has *lost his manhood*. Reduced to an obliging shell, he looks with awe at the white power structure and accepts what he regards as the 'inevitable position'. Deep inside his anger mounts at the accumulating insult, but he vents it in the wrong direction – on his fellow man in the township, on the property of Black people. […] His heart *yearns for the comfort of white society* and makes him blame himself for not having been 'educated' enough to warrant such luxury. All in all the Black man has become a shell, a shadow of man, completely defeated, drowning in his own misery, *a slave*, an ox bearing the yoke of oppression with *sheepish timidity* (Biko 1978: 28–9, my emphasis).

On both sides of the Atlantic, the *Black man* is a political subject fighting for his humanity, 'deballed', with the 'knees of [his] soul numbed by endless kneeling to catch the crumbs from [his] master's table' (Kgositsile 1971: 64)). He swallowed his balls and his conscience and has now become a shell, a shadow of a man, a slave who is politically ineffective. The androcentric nature of these passages cannot go unremarked. One notices it in Kgositsile's congregating of native sons, and not native daughters. While Kgositsile is invested in duly performing the important work of faithfully witnessing the matriarchive, of responding to its demands to transform fire into action, his position and privilege as a Black man in these circuits of exchange at times occasion myopic limitations to his poetics, as seen in 'Towards a Walk in the Sun'. Even when there is an active absence of the matriarchive consciously woven in his message, Kgositsile's gendered language falls into the traps of reproducing the preoccupation with the symbolic castration of Black men by white power, dominant in this milieu. This was the case not only in the Black Arts, Black Power, and Black Consciousness Movements, but pervasive in post-independent and postcolonial political philosophy.

BCM scholar Vern Cromartie convincingly argues that Biko must have read Kgositsile: 'Kgositsile was a key figure in the Black Arts Movement in the USA and a native of South Africa. It is highly unlikely that the well-read Biko did not know of Kgositsile's impressive body of literary work' (2018: 130). Biko's seminal *I Write What I Like* (1978) brings the voices of Frantz Fanon and Kgositsile, among others (such as Ralph Ellison), into conversation to underscore the global nature of Black oppression. When we read Biko's definitive manifesto of the BCM, his theories bear resonances of Kgositsile's 'Towards a Walk in the Sun'. As a political theorist, Biko seeks to make the Black man return to himself; as a poet of revolution, Kgositsile is concerned with the same; their prognoses align:

> The first step therefore is to make the Black man come to himself; to pump back life into his empty shell; to infuse him with pride and

dignity, to *remind him of his complicity* in the crime of allowing himself to be misused and therefore letting evil reign supreme in the country of his birth. This is what we mean by an *inward-looking process*. This is the definition of 'Black Consciousness' (Biko 1978: 29, my emphasis).

Kgositsile uses this methodology in 'Towards a Walk in the Sun', rejecting any convenient fallacies that might be used as balm in this battle, such as 'I have a glorious past'. He lambastes escapist rhetoric to strip the community bare of its protective narratives, in favour of a naked truth: we need to end this world, NOW. The end of the world is the call to decoloniality, to ending the system of relation based on domination, exploitation, and obliteration of Black people under the auspices of a teleological progress narrative; it must be exploded! The second part of the poem is a steady road to this climatic end, with the turning point of the poem asking again as he did at the beginning, 'who are we?', now quivering and confrontational as we collectively stand facing the naked truth of our realities. Adopting an 'I' pronoun for the first time in the poem to express his despair, intricately linked to the collective despair – 'I listen ... I yearn' – the poet laments the dream that might become a nightmare. These desires are tied to memory and keep him up all night listening to the haunting sounds of history's demands, the demands of the gods 'soaring like the tide'. The line 'All night long I listen to the dream' is a direct reference to the 'new dawn' mentioned earlier, and the 'newborn fire' that the *son* must be rebirthed with as the *sun*, to burn down the dominant culture and political paradigm. The question 'where are we' punctuates the second part of the poem with alienation and dispossession brought about by slavery and enforced exiles, leading into the choreographed song and dance of the poem's climactic ending:

> THE WIND YOU HEAR IS THE BIRTH OF MEMORY
> WHEN THE MOMENT HATCHES IN TIME'S WOMB
> THERE WILL BE NO ART TALK. THE ONLY POEM
> YOU WILL HEAR WILL BE THE SPEARPOINT PIVOTED
> IN THE PUNCTURED MARROW OF THE VILLAIN; THE
> TIMELESS NATIVE SON DANCING LIKE CRAZY TO
> THE RETRIEVED RHYTHMS OF DESIRE FADING IN-
>   TO MEMORY (1971: 64)

The poet attunes his African American readership to the wind that is caressing the eve of the new dawn, carrying a dream, flowing and coursing through their lands, continents, and bodies, announcing its birth. He centres the wind through the ecosomatics-geopoetics matrix to position himself as possessing and being possessed by the spirit, breath, and air from the bodies of the mothers, bodies of the land, bodies of knowledge, and celestial bodies.

From that position he commands his community to be party to the collapse of this regime and the birth of a new dawn that can only be possible through the ending of all talk, of all poetry, and taking up arms. The wind operates within a poetics of suture, felt not only by him but by the 'timeless native son' in America, entangled with roots that defy death, that continue to weave him into a strong tapestry of song to which he must now dance, in unison with this poet, towards the enemy, armed with retrieved rhythms of spears of the gods as they collectively launch into the enemy, like Moruakgomo's descendants. This collective action by native sons is crucial as it is underwritten by accountability to one another, to history and the future. To this declaration of the end of art talk, David Nelson responded 'therefore we are The Last Poets of the world' (in Oyewole 2014), taking the message to his fellow poets and ending their search for a name.

Kgositsile: 'The Original Last Poet'

In the epigraph to his *Branches of the Tree of Life* (2014), in a poem/supplication titled 'Invocation', Abiodun Oyewole expounds:

>And a South African poet named Kgositsile said:
>
>THE WIND YOU HEAR IS THE BIRTH OF MEMORY
>WHEN THE MOMENT HATCHES IN TIME'S WOMB
>THERE WILL BE NO ART TALK.
>[...]
>Therefore we are The Last Poets of the world
>Said David Nelson, Gylan Kain,
>Felipe Luciano, Umar Bin Hassan, Jalal Nuriddin,
>Suliman El hadi, Abiodun Oyewole, and
>The heartbeat Nilija (Obabi)
>[...]
>We, The Last Poets, are the seeds
>For the rap artists to grow a garden
>And yet we are only a branch
>From the tree called Griot

David Nelson, Gylan Kain, Felipe Luciano, and Abiodun Oyewole heard the messages in the wind, felt their urgency, and entered a timeless multidirectional dialogue across the Atlantic. Oyewole reflects: 'we liked the name and felt it would suit our purpose' (2014: xx); and he notes that 'it gives you something to strive for when you have a meaningful name'.[2] Names, as stated in the previous

---

[2] Author interview with Abiodun Oyewole, New York, August 2014.

chapter, mark rites of passage in which the old dies and the new is born; they mark a rebirth. Further, they index a lineage, marking belonging and mapping particular historical, cultural, and geographical events. They also advance the mission of the lineage, working within their tradition and driving their purpose forward. As Oyewole understands, 'the poem stated clearly our position as a people in a struggle and made a direct statement as to the future of our struggle and our imminent victory'.[3] Kgositsile's clear vision of decolonization and commitment to social transformation entangles the mission of his homeplace, the national liberation movement (uMkhonto we Sizwe), the family, and wider community within which the new members of The Last Poets are registered as part of the lineage.

On 'collaborating' with Kgositsile, Oyewole asserts that 'it meant everything to connect with the mother, with mother Africa, period. The one thing they tried to do was cut the umbilical cord [...]. It can never be cut'.[4] This type of gendered assertion of identity and roots has been critiqued by scholars such as Florence Stratton (1994) as problematic, and it is, considering the gender parities of the Black Arts Movement at the time. Nevertheless, the communal relationship extended by Kgositsile's poem to these four men offered them a meeting place where they could encounter otherwise possibilities. Paul Gilroy reminds us:

> The intense and often bitter dialogues which make the Black Arts Movement move offer a small reminder that there is a democratic, communitarian moment enshrined in the practice of antiphony which symbolizes and anticipates new, non-dominating social relationships. Lines between self and other are blurred and special forms of pleasure are created as a result of the meetings and conversations that are established between one fractured, incomplete, and unfinished racial self and others. (1993: 79)

When I interviewed Oyewole in 2014, he revisited the 1960s with nostalgic fervour, reciting and chanting that stanza from Kgositsile's poem, almost thirty years later, verbatim, from memory, singing the praise song of The Last Poets' lineage. As he calls it 'Invocation', it is the prayer, the summoning, the petitioning of presence, it is to ritually invite the presence of ancestors, to appease, entreat, and supplicate his lineage for fortitude, protection, and resilience. The symbolism of the umbilical cord is not unlike how Kgositsile reaches into his navel for the soil that buries his mother to retrieve a 'fire song' – it is a relational poetic that positions all as equally incomplete, as 'fractured, incomplete, and [racially] unfinished', seeking a return to the whole, even when

---

[3] Ibid.
[4] Ibid.

their historical, linguistic, and geographical differences distinguish them. The Black sonic metaphor of heterophony generates what Fumi Okiji refers to as an 'empathetic mode of sociality' (2018: 6) in which 'the parties involved approach or adapt to each other in a manner that supports the retention of their particularities' (73). I stress radical empathy as productive of this retelling, recitation, resounding, repetition, and reworking that inherently invites further adaptation and reimagining. Empathy has its foundation in the homeplace first, in the formative years, before expressing itself in the community and larger society.

In the crucial moment of packing Raditladi's *Motswasele II*, of impending and indefinite exile, Kgositsile could not have envisioned that it would be transformed to a resource base for African American cultural production and a crucial foundation of their countercultural moment. To continue in Oyewole's metaphor of The Last Poets as 'the seeds / for the rap artists to grow a garden', Raditladi's drama *Motswasele II* is a tree nourished by the roots of Setswana orality and orature, mythology and symbolism. The text represents spores which the wind, Kgositsile, carried across the Atlantic to new lands. This is metonymic of diaspora – whose Greek botanic etymology refers to the scattering or dispersion of botanical spores, reminiscent of Kgositsile's imaginings of the diaspora as branches of a tree with roots in Africa. These spores and/or branches are from 'the tree called Griot', growing in adverse new conditions, adapted into the poem 'Towards a Walk in the Sun'. The spore of Kgositsile's poem, from the griot tree, cultivated The Last Poets' poetry/rap across the Atlantic, which subsequently grew the garden of rap. If The Last Poets are the purported grandfathers of rap, then Kgositsile is symbolically an ancestor of that Black expressive tradition in a cultural continuum with the griot. This is how The Last Poets cannot sing their name without looking to Southern Africa, paradigmatic of how the historiography of the Black Arts Movement is incomplete without Kgositsile, and the mapping of BAM exclusionary without detouring to South Africa.

So much did they love their new identity that they titled their debut album *The Last Poets* (1970). The album reached the US Top Ten Chart, unusual for such an unpopular genre referred to as 'chanted rap poetry classics' (Powell 1991: 246). On the album cover, they are adorned with afros and dashikis, posing with their conga drum on a sidewalk that could very well be any Black ghetto on the African continent or its diaspora. Their self-styling represents the move from the misnomer 'negro' to the signifier 'Black' and 'African', precipitated by the Black Power Movement and espousing an African sensibility. As proponents of the Black Arts era changed their names respectively from LeRoi Jones, Don Lee, Rolland Snellings, and Paulette Williams, to Amiri Baraka, Haki Madibhuti, Askia Toure, and Ntozake Shange, in their efforts to denounce their 'slave names', Kgositsile seems to shout, as Margo Crawford argues, 'I was born in the ground you claim'; Crawford goes on to say that Kgositsile 'emphasized that he represents the materiality of Africa sometimes effaced in African-American fantasies of the motherland' (2007: 113). In encountering Kgositsile's work, the motherland shifted from the fantasy of a romanticized, glorious past of great civilizations to a coeval continent under colonial siege. The name 'the last poets' can be seen as emblematic of this: the last shall be first, the last being the first poets, the griots, imbongi (praise poets), and bards, continually materializing with a living history now presented by Kgositsile.

Dorian Lynskey rightly situates The Last Poets 'at the nexus of Black America's two most radical art forms: poetry and jazz' (2011: 181). In addition, they crucially bridged the Black expressive cultures of the 1960s and 1970s – explosive speeches, spoken word poetry, jazz, bebop, soul – with the emergent tradition of rap. Earl Stewart and Jane Duran argue that 'rappers are more closely allied to the Black poetic tradition than the tradition of Black music' and that 'their art must be seen as yet another manifestation of the conjunction of Black poetry and Black music, a conjunction which [...] has deep historical roots' (1999: 51). These roots are elucidated by Kgositsile as follows:

> When rap started in the States [...] they were consciously attempting to reclaim that African oral tradition. And today the more serious rappers, the ones that the industry will not try to promote to shove down people's throats all over the worlds, is still trying to do that, and when you read it on the page, it is poetry by any standard.[5]

Rather than rehashing the argument that rap is poetry, here my focus is on mapping genealogies and trajectories of these expressive cultures and Kgositsile's pivotal position therein. This emphatically recasts multiple locations of the Black modernity they engender, not solely and exclusively in North America, not wholly defined by routes, and not arrived solely via the Middle Passage.

Timeless Songs in the Wind, in the Bloodline

Motswasele II formed the foundation for the poem 'Towards a Walk in the Sun', which is itself invested in futurity, like a relay marathon, in which Kgositsile passes the baton he received from Madikeledi who encouraged him to read in Setswana to members of The Last Poets. That baton was then passed to a generation of rappers, continuing to find relevance, resonance, and strategic transformation in the contemporary hip hop age. We have seen the value of this intergenerational inheritance, theorized as a Black sonic practice of 'digging in

---

5   Author interview with Keorapetse Kgositsile, Pretoria, April 2014.

the crates', in which rap's self-referential method and citational practices that sound the collective utterance is history-making, while simultaneously future-making.

Drawing attention to intergenerational dialogues, I turn to the Johannesburg-based hip hop outfit 'Tumi and the Volumes' (T&V), the first in South Africa to perform with a band, exploring the influences of jazz, funk, and blues. Just like The Last Poets, T&V's lead, Tumi Molekane, is affiliated more to the Black poetic tradition than the tradition of Black music, and was introduced to the Johannesburg spoken word scene as a member of the nine-member poetry outfit PERM. Molekane was born to exiled South African parents in Tanzania and 'returned' to South Africa to settle in Johannesburg, becoming a permanent feature on the spoken word scene. His work explores issues of identity and belonging, and his upbringing is central to his artistic sensibilities and diasporic consciousness. His art represents the conjunction of Black poetry and Black music, illustrated in him featuring performance poet Lebogang Mashile, as well as Kgositsile, on his albums; poets who have both taken to the jazz form as a vanguard that grounds their poetic in a larger Black experience.

The tradition within which Kgositsile worked attracted Molekane, who invited the elder poet to appear on the hip hop album *Tumi and the Volumes* (2006). Molekane believed that 'we need to treasure [artists like Kgositsile] by creating systems that promote the passing down of their genius. It is the tree from which today's talent picks from' (Mazaza n.d.). The metaphor of the tree is once more invoked, and has, in the example of Kgositsile's life and work, grown in different directions, with branches clasping diaspora skies and growing new fruits there while he was in exile, simultaneously nurturing the Black Consciousness era in apartheid South Africa, and later nourishing Black youth culture in post-apartheid South Africa.

Kgositsile's collaboration with T&V produced the track 'Johnny Dyani'. The track draws from the poem titled after the eponymous jazz double bassist from legendary exiled South African jazz band The Blue Notes. On T&V's album, the track features Kgositsile's melodic and jazzy voice reciting over an outstanding bass line from the band's bassist Dave Bergman. Kgositsile, Dyani, and Molekane, three South Africans in exile, converge on this track, with the younger wordsmith retrieving Kgositsile's and Dyani's 'rhythms' out of the otherwise shelved archives into the collective memory of post-94 youth culture. This is the work of 'digging in the crates' that perpetually waters the Black expressive cultural continuum. Lifestyle journalist Percy Mabandu writes that all jazz records are connected, 'plugged into one another through an infinite web of band membership, themes, and composition revisitations' (2014). Similarly, Kgositsile's poem on T&V's album weaves an infinite web of transnational jazz figures, ensembles, and compositions: a key site of stereomodernism (Jaji 2014). Mabandu meditates on the 'excesses of Kgositsile's poem' on the T&V album:

> Consider, for instance, that moment you first encountered the name of the great jazz bassist Johnny Dyani through a poem by Keorapetse Kgositsile off Tumi and the Volume's eponymous album. Your curiosity whet, you type Dyani's name into Google. The search engine returns a number of his albums, including the 1978 SteepleChase release *Song for Biko*. Snagged by that revolutionary's familiar name, you check out that album to discover a tune titled *Joburg – New York*. While listening to it, you might be struck by a trumpeter called Don Cherry. […] This discovery brings you back to the home circuit, where more records sustain the elaborate network and economy of meaning. (2014)

There is much more one can add to Mabandu's exploration of the Black expressive terrain mapped by Black South Africans' collaborations with Black Americans: for instance, digging in the Don Cherry crate reveals another album, *Blue Lake* (1971), recorded with jazz pianist Abdullah Ibrahim, who was introduced to Duke Ellington by Sathima Bea Benjamin, Ibrahim's wife, whose name 'Sathima' was bequeathed by Johnny Dyani. And the web grows even greater. T&V's song and Kgositsile's poem open a world of meaning, a transnational figuration of rap, jazz, and poetry in the stereomodern twentieth century that continues into the twenty-first century. Naming and other forms of association create vibrant and codified circuitries of meaning: Dyani's *Song for Biko* gives a frame of reference to the spirit of that album, and an understanding of who Stephen Biko was, and what he stood for certainly adds to the appreciation of the music.

Similarly, the name 'The Last Poets' opens up an elaborate network of meaning that might help to contextualize their politics. Typing their name into Google, the search engine returns a number of articles that point to Kgositsile as the source of their name. Dyani's composition 'Joburg – New York' frames Kgositsile's journey and relationship with Black America, resounded by Gil Scott-Heron – whom Google would have certainly brought up with The Last Poets – in his album *From South Africa to South Carolina* (1975). This remaps feeling/listening and phonography as a geography of shared anti-Black struggle in both countries. Scott-Heron's song 'Johannesburg', for example, ends with the declaration, 'L.A.'s like Johannesburg / New York's like Johannesburg'. Such is the power of naming and cross-generational homage through historical references and cultural archaeology.

The intergenerational dialogues fostered by Molekane are crucial to the work of retrieval, particularly reworking through reclaiming lost archives of exile. Featuring Kgositsile is both a homage to the elder statesman's role in the anti-apartheid struggle and Molekane's mother's participation[6] therein – stories of exile that never quite made a 'return'. The song and struggle are everpresent in the blood, passed from generation to generation in the Black family tree. His specific form, 'jazz rap' or 'jazz hip hop' is spearheaded by the likes of A Tribe Called Quest, whose second album, as Joseph Patel observes, establishes 'a consummate link between generations, taking the essence of jazz and the essence of hip hop and showing they originated from the same Black centre' (2003: 25). An often-cited rhyme on the track 'Excursion' from A Tribe Called Quest's 1991 album *The Low End Theory* speaks of the mutual influences between Black expressive cultures. Here, Q-Tip raps about when he, as a teenager, listened to hip hop: 'My pops used to say it reminded him of bebop / I said "well daddy don't you know that things go in cycles?" / "Way that Bobby Brown is just ampin' like Michael [Jackson]"'. 'Excursion' cites a dialogue from The Last Poets' track titled 'Time' from their 1971 album *This is Madness*, the title track of which features tenor saxophonist Pharoah Sanders, whose album *Thembi* (1971) contains liner notes in the form of a poem written by Kgositsile ('Pro/creation', 1974b).

'Pro/creation' speaks to intergenerational citational practices in Black expressive cultures: in the process of creating one is always procreating, as Kgositsile believes, drawing from the collective reservoir and sounding the community in that heterophonic sense. The title speaks of continuity and re/birth in the cycles, which can be studied between the hip hop generation and those of jazz and poetry. Q-Tip of A Tribe Called Quest tells us that he grew up in a household 'filled with music [...] My father listened to Duke Ellington, Miles Davis and John Coltrane' (in Murph 2002), demonstrating a musical lineage of jazz and hip hop: 'from a practical standpoint, the artists' parents and siblings often had record collections that were readily available and could be used to sample' (Williams 2010: 441). The introduction and access to their parents' physical archives of records by the next generation transported them as listeners to different eras, sounds, dialogues, and histories. In her DJ scholarship, Lynnée Denise (2013) offers four critical components of this dynamic: chasing sampling, digging through the crates, album cover art, and liner notes as sites of multiplicity in which sonic registers of Blackness across generations, genres, and socio-political histories can be studied. We can locate physical matriarchives in the form of these inherited record collections.

In a conversation between Mark Anthony Neal and Fred Moten, Neal argues for the place of Blackwomen in Black history and culture by referring to Afrika

---

[6] 'I was in Morogoro. My parents were terrorists you see. So that's where they had all the babies and the kids were born', he tells *MindMap* magazine (in Mthembu 2012: 19). His parents were in Morogoro, Tanzania, where that government had given the ANC a plot of land from which to run their affairs.

Bambaata's claim that the first two hundred albums he owned were from his mother's collection: 'So if we are asking where are the women in this tradition *they are in the crate*. It was his mother's curating of the crate that drew him to the music'. Moten adds:

> That's my collection too; they are my mom's records. I remember when she had some health issues when I was a young adolescent, she was just out of surgery and sensed that there might be malignancy; it turned out not to be the case. But she wrote letters to me, she said if you want to understand who I am you have to listen to the records. And it was not just to understand who she is, but *who we are* and *what we are*. (2018a, emphasis in the original)

The conversation between Moten and Neal poses a productive task to look against the grain and engage our multisensory perception in locating Blackwomen in the archive and understanding who and what we are. Moten here sounds the matriarchive, eloquently asserting, 'Black culture is in many ways a maternal culture. It is a maternal insurgency!' (2018a). In many ways, the nature of inherited records as forms of heirlooms, capacious archives that root us in a tradition by introducing us to others who like us have imagined the world differently during their time, who have fashioned subversive forms of racial and gender subjectivities to affirm their lives and those of their communities. These archives are always an invitation to comprehend the potential of history in shaping the future, with us, inheritors of the tradition, as active agents. The archives invite intergenerational dialogue through sampling, intergenerational collaborations in the visual and literary arts through the art cover and liner notes, and access to alternative socio-political histories not found in dominant history books or school curricula, thereby having pedagogical elements, too. In the next chapter, for example, we will consider Jamal Cyrus' record installation, which repurposes Kgositsile's 'Towards a Walk in the Sun' as one of many records inherited by this generation, locating the archive of the Black Arts Movement as a vital and vitalizing one for this generation and many to come.

Here, the coming together of Black arts in the States with South African culture is very important in these histories. It seems that any record of 1960s and 1970s Black culture in America will inevitably have the footprint of those South Africans who were in exile. Recently, two important documentaries were released, one titled *Ailey* (2021), on the prolific, pioneering African American dancer Alvin Ailey, and the other one titled *Summer of Soul* (2021) on the 1969 Harlem Cultural Festival. Both reference the music of Hugh Masekela as expressive of a global Black experience. I was also amused to learn that one of my favourite writers, Kiese Laymon, has recently begun publishing under his full name Kiese Makeba Laymon, after the South African singer

Miriam Makeba. There are many such examples. When, in 2020, The Last Poets celebrated their fifty-year anniversary, artists such as Erykah Badu and the poet Aja Monet took to social media to write about the legacy of The Last Poets, pointing to Kgositsile in detailing their genealogy. Perhaps more pertinent is the intimate intergenerational dialogue between Keorapetse Kgositsile and his son, rapper Thebe Neruda Kgositsile (Earl Sweatshirt). He exemplifies an artist whose longevity and mainstay will be ensured by grounding his work in the rich tradition from which he emerges.

Already hailed a supreme lyricist and the most talented member of his Los Angeles-based hip hop crew, Odd Future, when he was just sixteen years of age, Thebe Neruda Kgositsile is a proponent of the rap genre purportedly birthed by the spoken word poetry of The Last Poets. He exemplifies the literal and metaphorical 'pro/creation' – the lineage, in the blood, is carried forward and generates points of departure and points of return, even across the ocean, in the tree branches of the diaspora nourished by roots in Africa. Named after the Chilean poet, whom the older Kgositsile considered the foremost poet of the twentieth century, the gifts of words dreamed for him by his parents – his mother Cheryl Harris is a prolific Law professor at the University of California in Los Angeles, and a writer – was doubly in the blood and in the naming practice. Born in 1994, the year of political rupture in South Africa, Thebe, Tswana for 'shield' – a shield that defends a warrior from launched spears – symbolizes continuity in Kgositsile's life and work, where the personal and the political coalesce. In granting his American-born son a Tswana name, he strove to 'shield' him from the alienation of natal deracination, imbuing him with a consciousness of the ongoing struggles of being Black in this world. 'Neruda' articulates the hopes for the bearer of the name to unapologetically launch dissidence against any injustice through words.

These hopes and dreams weave memory with desire, the past with the future, and ultimately, (South) Africa and the Black diaspora. The dreams, rooted in history, are articulated by Kelefa Sanneh for *The New Yorker*: 'Thebe Kgositsile had a shadow life as a literary character, a projection of other people's enthusiasms and imaginings, long before Odd Future came into existence. [...] This is a baby imbued with the spirit of South Africa's martyred heroes [...]' (2011). This excerpt speaks to the idea of 'pro/creation', that the dreams and vision of a people are couched in song, names, and places, which renders them 'everpresent' 'in the blood', always available for the bearer of the name to access through rituals of re-membering. For Thebe Neruda, working within the tradition of the Black sonic made these memories always already accessible, even when his relationship with his father was strained. Digging in the crates of rap will always bring up the relationship between Kgositsile and The Last Poets, between spoken word and rap, and between spoken word and the oral traditions of African griots and imbongi – a family tree that bears Thebe Neruda on one of its branches. This relationship is emphasized and celebrated in Kgositsile's poem to his son, 'Rejoice' (2002), in which the poet sings a praise song for the veritable presence of the ancestors in the gifted voice of his son. In his 'Rejoice', the older Kgositsile takes it all the way back to the gifted bards of rural South Africa, dubbing Thebe Neruda the 'dreamkeeper' whose 'spontaneous song' and dance pulsate with 'the force of my people's ethos' (2012: 102).

Earl Sweatshirt is deemed by his father to be the 'dreamkeeper', a praise that Kgositsile in the past, in the dedication of his *The Word is Here* (1973), reserved for Langston Hughes, Zora Neale Hurston, Can Themba, Jiyane Magoloane, and Chris Okigbo – all foremothers and forefathers of lived expression that continue to lubricate the churning engines of our collective movements against forces of oppression, in 'spontaneous song' and dance of resistance, joy, belonging, and revolt. The dynamics of the spoken word that evolved from Magoloane – 'the greatest poet of the nineteenth century' (Kgositsile 1973: 3) – evolved to written epics, to other literary forms like the novel and drama, and into rap, persisted through the commitments of dreamkeepers, proponents of 'the word' here to continue in the tradition of their predecessors. Kgositsile locates Earl Sweatshirt in this weave, 'pulsating with the force of my people's ethos', as 'beneficiary of the fruit / harvested from my people's memory', the fruit of the tree, the family tree, the bloodline, the lineage, and the Black collective (2012: 12). The senior praise poet concludes his honorific in the standard formula of that Tswana genre:

> Poet leave him
> Leave him alone
> You have praised him
> You have praised him
> Without knowing his name
> His name is Mouth-that-tells-no-lie (2012: 12)

Again, the poet speaks not as an individual but with the distilled voice of the community representing his predecessors who have made these gifts possible. He writes not as a father, but as a voice of admiration for the preservation of the people's 'memory', which is now giving momentum to a following generation, functioning within a different historical imperative. He does not stake any claims to his rapper son's talents just as he has never articulated any ownership of his own; he believes the word was here long before he was born, and will outlive him, a position that comes with the responsibility as keeper of ancestors' dreams to dispense the word in service of community in the poet's lifetime, to pass the baton and ensure continuity. He concludes the poem on a more personal note with 'mouth-that-tells-no-lie', drawing from one of the five lessons instilled in his grandmother's household, which he went on to impart to his children: to always tell the truth and, in turn, to always be believed. As his daughter

Ipeleng informed me, 'it was a principle, a rule in the house that supported us to stand in our truth'.[7] This intergenerational lesson is the door that sets the next generation on a path to self-trust. It is one of the many immaterial objects from the matriarchive, now in the Black arts archive.

Thebe Neruda's evolution from teen sensation to an adult rapper was underpinned by 'return'. He has found infamy amongst his listenership through incensed and resentful lyrics peppered with misogyny and pubescent angst as part of the group Odd Future, and, at 16, was 'rapping gorgeous scenes of mutilation with the coldness of a bloodless sociopath' (Pearce 2019).The anger was directed towards his mother, too, who ultimately made the decision to send him to remedial boarding school in Samoa, a decision that threw her into the angered awareness and vexed vitriol of her son's fans, for whom he had become a 'profane patron saint' (ibid). His transformation was precipitated by being raised by educators, with his mother educating him on Black history and white supremacy. Here he found his purpose, moving from the alienation and blind rebellion akin to the one that plagued Bigger Thomas, into becoming a responsible and informed member of society in the tradition of the Black collective. Meditating on his album *Some Rap Songs* (2018) he stated, 'I'm trying to communicate myself using sacred theme music for my soul and for people's souls, […] I'm trying to submit this as my contribution to the tapestry. I spent time making sure that it stands out but still fits into something that's bigger than me' (in ibid). This is the desire and hope of a dreamkeeper, a socially responsible bard who accepts their gifts as not theirs alone, but as fruits to nourish the collective.

The politics of love, care, and empathy ground the bearer of gifts in the family and community they are born into and that are ultimately repurposed to fashion culture and revolution. Thebe Neruda's transformation to a dreamkeeper participating in the politics of 'contributing to the tapestry' by serving 'something that's bigger than me' was necessarily a return to Mother, to the matriarchive. In *Some Rap Songs* he makes this clear, acknowledging how the women in his life cared for him during the bad times: 'My cushion was a bosom on bad days / It's not a Black woman I can't thank'. This show of vulnerability also sees the young rapper sharing details of his depression, grief, and sadness, particularly around the death of his father in 2018, three months before the album was released. On the track 'Possum', he produces a sonic bricolage of his mother's keynote address in which she calls Thebe Neruda a 'cultural worker', sewn into a conversation with his father's poem 'Anguish Longer Than Sorrow'. Cheryl Harris used the phrase 'cultural worker' purposefully to link her son's gifts to those of his father. Kgositsile had deployed this phrase, popularised in

---

[7] Personal conversation with author, Johannesburg, 2016.

his 'Culture and Resistance' keynote address in Botswana in 1982, to shun any artist who deviates from their social responsibility; a cultural worker is as vital to society as a nurse and a teacher, there to serve their communities. Here, mother redirects son's energies towards the collective. The album concludes with the track 'Riot', which samples his 'uncle' Hugh Masekela's song. These two tracks locate South Africa in America and assert his South African identity from the position of the Black diaspora. In Sheldon Pearce's words,

> Keorapetse Kgositsile had a great respect for jazz, and he treated it as a sort of entry point into the Black American experience; in a poem for legendary drummer Art Blakey and his collective the Jazz Messengers, Thebe's father once wrote, 'For the sound we revere / we dub you art as continuum / as spirit as sound of depth / here to stay'. In a way, *Some Rap Songs* honors this lineage, serving as a bridge between the jazz of two nations, treating rap as a medium, and serving as a tie-in to his South African heritage. Fittingly, the hard-looping album seems to be closing a few loops of its own: not only linking generations of Black music and finding its place in the continuum, but also tracing Thebe's genealogy. (2019)

This is what the Black sonic can hold in its durability. The sonic – oral, aural, auditory, echo, reverberations, heterophony, ensemble, chorus, digging in the crates, sampling, liner notes, song, and dance – is expressive of forms of relation, solidarity, kinship, community, familial, and intergenerational dialogue underwritten by the politics of Love and Care. Thebe Neruda's next album *Feet of Clay* (2019), a turn of phrase taught to him by his mother, fortifies his conciliatory tenor and heralds a renewed appreciation of the politics of love in which he seeks to ground his work. It deepens his identitarian and aesthetic roots, prompting Craig Jenkins to assert: 'as a poet's son, Earl is serious about the stewardship of the oral tradition. Rappers are descendants of the African griots, Sweatshirt reasons. He worries about the ramifications of the generational disconnect […]' (2018). The 'mouth-that-tells-no-lie' is one that stands in its truth without fear. Bearing this name, carrying this tradition and bloodline, and with roots redirecting the fruits he will bear, we can only look forward to the contribution he seeks to make to the tapestry.

The cosmological outlook in Kgositsile's work aligns with his mission to write poems imbued with African philosophical orientations, ritualistic in their content to sound music and sonic patterns of the collective. This sharp ear towards the Black sonic is an affirmation and assertion of his humanity and sense of belonging in the immediate community and wider society underscored by connectedness to the inner circle of his family, the collective circle, and the global Black community without sacrificing either his roots or the realities of the present. He insists on a humanity that is inclusive and spacious enough for all particularities, one that is not spiritually bankrupt or devoid of love, thereby imbuing his revolutionary politics with a love ethos, transforming the political into the spiritual.

In 2012, a Houston-based art collective comprising three native sons, Otabenga Jones & Associates, through their own act of digging in the crates, found Kgositsile's poem – it could have been via The Last Poets' *Holy Terror* album, or *Black Fire,* the anthology of the Black Arts Movement, or through Kgositsile's own oeuvre; either way, it is through Black music's act of referencing its own history that the terrain of geography as phonography can be mapped, and a historiography documented. The collective was inspired by 'Towards a Walk in the Sun' and collaborated on a project of the same name, which includes an eponymous rap song, record art in the form of collage, and a comic. The next chapter studies the practices found in Otabenga Jones & Associates' work.

4 Spaces: Twenty-First-Century Suns/Sons Must Rise Again

> No futurism is worthwhile
> unless it includes indigenous
> knowledges.
> *Kodwo Eshun*, 'The Algorithmic Poetics'
> (2017a)

Kgositsile's 'Towards a Walk in the Sun' (1971) is a future memory. The poem interweaves and enfolds indigenous knowledges from Southern Africa with new political and aesthetic imperatives of exile in the Black world to produce otherwise possibilities. The 'otherwise' 'bespeaks the ongoingness of possibility, of things existing other than what is given, what is known, what is grasped' (Crawley 2016: 24). Kgositsile harnesses the otherwise from the Tswana literary corpus in his care, which enshrines the cosmologies, languages, mythologies, forms of being and relating, and terms of humanity, which he in turn refashions and transforms to reconfigure the political present in Black America. This chapter focuses on the cosmology of the sun and the native sons to reveal the infinitely generative nature of the Black Arts Movement archive in twenty-first-century African American social movements. In their quest to construct continuities between the past and the future, to walk in the footprints of their predecessors, twenty-first-century Black movements mine the Black arts archive in fashioning a radical imagination that responds to the unfinished project of white supremacy and Black liberation.

It is within this context that the Houston-based arts collective Otabenga Jones & Associates (OJ&A) retrieved 'Towards a Walk in the Sun', adapting it to operate within the realm of visual and material culture, as well as the sonic archive. The poem's radical convergence of two world systems – South African and African American literary classics, aesthetics, and oralities — spurred on that art collective's responses, which are generative and offer new reflections on discourses of Afrofuturism. Further, in framing OJ&A's work as part of dreamkeeping, a practice of intergenerational and ancestral dialogue that converges pastpresentfuture, here I theorize dreamkeeping as a musical practice of 'digging in the crates'. Within this practice, rap's self-referential method and citational practices function as a naming device indexical of Black alternative histories of thought, sounding the antiphonic utterance across space and time. Members of the arts collective respond, as members of The Last Poets did forty years ago, to Kgositsile's call, dancing to his choreographies of transnational native sons, armed with spears to move to the rhythms of retrieved memories from Africa carried by the wind.

The visual adaptation of the poem into an Afrofuturist comic and collage by Robert Pruitt and Jamal Cyrus, respectively, and into a sonic installation by Cyrus presents an opportunity to study the translation and transfiguration of the poem into different media. I return to what Kgositsile said about the native son Bigger Thomas in the previous chapter and in the final stanza of 'Towards a Walk in the Sun':

> Although we have a lot in common in general, brought about from external forces that messed up our development under slavery and colonialism, there are *different histories*. Then the specific or practical hells we inhabit, that we resist against are not identical. But if we understand a Bigger Thomas in Chicago, we are equipped to grasp their South African counterpart (in Taylor-Guthrie 1996: 37, emphasis in original).

Kgositsile highlights and affirms the commonalities that would compel him to foster solidarities with African American struggle – the shared racial struggle – but at the same time wishes to not overlook the 'different histories' that also shape the way 'we resist' and perhaps inform desires for different presents and futures. While the common desire for the end of white supremacy and Black subjection is undeniably the unifying force, the methods and approaches towards those ends are different. In this chapter I investigate differences in solidarity, the disjuncture or 'disarticulations', as referred to by Brent Hayes Edwards, that generate a sense of *décalage* – 'gaps, discrepancies, time-lag, or interval' (2003: 13) – across communities of the Black diaspora marked by difference.

The translations by OJ&A of 'Towards a Walk in the Sun' into visual and sonic cultures in 2012 provide a site in which to analyse these disarticulations. In *Black Post-Blackness*, Margo Crawford contends that when the BAM repudiated the label 'negro' and embraced the identity 'Black', its members were involved in a practice of anticipating the *unthought* – the 'not yet here' (2017: 3, emphasis in original). Crawford's book thereby 'opens up a space in which the not yet here of the 1960s and early 1970s Black Arts Movement converges with the not yet here of early twenty-first-century African American literature and visual arts' (3). She thus imbues the BAM's aesthetic and politics with an anticipatory currency, which is 'deeply tied to the future' (31). The socio-political currency of the *unthought* is crucial in both eras. I suggest here that we read Kgositsile's 'Towards a Walk in the Sun' as attempts to achieve the unthinkable: to explode the limits of possibility through weapons fashioned from elsewhere, and attain the unthought. The poem is an attempt to rejuvenate the Black liberation struggle in Black America with otherwise possibilities, arming native sons with visions of the future shaped by living histories and 'memories deeper than the ocean' (1971: 81), enshrining alternative forms and relationalities tied to African languages, philosophies, mythologies, and cosmologies, positing alternative ways of relating to self, others, and the living environment. In this poem he sought to make Black Americans feel differently about themselves, turning them towards recovery and repair. This is the unthought that gives primacy not to the white supremacist capitalist machinery, but to the preservation of ontological and historical totality.

Which Sons, What Sun?

Kgositsile never tells us in the poem what 'Towards a Walk in the Sun' *is*. The word 'towards' gives us a sense of the preparatory, presupposing an initial stage towards another stage when this walk would be possible. It is important to bring together poems and short stories in which he unpacks this notion in order to elucidate the clarity of his vision. What he does offer in the poem is 'snow', which is presented as antithetical to 'sun': 'where are / the men to matches / the fuse to burn the / snow that freezes …', from the opening of the poem, and 'your sight is colored / with snow' in one of the conclusive stanzas which lead to the climatic crescendo of the final rallying call (1971: 64). These two stanzas invoke lines from an earlier poem dedicated to Rap Brown, 'When Brown is Black', in which Kgositsile calls for ice-cold America to be blown up, with Brown

> blowing up white myths
> which built up layers of mists
> which veiled the roads to the strength
> of our laughter in the sun (1969c: 10)

In the poem Kgositsile riffs on the refrain, 'what does a penny buy', a question asked by Rap Brown in his time, to which the response was, a box of matches. This refrain is transplanted in 'Towards a Walk in the Sun', where the poet searches for men to light the matches to ignite the fuse, thus exploding, perhaps in the Hughesean sense, white America and its myths, giving way to 'our laughter in the sun'. White myths built up layers of ice or mist that colour Black sight with snow, blinding Black pathways of liberation. For Kgositsile, that is why 'towards a walk in the sun' is necessary, to burn the matches that will melt the snow and return the power of sight to his people. He seeks to melt the snow-white myths by fashioning a Black mythology that will unveil the roads and strengthen the masses. Kgositsile's Black mythology enshrines forms of self-narration that are otherwise to constructions of Blackness in the white imagination.

Kgositsile's short story 'The Ab/original Mask', published in the *Negro Digest* of October 1969, elaborates these ideas further. In 'Ab/original Masks', a woman called Balese meets a diasporic man called Reaitse on a winter's night in snowy New York City, and the two fall in love. Balese seems to be an American-born Tswana, born to exiled parents, while Reaitse (Tswana for 'we are the knowers' or 'we are the ones who know') is in New York due to some form of exile from a region on the African continent called Sun Valley. He tells Balese:

> 'Some day I'll take off to the sun with my son. He loves to play with the sun.'
> 'How come?'
> 'He believes he's a god like the sun.' (1969a: 59)

In this short story, Sun Valley remains a desired place of return, here invoking Kgositsile's self-understanding of his exile as *the son who sets in the west to rise again like the sun with newborn fire*. The relationship between the god and the sun was explored in the last chapter, but here the sun carries the double meaning of being a god like the sun, who rises again, signalling continuities in the lineage and totality in the onto-triad where the living dead and the living are intricately tied to the not-yet-born – a deep responsibility to the past and future converging in the NOW as pastpresentfuture. The Christian figureheads of the father and the son are overturned by the active absence as well as the materializing and entangling presence of the matriarchive which instructs his fire and is the impetus behind the desire for return. Reaitse offers a brief history of Sun Valley to Balese:

> Some day another tribe had come in from the sea. They had imposed their gods and their traditions on the people of Sun Valley. They had cut up the land as they pleased, deposed the kings of the Valley and held the Sun Valleyians in bondage. And now we laugh less and less, […] and you do not even have memories of tales told by the fireside. (1969a: 57)

I have summarized this short story drastically to highlight important factors related to 'Towards a Walk in the Sun': the poem encapsulates the desire by the son for return to a future *place of the sun* where laughter will be restored. It is a blues for lost *gods, traditions, land,* and *bodies of knowledge* – the cosmologies of the *land of the sun*, which Kgositsile reimagines and refashions in the poem, adapting it to the Black world as attempts to return those cosmologies to African Americans. The poem then presents the first stage that is necessary for a return of these elements – a physical return for Kgositsile to apartheid South Africa to wage a bloody war towards the liberation of his people, towards the restoration of their laughter. This is the unthinkable in Kgositsile's political and aesthetic arsenal. The sagacious approach of not alienating or disregarding the imperatives of their lived experience in the New World, not dealing only with their 'glorious' parts, locates the poem within a politics of Love and Care, of conviviality and solidarity. It becomes capacious enough for African Americans to assemble the necessary tools for their own imagined return, adapting them to their relevant context. As such, for the Black arts era his work is the seam where revolutionary possibilities pulsate, to which African Americans seek to suture their own.

OJ&A's translation of the poem in their visual and sonic works presents an iteration or transliteration of that imagination. Their work is generative in that it allows me to speak to radical traditions from two milieus, the Black arts era and the twenty-first-century era on the cusp of the Black Lives Matter movement. The Afrofuturist aesthetic produced by OJ&A in their translation of 'Towards a Walk in the Sun' is in the tradition of Black arts figure and futurist Sun Ra, whom one of the members, Robert Pruitt, engages in his 'comic adventure' *Towards a Walk in the Sun*, an Afrofuturist visual rendering of alternative worlds in space, which Sun Ra would have called 'Alter-Destiny'. Brent Hayes Edwards argues that during the BAM, the intergalactic and interplanetary in Sun Ra's work 'evidenced Ra's continual vigilance towards the *impossible*, the *unthought*, the *unconceived*, the 'not', the 'alter' [...] an attempt to break the limits of what can be thought [...]' (2017: 125, my emphasis). Sun Ra sought to produce a poetics of possibility through 'myth-science' as a critical strategy to break with the white supremacist paradigm of imperialist America. In his work, the alter is in another place, an elsewhere in space; for members of OJ&A, that alternate place is also imagined in space, as will be shown in this chapter. For Kgositsile the alter is an otherworld whose existence and location is known through socio-cosmology, lived and living, coeval and synchronous with this moment, productive of material, psychic, and spiritual matter to conceive the unthinkable: liberated futures.

In 1970, Kgositsile wrote a poem dedicated to Sun Ra titled 'Introduction to a Future History Book', which was previously unpublished until very recently.[1] The poem provides further elucidation of the desired destiny that is alternate to the status quo, and Kgositsile depicts that destiny as inevitable, depicted in future history books:

> Dark clouds race across the earth
> for the final flood. Beat
> the frenzied rhythm
> give birth to Life
> stop the years from groaning. (2023: 254)

---

[1] The poem first appeared in print in 2023 in the posthumously published volume, *Keorapetse Kgositsile: Collected Poems, 1969–2018*.

This opening is in dialogue with 'Towards a Walk in the Sun', and it deploys natural phenomena, in the fashion and likelihood of Moruakgomo from *Motswasele II*, and in the oratory tradition of Batswana, to speak to this monumental historical force: 'dark clouds race across the earth / for the final flood', with a pun on 'race'. It would seem the wind that caressed the eve of a new dawn has achieved its agenda by choreographing native sons to dance in unison to a frenzied rhythm, ending a global anti-Black colonial capitalist modernity. The rhythm is a vital force of life, growth, and continuity through all that was, is, and will be: 'the smallest cell remembers a sound' (Philip 2014: 37). The final flood is biblical but also biological, for all life comes from the waters of life: the amniotic fluids of creation. Water represents the principles of destruction and creation, endings and beginning, death and rebirth. The poem continues:

> […] I
> have known unseasonable filth
> fly with Sun Ra
> to sunlit regions cleansed by soul units
> turn mythscience into a reality. (Kgositsile 2023: 254)

The poet testifies to the unspeakable filth from the groaning years, before the world's ending, the 'unseasonable' period of darkness and coldness. 'Unseasonable' is a pun that plays on the protracted season of suffering that was unbroken, without seasons; it also alludes to bitter years that could not be seasoned to alleviate or improve the taste. The necessity to fly to sunlit regions is acknowledged and throws into relief those lines from the opening of 'Towards a Walk in the Sun': 'where are / the men to matches / the fuse to burn the / snow that freezes some / wouldbe skyward desire' (1971: 64). The freeze required blasting and blowing up towards sunlit regions. However, this is where Sun Ra and Kgositsile part ways – Kgositsile seeks to 'turn mythscience into a reality' by returning with what he refers to as 'furor' (1973a: 65): 'carry[ing] your heat' (2023: 64), an African American colloquial moniker for a gun, but heat also referring to the passion and anger, the love and care that are at the root of rage and revolt. These are the guns that have been transformed from spears, which we can presume he retrieved from the sunlit regions, used to, as 'Introduction to a Future History Book' continues, 'burn every infernal chain in the furnace of your life'. For Kgositsile the sunlit regions equipped the son with 'newborn fire' which he now uses to break dawn in the west, journeying like the sun to the east where he shall be reborn. The fire of destruction and conflagration ends the groaning years of exile to birth something else. When that time is here, Kgositsile seems to be saying to Sun Ra, 'do not go west'.

Kgositsile's poem to Sun Ra resounds in the work of one of the OJ&A's members. Kenya Evans (Mumblz Medina Evans), a rapper and collaborator in the art collective, recorded a rap song titled 'Towards a Walk in the Sun' (2012), which is available on his Bandcamp page.[2] The chorus of the rap song is as follows:

> Towards a walk in the sun
> The view is cinematic
> Feel the heat when we run
> The glow is pure magic
> It's a soul classic
> We've outlasted days in a slum
> Ways of the gun
> Raising a son
> I gots to have it

This chorus demonstrates a literal interpretation of 'a walk towards the sun', flying to 'sunlit regions', and being cleaned by the 'soul units' of Kgositsile's poem, providing a sonic cleansing by a 'soul classic'. In both Kgositsile's poem and Evans's chorus, the sun is a place of ritual where they undergo a rite of passage that transforms them through a cleansing song and rhythm. The walk towards the sun brings relief from the ice-cold realities of an anti-Black America and its gridlocked existence in the filth of the 'slum'. Outlasting days in the slum that is America marks Black life as Black survival, branded by carceral realities and premature death. Flying out of this slum reveals a cinematic view, ending periods of alienation and dehumanization, to experience a glow that is 'pure magic'. Evans's is a poetics that generates its own sense of repair, albeit divergent from Kgositsile's own yearnings. However, Kgositsile teaches us conviviality and capaciousness: all forms of radical imaginations towards Black liberation are important and necessary, affirming life as creative force. Kenya Evans brought 'Towards a Walk in the Sun' to the attention of the collective, which became generative in their attempts to articulate the struggles of their time.

In their Afrofuturist translation of Kgositsile's 'Towards a Walk in the Sun', Pruitt and Cyrus locate Kgositsile in a particular African American historical dialogue with Nat Turner, the Black Panthers, Octavia Butler, Sun Ra, and James Brown, as a practice that sutures past, present, and future, slave rebellions with the Black Arts and Black Power Movements, as well as with the burgeoning Black Lives Matter movement. Due to deracination from the African continent occasioned by the Middle Passage and the inaccessibility of existing synchronous, coeval African languages, customs, and cultures, they forage the Black arts archive as well as look to Africa. Kgositsile's ubiquitous presence

---

[2] 'Towards a Walk in the Sun', https://mumblzmedina.bandcamp.com/track/towards-a-walk-in-the-sun-2 [Accessed 16 September 2015]

in that archive reconfigures and rezones space, time, history, and geography, locating the art collective's work in a 'trans*' poetics. Christina Sharpe offers 'trans*' from 'Trans*Atlantic' to think of 'a variety of ways that try to get at something *about* or *toward* the range of trans*formations enacted on and by Black bodies' (2016: 30, emphasis in original); she explains:

> I am thinking the trans* [...] as a means to mark the ways the slave and the Black occupy what Saidiya Hartman calls the 'position of the unthought'. The asterisk after the prefix 'trans' holds the place open for thinking (from and into that position). [...] The asterisk speaks to a range of configurations of Black being that take the form of translation, transatlantic, transformation, transmogrification, transcontinental, transfixed, [...]. (ibid.)

The variety of ways in which this art collective from Houston attempts to get at something *towards* transformation constitute an act of reaching out, a yearning to continue in the lineage, a desire for dreamkeeping through which they may transmute their unthought position. They reach across time, histories, and geographies, claiming through translation, aesthetics, and poetics from the collective Black archive of Africa and the diaspora. Kgositsile's 'towards' is also a form of reaching out, a call, a future petition, and a conjuring of transformation of the unthought through the unthinkable. It is a spell for the future; it imagines and commands stage two of the plan: adrienne maree brown teaches us that 'all organizing is science fiction'; it is speculative, dreaming up, and acting from the *not yet here*, 'imagining a world we have never seen before' (2015). Kgositsile's poem operates within that dynamic, on the one hand imagining a decolonized and liberated South Africa that he will bring into being through 'newborn fire' upon his return, and on the other hand tilling a seedbed for African Americans upon which they may sow their own imagined liberated worlds. His 'towards' opens that space for thinking from and into the unthought, to expand and rupture it. 'Towards' is an offering to the collective in their unfinished struggle, a gathering place from which to imagine otherwise. It issues an invitation to translation, the ongoing process of crossing over, which in Kgositsile's life was marked by traversing spatial, linguistic, temporal, cosmological, and customary borders. This invitation is taken up as an intergenerational offering in the twenty-first century's ongoing Black liberatory struggle.

Reeding Sound Knowledges, Riting Futurist Imaginations

There is a potent relationship between words, sounds, and images that attends Kgositsile's process of writing, emerging out of wandering in the process of 'taking a solo'. The jazz solo metaphor signals both the sonic and the ensemble, the presence of community and its sound knowledges. Here we must recall the agential nature of elsewhere, often possessing him, or as in the case of 'Towards a Walk in the Sun', bringing sound knowledges to him via the wind. As he relayed to Danille Taylor-Guthrie, 'I think in images. My images aspire to be clear pictures carved out of sound' (1996: 36). These sounds, whispers, echoes, and reverberations are active materializations of elsewhere worlds acting upon him, and whose knowledge he strives to capture by moulding his language in order to sound those worlds he seeks to signify. In his own words, 'I tame English to sing who I am'.[3] This is the process of 'writing as riting': capturing or apprehending the sonic to be scripted into words. The image is what he 'sees' or *reeds* 'there', reeding understood to be multisensorial – 'I see with my skin and hear with my tongue' (1975: 22) – and what he retrieves from there he transcribes or *rites* into that singing language.

Kgositsile contends that poetry at its best is music; indeed, Amiri Baraka proclaimed that poetry is 'speech musicked' (1968: 243). Both Kgositsile and Baraka address the Black arts ethos according to which Black music is the most successful expression of the Black experience. For Kgositsile, Black music extended deeper into the sound knowledges of the community in Southern Africa; that is, the Black sonic over-exceeds Black music to also include oralities and auralities of his cosmological orientation. Sound for him then functions as a medium and bridge between worlds, at an aesthetic level, suturing words and images from elsewhere into his poetry. Sound is central to the literacy system of *reeding* and *riting*, undergirding acoustemology or a knowledge of the world through sound.

Sound as modality for being and becoming in relation with the living world, for grasping living and actively materializing elsewhere from his 'old roots that defy death' (1971: 71) is a tool of enlivenment that rejuvenates the English language from its stasis by refracting it with images from indigenous and cosmological worlds. These images contain their own systems of signification depicted in symbols, signs, and codes. In the hands of a capable writer concerned with taming the English language, these symbolisms are transliterated into the English language, expertly bridging the two worlds through carrying symbols from one to the other to bear upon the world of English. Chinua Achebe extols Mazisi Kunene – for whom Kgositsile had 'a whole lot more respect than any other contemporary writer from anywhere on this planet' (Rowell 1978: 37) – as one such capable writer functioning at this nexus. In his *Anthills of the Savannah*, Achebe writes:

> As Africans today we should make it habit of invoking these powerful images from our history, legend and art. [...] You don't have

---

[3] Author interview with Keorapetse Kgositsile, Pretoria, April 2014.

to repeat everything that Kunene said, but just mention the keyword, the password, and the whole image is called up in the imagination of those who know, who are aware, who are literate in our traditions. I think this is very important (1987: vi).

The literacy of our tradition is what prompts me to offer *reeding* and *riting* as a signification system. While Kunene achieves this through writing in isiZulu first, then translating his work into English to capture those 'powerful images from our history, legend, and art', Kgositsile embraces the all-encompassing Black sonic as modality, as an alternative route to the same end. This is crucial as it offers us an opportunity to ground the Black sonic – bebop, rap, spoken word poetry – in the aural/oral practices of the community, of the matriarchive, of the ceremonies and rituals in Africa, or rural country sides, and of the collective. The Black sonic, when considered in this long arc of history, emerges from the people's collective genius, their own imaginings of the world, the storied lives they produced, and the transformation of those stories, images, and signs into tools of resistance. Jazz as modality in Kgositsile's life and work offers us the opportunity to map the sonic from home languages to the community songs shared when tilling the soil or gathering for funerals and weddings, to workers' songs in the mines and songs of domestic workers, to protest traditions, and to the avant-garde. Throughout history, their survival and longevity, maintained through creative and strategic transformation, continue to move us, the community, to move the artists and writers to aspire to words that live and sing.

This book offers *reeding* and *riting* as method and praxis of recuperation – implying both retrieval and convalescence or repair – an approach for those actively engaging the elsewhere and unknowns into this 'here' world. Through *reeding* and *riting*, Kgositsile's aesthetic in 'Towards a Walk in the Sun' 'recovered the histories of counter-futures' (Eshun 2017b: 301) from elsewhere. These counter-futurist imaginaries include the *terrafirmament*, the mythic language of the *sun* and the *son*, grounded, landed, and earthly, not in space.

Terrafirmament draws from indigenous creation narratives of Southern Africa, in which the people originate from the skies or heaven. In their languages, too, the elements of celestial phenomena pepper and populate their everyday speech, as seen briefly in Moruakgomo's speech act in *Motswasele II*. This orientation is what enables Kgositsile to fashion the language of him being the son that sets in the west and rises in the east like the sun. That phenomenon takes place not in space but in his life and lived experience. Here we could appreciate Kodwo Eshun's contention that 'no futurism is worthwhile unless it includes indigenous knowledges'.[4] I understand this to also mean that any futurism imagined from within the logics of Euromodernity is not worthwhile

---

4 'The Algorithmic Poetics', RAW Academie Lecture, 26 April 2017.

as it traps us in binary logics that bifurcate the heaven and earth, skies and land, celestial phenomena and animal/human life. Kgositsile repudiates this and draws on the complexity of his people's narration of their own lives, relations, and materialization. Further, he finds this an archive that must be 'unveiled and unleashed' (1975a: 17) on the white world. This is his 'alter-', operative within the Black sonic, but one rooted in the *long durée* of sound, lived and known, living and unknowable. This is the 'alter-' from which he imagines his alter-destiny, rooted in indigenous knowledges. Desire is entangled with memory.

It is my view then, that Afrofuturism is not the term that encapsulates the 'not yet uhuru'[5] or *a luta continua*[6] *of artistic expression by Africans living on the African continent.* A leading proponent of the movement, Nigerian American author Nnedi Okorafor rejects the label Afrofuturism and classifies her work as Africanfuturism or Afrojujuism, subcategories of science fiction and fantasy, respectively, 'that respectfully acknowledges the seamless blend of *true existing* African spiritualities and cosmologies with the imaginative' (2019). Africanfuturism is 'specifically and more directly rooted in African culture, history, mythology and point of view as it then branches into the Black Diaspora, and it does not privilege the West' (ibid.). In her popular essay 'Afrofuturism is not for Africans living in Africa', the South African writer Mohale Mashigo offers: 'Our needs, when it comes to imagining futures, or even reimagining a fantasy present, are different from elsewhere on the globe; we actually live on this continent, as opposed to using it as a costume or a stage to play out our ideas' (2018b). Works that clearly demonstrate an 'alter-' imagined from lived, available, materializing, and existing mythologies, folklore, and legends necessitate other theorizations.

In his imagining of the 'alter-', for instance, Sun Ra draws from Egyptian cosmology and mythology, an Egypt of 'ancient civilization', of 'glorious past' (Kgositsile 1971: 64). This is where Kgositsile parts ways with him as Kgositsile is engaged with an Africa of contemporaneous times, embattled in its own struggles with colonialism and apartheid. I do not discount the value of Afrofuturism but rather argue, like Mashigo and Okorafor, that it would be parroting African diasporic culture if South Africans or Africans on the continent adapted this label while our own history and languages are available to us. It would serve us if Africans living in Africa had names for their own creative practices in which they imagine futures or reimagine the present. Okorafor calls her practice Africanfuturism, with the prefix 'African' signalling her position as a Nigerian

---

[5] As Letta Mbuli laments in her album *Not Yet Uhuru* (1996) – 'Not yet freedom' – in post-apartheid South Africa.
[6] Inspired by the FRELIMO slogan that means 'the struggle continues' and popularized in larger francophone and anglophone Africa by Miriam Makeba, this phrase has come to signify and lament Africa's unfinished revolution following independence.

living in the States. Kgositsile's position as an exiled South African living in the States, however, produces the generative concept of future memory: memories of the future.

It becomes imperative then to question any practice on the continent that prefixes itself with 'Afro'. This, for the African referring to herself, seems a tautological self-reference that exposes a self-understanding through western eyes, or even through the eyes of the Black diaspora. It underlines our colonial alienation, where we were taught and have internalized that our traditions and cultures cannot produce anything of value. The 'Afro' in 'Afro-surrealism' or 'Afrofuturism' is a prefix that underscores a view of and engagement with Africa from outside, with Africa as external reference. Afro-surrealism locates the centre of surrealism elsewhere outside Africa, whereas the 'African influence on the founders of surrealism was evident even before they called themselves surrealists – that is, before the formation of the movement in 1924' (Rosemont & Kelley 2009: 6). And Afrofuturism addresses an African-oriented future from the positionality of diaspora. As Jayna Brown observes:

> The concept is often masculinist: Afrofuturism, and studies done under its aegis, have given us a host of beloved brothers and patriarchs. From Sun Ra to George Clinton, the Mothership is manned, so to speak. The (feminized) ship is the ultimate symbol of the diaspora and of […] the mode of transcendence into the galaxy, away from the limited human idea of Earth – but it is men who direct this ship. (2021: 16)

When the continent is experienced psychically, historically, politically, ancestrally, generationally, spiritually, and mythologically, it is known to us, and informs how we know ourselves, each other, and the living world. This would produce such a poetics as *terrafirmament* which is very clearly articulated by Kgositsile as grounded and landed, with the landedness and placeness entangled with the umbilical cord and feminine principle that makes the fight for land as spiritual as it is political. The body of the mother, his body, the body of land, and celestial bodies are interconnected and interdependent. His orientation to the elsewhere and its sound knowledges and ontological totality reshapes, reorders, and reconstitutes that 'limited human idea of Earth', opening other ways of being, knowing, and doing a life of resistance fanned by politics of Love and Care. Even when the heavy masculine language of 'native sons' that fashion the future in Kgositsile's poem tends to fall into this trap, he constantly reminds us that sons come from mothers, no matter what the holy trinity would have us believe. The keywords and passwords of 'wombs for rebirth' in the poem assure us there is no ending this world and birthing another without the feminine principle.

The deft adaptation of 'Towards a Walk in the Sun' by Cyrus into an Afrofuturist aesthetic rightfully addresses itself to the States by weaving Kgositsile's poem with Henry Dumas' mythopoesis, while Pruitt's adaptation of the poem into a comic interweaves Kgositsile's poem with Sun Ra, Octavia Butler, Nat Turner, and James Brown. This is a celebration of the Black genius, the openings that Kgositsile's poetics of possibility offer, bridging of their desire with the not yet here, the coming to terms with their unthought. Theirs is a futurist radical imagination bound up with African American memory, with deeper histories of reimagined African roots enabled by Kgositsile's ubiquitous presence in the BAM archive.

Introducing Otabenga Jones & Associates

The Houston-based arts collective Otabenga Jones & Associates comprises of Robert Pruitt, Medina Kenya Evans, and Jamal Cyrus and has a mission to educate young African Americans about the fullness of the African American experience through preserving and promoting the core principles of the Black radical tradition (Creativetime n.d.). This logically led them to dig into the crates and archives of African American history. Their iconographies and repertoire are evidently inspired by the Black Power Movement (BPM) and the Black Panther Party (BPP). On 28 February 2014, they premiered 'The People's Plate', a collaborative art project and public health programme addressing the ongoing crisis of obesity and its related risks in their communities. They were modelling it on the Black Panther Free Breakfast for School Children Program, which saw the Panthers cooking and serving breakfast to poor inner-city children. OJ&A sought to provide at-risk community members with a set of tools that might encourage self-sufficiency and empowerment in maintaining their own health through food choices while building community. They assembled lunch kits made available to participants of the workshop. Each lunch kit carried an illustrated image originally made by Emory Douglas, a graphic artist who created much of the iconic artwork and graphics for the BPP, and who became known as the BPP minister of culture. In conjunction with this project, a wall mural of the same image – titled 'Dare to Struggle, Eat to Win' – by Douglas was painted as a community project in the Lawndale neighbourhood of Texas. The visual artists in the collective often deploy Douglas's images to speak to the politics of the day.

The Black radical tradition they seek to promote is evinced in their name, Otabenga. Ota Benga was a Congolese pygmy man who formed part of the perversity that was human zoos, in/famous in the nineteenth century. He survived the pygmy genocide carried out by armed forces loyal to Leopold II, the king of Belgium and ruler of the Congo Free State. Benga was originally bought by Samuel Phillips Verner, a missionary and anthropologist from South

Carolina, who was hired to find pygmies and other Africans to take them to St. Louis for an anthropology exhibition at the 1904 World's Fair. There he would be exhibited alongside other aboriginal first peoples and was not allowed to return to Africa after the fair. He was exhibited at the Bronx Zoo in New York right up until 1906, the main feature of 'his' show being his precise existence: his body, his sharp-pointed teeth (filed to sharp points in the customary way of his people), his height, and his proficiency with a bow and arrow, which he displayed through shooting a target. The racial science of Western 'civilization' – its obsession with categorization, classification, statistics, and eugenics – was the driving force behind these human zoos, which were meant to concretize white supremacy through difference between the west and darker continents, human and animal, and Black and white. Ota Benga was exhibited in the Monkey House of the zoo, where he was often placed with an orangutan, not for company, but for comparison and effect. He committed suicide by shooting himself in the heart in March 1916. The Otabenga Jones & Associates collective resurrects him to humanize him and bring to light this dark history.

Speculative Futures through the Black Sonic

In 2011/2012, OJ&A collaborated on a project titled 'Towards a Walk in the Sun', rendered through three mediums: a rap song, a comic book, and a vinyl cover collage. Earlier in the chapter, we briefly explored Kenya Evans's rap song; what follows is an investigation into Jamal Cyrus' collage that forms part of an installation organized around what he calls the 'phonic substance'. Here, he gathers 'from a non-linear view of history, identifying the concrete and corporeal intersections between diverse cultures' (Castro 2010), in this instance cultures within the Black radical tradition. As detailed in the write-up of another exhibition that focuses on his explorations with sound, 'the origins and progression of music […] act as Cyrus' thematic embarkation to explore their functions and influences between […] cultural interactions' (Castro 2010). His preoccupation when creating this collage was the relationship between the Black arts milieu and twentieth-century Black art production.

Cyrus works with the medium of Black music from the golden pioneering era of the 1960s and 1970s as muse. The 2013 exhibition of his work features the installation 'Pride Records', a display of records from a fictional 1970s record label, with record covers bearing artistic expression in collages or drawings that chronicle the Black experience through music. In Cyrus's conceptual project, 'Pride Records was closely monitored by the FBI for releasing records deemed subversive by the agency' (Whitney Biennial 2006). On this shelf, we find reworked existing real records coexisting alongside entirely fictional records. The records include Nikki Giovanni's *Truth is on its Way*, Shaniqua Hameed's *The ABCs of Revolution*, Uhuru Splatter's *The Visions of African Mystics*, Rev.

Hue L. Black's *All Suffering is not in Defeat*, Sub-Terror's *The Runaways*, Amiri Baraka's *6 Minutes Till Nation Time*, and, finally, The Dowling Street Martyr Brigade's *Towards a Walk in the Sun*. By enabling a cross-pollination between real and imagined records, Cyrus enters into a dialogue with the earlier era that not only addresses gaps in the Black archive, but also inscribes historical fiction through the medium of Black music, where boundaries between real and unreal are blurred.

The Nikki Giovanni vinyl is a real historical record from 1971, in which Giovanni reads her selected poetry to the sounds of The New York Community Choir. Amiri Baraka's 1972 record *It's Nation Time*, recomposed as *6 Minutes Till Nation Time* by Cyrus, is also a real record. It is noteworthy that the trend of recording poetry albums was pioneered by Detroit-based Broadside Press, which issued tapes of poets reading their own books that the press had published – among them Kgositsile, who recorded his debut collection *Spirits Unchained* (1969). The pressing of poetry readings onto vinyl popularized poetry, in turn producing poetry-music groups such as Gil Scott-Heron and The Last Poets. Rev. Hue L. Black's album is fabricated by Cyrus and features a sermon 'All Suffering is not in Defeat' to mimic Motown Record's spoken word imprint Black Forum which, from 1970s onwards, pressed and published poetry and popular speeches from the Black power and civil rights era. One of the records from the Black Forum – a 1967 speech by Martin Luther King, 'Why I am opposed to the war in Vietnam'[7] – was published in 1970 and nominated for a Grammy Award. The other album from Black Forum, *Free Huey*, features a speech by Stokely Carmichael advocating for the release of BPP founder Huey P. Newton. This real-life record is one that Cyrus invokes through the name Rev. Hue L. Black.

Shaniqua Hameed's *The ABCs of Revolution* is reproduced by Cyrus and repositioned in his installation as a cultural rarity, as a 'vinyl shop discovery', and speaks to the limited numbers of records that used to be produced in the 1960s, especially of spoken word poetry and an artist singing 'the ABCs of revolution'. The record was released in 7 inch and, speaking to its peculiarity in today's recording industry and popular culture, Cyrus states: 'imagine Amiri Baraka or Maulana Karenga as a guest star on early Sesame Street', presumably to sing the ABCs of revolution (in Lucas 2016). Thus, Cyrus functions within the speculative, recreating histories that include alternative traditions of thought and reimagining them as counterpublics then and today. Peter Lucas writes that the 'covers on display are the only ones in existence and the recordings themselves can only be heard in inner echoes between existences' (2016).

---

[7] The speech, because of its radical nature, purportedly led to his assassination, and was not cited by white America at the time, as it goes against its integrationist image of Dr King as a model for nonviolence.

Through the practice of digging in the crates, Cyrus listens to history and retrieves discoveries that allow him to reshape the present.

His practice functions at the nexus of spoken word poetry/speeches, visual culture, and Black music, mirroring the word-sound-image relationship that underwrites Kgositsile's otherworld wandering. I read Cyrus's digging in the crates as an aesthetic parallel to wandering to 'otherworlds' of the 1960s and 1970s to retrieve politics, poetics, and otherwise possibilities from there to disrupt and rupture the enclosures of the dominant paradigm. In his wanderings, he encountered Kgositsile's 'Towards a Walk in the Sun', presumably in the anthology *Black Fire: Anthology of Afro-Asian Writing* or in Kgositsile's collection of poetry *My Name is Afrika*, or on The Last Poets' album *Holy Terror*. Whatever the source, the circulation of the poem demonstrates the prevalence and primacy of the sonic in practices of reordering history and the future in the now. The sonic becomes a place where 'vinyl shop discoveries' and rarities can open up whole worlds of alternative histories of thought that are trans*formative.

In Cyrus's conceptual project, Pride Records signed a fabricated band, The Dowling Street Martyr Brigade, whose debut album was titled *Towards a Walk in the Sun*. Cyrus designed the album cover of this band through the medium of a collage that is superimposed on the album art of the British rock band Cream's 1967 album *Disraeli Gears*. The hallucinogenic hippie imagery with a neon flowery motif from the Cream album is used as a background upon which cut-out images of funeral proceedings are placed. Dowling Street also refers to a real street in Lawndale, Houston, a hotbed of activism during the 1960s and 70s. The coffin is carried by a group of militant members donning afros, berets, and the customary leather jackets with their Black fists raised in a Black power salute.

The funeral signals Black death at the hands of the state while the psychedelic colours represent a parallel movement that rebuked mainstream American values and fought for free will and free love. In placing the two images side by side, Cyrus reminds us that, in 1967 and 1968, Black people were systematically mowed down by the state, from Martin Luther King to Bobby Hutton and Henry Dumas, while the free love movement declared 1967 to be 'the summer of love', celebrating nihilism against the state and newly asserted autonomy. In this light, the band's name 'Dowling Street Martyr Brigade' is bitterly ironic, since martyrs from the two worlds are contrasted through one being metaphoric and the other being too literal. The collage's final message, the name of the band's album *Towards a Walk in the Sun*, reveals this contrast: the hippies attain the fantastical golden rising sun depicted in the collage in optics that invoke the pot at the end of the rainbow, while for the BPP the sun seems to be the galaxy depicted on the coffin. The hippies can 'space out' in bliss while the BPP have to imagine literal space travel to escape their inevitable death. Cyrus makes a statement about Black freedom: it is ironically marked by death. Further, Black death does not assure Black freedom. If all these Black martyrs died in the 1960s and 1970s, and freedom is still elusive in the twenty-first century, then freedom, it seems, cannot be attained within the strictures of America, hence imaginaries of the 'alter', of outer space.

The write-up for the collage states that the coffin 'represents writer and poet Henry Dumas' mythological "Ark of Bones", commemorating those lives lost in racists acts (Dumas himself was killed in a confrontation with New York Transit Authority police in 1968)' (Whitney Biennial 2006). Dumas was

Figure. 1. Jamal Cyrus' 'Towards a Walk in the Sun'

shot seven weeks after King. In Dumas's short story 'Ark of Bones', Headeye takes Fish-hound on a short journey into a boat floating on the Mississippi River which contains bones: 'a soulboat' (1974b: 17). The captain of the ark explains that the bones contained therein make the ship 'a house of generations', and that 'every African who lives in America has a part of his soul in this ark' (20). Those who are 'called' to their work and purpose must fetch their souls from this ark. Thus 'Ark of Bones' is a redemptive promise: those in the diaspora can reconnect with their past and future through retrieving their souls captured in the Middle Passage. Through the ark of bones that contains their history and future they may be redeemed and awakened. The ark is the 'arkive'.

Reading the coffin in Cyrus's collage as the ark in this short story produces several meanings: the dead are not dead but lie in the ark of the coffin and their spirits can be called upon to give the living purpose to continue the Black struggle against white supremacy. Also, the 'ark of bones' is timeless, or rather 'timeful' – pastpresentfuture – as it contains the bones of those who were, and are, an 'arkive' for a future, able to bring to life those who respond to their 'calling'. It is an 'arkive' of Black death, but also of life, continuity, redemption, and transformation. The notion of 'fetching yourself' from the ark has tonal parallels with responding to the antiphonic whistling of the wind, the 'birth of memory' which brings the chorus of the living dead to life, opening the future memory ensemble for the living and not yet here – to voices such as those of Kgositsile and Dumas.

Dumas's work calls diasporans to undertake ritual work, towards African American Southern traditions and beliefs, their mythologies in the New World fashioned from within the cauldron of slavery and reconstruction. I cannot overemphasize the importance of noting these differences of Black experience in global Black solidarity politics. Cyrus asserts a relation to the coffin as ark and arkive, as a ritual archive that gathers the past with the future through Dumas's radical imagination in his short story. When thought of in these terms, speculative and Afrofuturist, the coffin tells us that death transforms those who live, that the living dead reconstitute the living and the not-yet-born, and that the memory of the living dead can be culled to fashion a poetics of continuity, totality, and future memory. In Cyrus' collage the 'panthers' are marching forward into the horizon carrying this arkive of future memory which twenty-first-century 'native sons'/'panthers' harvest to know their names and purpose. The 'towards' in Kgositsile's title capaciously holds these multiple meanings and temporalities.

Dumas earned the title as 'an underground deity' from Amiri Baraka (1988: 161), who also asserted that Dumas' aesthetic is 'Afro-Surreal Expressionism' – a genuine embodiment, according to Baraka, of the Black aesthetic. Wright observes that in stories such as 'Ark of Bones', Dumas is 'engaged in the conscious fabrication, or re-fabrication of myths, an effort to "re-mythologize" human experience in reaction to the forces of dehumanization' (2003: xx). When we think of Baraka's line, 'At the bottom of the Atlantic Ocean there's a railroad made of human bones' (2002: 7), invoked by Dumas's work here, we see the common struggle in Black art, to re-fabricate and re-mythologize the world in response to anti-Blackness: Kgositsile used available and accessible mythologies from Setswana; The Last Poets creatively adapted it to the States; Dumas strategically transformed southern folklore, spirituals, space science, and literature in his practice; and Cyrus's Pride Records blurred real and unreal histories of Black music to shape speculative futures. In mining the Black arts and Black power archive and using a speculative poetics to redirect the future, Cyrus anticipated and threaded Black Lives Matter with the tapestry woven by Dumas's 'Ark of Bones' and Kgositsile's 'Towards a Walk in the Sun'. They all coalesce in the quilt of Black expressive cultures that will be continuously generative in the unfinished project of Black liberation.

Space is the Place?

Robert Pruitt's adaptation of Kgositsile's 'Towards a Walk in the Sun' into a comic adventure titled *Towards a Walk in the Sun*, was published in the Summer/Fall 2012 edition of *The Studio Museum in Harlem* magazine (62–5). Pruitt's oeuvre 'layers science fiction, hip hop, comic books, and Black political and social struggles' (Francis 2012) to exhibit the complexity of Black identity. The cover of the comic adventure has in its centre a masked man surfing space on a skateboard in typical hip hop/skater street style of sneakers, jeans, and a hoodie. It carries the name of the comic book, *Towards a Walk in the Sun*, and the subtitle 'A Comic Adventure by Robert Pruitt in collaboration with Otabenga Jones and Associates'. The cover also announces:

This comic is a collaborative effort between the members of Otabenga Jones and Associates. All text for this work was taken from the song 'Towards A Walk In the Sun' as performed by mumblz medina (Kenya F. Evans). His song was inspired by artwork of the same name, created by Jamal D. Cyrus, which was taken from a poem also of the same name by South African poet Keorapetse Kgositsile. Listen to Kenya's song and see Jamal's work here: http://mumblzmedina. bandcamp.com/track/towards-a-walk-in-the-sun-2

The theme of the comic adventure is also stated on the comic cover, directly drawing from the rap song composed by Kenya Evans/mumblz medina discussed earlier in this chapter:

> The view is cinematic
> Feel the heat when we run
> The glow is pure magic
> It's a soul classic
> We've outlasted days in the slum
> Ways of the gun
> Raising a son
> I gots to have it

In the comic adventure the skater feels the heat – slang for guns or criminality: to 'pack heat' is to carry a gun, and to be hot is to be wanted by police. The comic addresses systemic socio-economic inequalities ascribed to projects or 'slums', the justification of police brutality against Black bodies, and the mass incarceration of Black men. It works with the themes of eluding state capture, resisting and refusing to be ensnared by 'the reach of the plantation into the ghetto', as Saidiya Hartman (2019, 29) poetically phrases it. The slum is understood as the 'third revolution of Black intimate life, the next major transformation of Black social life after the ship and the plantation', an 'open-air prison' (Bradley 2019) that feeds the plantation-to-prison pipeline, marked by historical continuities. Pruitt's comic stages an escape from that 'carceral continuum', where, as Loïc Wacquant argues, African Americans dwell in 'the first genuine prison society of history' in which punishment does not end with the prison term but locks Black bodies in a carceral cast that determines their captive futures (2001). The 'carceral cast' extends beyond served time, to post-detention supervision, post-prison supervision, and general 'prisonization' of public housing and schools in poor inner-city settlements. For the Black body, the entirety of the United States of America is a prison, and Kgositsile's 'Towards a Walk in the Sun' offers a poetics of escape.

Fig. 2. Robert Pruitt's comic cover

The comic cover locates the main character in space, skating instead of walking towards the sun, supposedly released from the grips of white supremacist surveillance and carcerality, floating freely. He wears a Dogon mask on his face, and we understand his skating device to be space technology in a manner similar to an astronaut's suit. The vitality and mainstay of Dogon cosmology within the African and Afro-diasporic imagination cannot be overstated for its productive powers to bind the earth and the cosmos. For example, Ethiopian (labelled 'surrealist') painter Skunder Boghossian learned 'the concept of the vital force and Dogon Cosmic religion' (Debela 2004) while in Paris studying Fine Arts. When he later moved to the States, he collaborated with Kgositsile, illustrating the covers of the latter's poetry collections *My Name is Afrika* (1971) and *The Present is a Dangerous Place to Live* (1974). The influences of Dogon cosmology can be noted in Boghossian's illustration for the 1971 collection.

Mali's Dogon people use masks to bind themselves to both heaven and earth, the cosmos and the land, and the past and future with the present. The mask is not only a portal to the spirit world but joins the vastness of the cosmos with the vastness of the human's inner world. In essence, masks are technologies of trans*, of expressing the porosity of the human body in its attempt to perform interconnection and interrelationality with other bodies: celestial, terrestrial, animal, and water bodies. Trans* is a poetics of suture. In African rituals, mask rituals and ceremonies collapse the borders between living and dead, seen and unseen, spirit and material, and past and future, suturing them together. Masks sublimate the human experience to seek totality, continuity, and enlivenment with the living world. Masks transform embodiment into enlivenment: the re-animation of the embodied trans*. Masks are therefore ritual technologies used to facilitate inhabiting the manifold of the onto-triad, of the living, the living dead, and the not yet here, enfolded in the quivering pastpresentfuture.

The experience of collapsed barrier between the living and dead, seen and unseen, spirit and material, past and future, and the cosmos and the earth in the Southern African context, where masking traditions are not common (even if Lefifi Tladi deploys masks and masking in his work, which I discuss in the next chapter), is activated and enhanced through ritual. In the Southern African context, the role of song in articulating ontological belonging to each other and the living world is important. In the languages of the land, the *ngoma*, *koma*, or *malopo* rituals enliven the livings' experience of the living dead, the not-yet-born, the living world, and the cosmos. The *ngoma* or *malopo* complexes are healing rituals that encompass totems, drum, dance, song, names, and *land* (names-songs-places matrix). They also place at their centre the figure of the healer, whose abilities are activated by both these complexes (*sangoma* or *lelopo* are both healing traditions). This healer is what Kgositsile calls the 'Motswana doctor', subject of the next chapter, but important in this chapter for his ritual technologies of the bones, which s/he uses to divine over physical, metaphorical, and spiritual ailments and to predict futures. Their bones, which Kgositsile calls on in the next chapter, are important in drawing parallels with the masks discussed here. I draw these parallels to elucidate productive differences in reading/reeding the cosmos in Kgositsile's 'Towards a Walk in the Sun' and in its adaptation by Pruitt.

Masks and bones represent *terrafirmament*: they abolish the binary between heaven and earth and sacred and profane, and this conjugation is articulated in indigenous languages, explored elaborately in the next chapter. The knowledge of self, each other, and the world in the cosmology of Southern Africa centres on the cosmos as omen and guiding force. The cosmos is the nucleus of most creation narratives of the region, where it is inextricably tied to human activities and all other forms of life. Many groups from Southern Africa trace their genesis to the cosmos. Zulumathabo Zulu explains that in the Sesotho (in the same language group as Setswana and Sepedi) language,

> planet earth is referred to as *Lefatshe* meaning the subset of the cosmos. This gives us an insight with respect to how and why they named the earth in this fashion. The Basotho were looking at the planet from the cosmic superset. This is a cosmocentric view of the universe [... and a] cosmocentric explanation of the universe. They command an impressive knowledge of the starry universe. Of particular interest to us are the stars that are not visible to the naked eye such as the star systems of Tosamasiu (Sirius) and the Tosa (Jupiter) star system. Both Tosamasiu and Tosa are visible to a naked eye but have orbiting satellite systems that are not visible to a naked eye. Tosamasiu refers to the ternary star system such as Sirius A, B and C respectively. Peomaha or Peo Ya Mahaha refers to the sacred seed named for the invisible star of Sirius B. The seed is Mabele (sorghum), a sacred crop among the Basotho. Lebeleha or Mabeleha refers to another invisible star of Sirius C. Lebeleha means the one who gives birth according to the seed of Mabele. The naming of star systems *uses the female principle* as is the case in the philosophical constructs of the Basotho. [...] *As the sons and daughters of the cosmos, they possess this astronomical knowledge without technological instruments because this knowledge is already part of their sacred mythology.* (2015, my emphasis)

Zulu makes crucial points here, but the most important point in connection with our discussion of Afrofuturism is that the act of engaging with the cosmos for Africans is an act of re-membering, of accessing and connecting with what is already a part of them. In this cosmocentric universe, the sense of symbolic being beyond the biological, the being tied to mythos and cosmogeny

(McKittrick & Wynter 2015: 34) constitutes the cosmos in the storied sense of a becoming-in-relation. Kgositsile's 'Towards a Walk in the Sun' does not look up to the heavens to locate the sun and the son connection; he expands into the language and the lived experience that create his storied being that enshrines sacred mythologies and song, proverbs, and philosophical bearings. Reciting the 'birth of memory' is an act of re-membering triggered by the wind that places the female principle at the heart of the process of ending and beginnings, of rebirthing and naming.

Pruitt would know from readily available sources that Dogon cosmology articulates the rapid rotation of Sirius B – the brightest star in the night sky – in fifty-year orbital cycles, with great accuracy, even when this star cannot be seen without the use of a telescope. In Dogon culture this cosmology and its story of creation served as a blueprint for all facets of society, from the ways to cultivate fields and build houses, to weaving, pottery making, drumming, and blacksmithing. Southern African sacred mythology is constructed around similar genealogies, with agrarian, ceremonial, and temporal organizations tethered to cosmological phenomena. Pruitt and Kgositsile both draw from the genius of the Black collective, but through approaches that differ in productive ways: repetition with difference. In illustrating productive differences in solidarity politics, here we learn of another important site of divergence: access to African languages. Masks become an apt technology in comics as they enable their wearers to bear supernatural powers; for the Dogon, masks are ritual technologies to assert and access existing otherworlds. For Kgositsile, the phenomena of *terrafirmament* gather subsets and supersets of the universe that he expresses in the names-songs-places matrix, in which places include the cosmos. His gathering work is underscored by sound knowledges – *legodimo lefase, lefase legodimo* – implying a mirroring or continuity between earth and the cosmos.

In Pruitt's comic the cosmos is out there. The first page of the comic depicts a police chase and shootout in space, a resigned comment on the inability to escape white America's state-sponsored police violence, which would follow you into the cosmos. The skater's hoodie – an item of clothing now racialized and criminalized, and therefore anticipating the Black Lives Matter movement that would be triggered by the shooting of Treyvon Martin in February 2012 in a saga that focused on his hoodie as suspicious – transforms our cosmic skater into a technologically advanced robot resembling the American science-fiction action figures, the 'Transformers'. The mask is a ritual technology that transforms the skater into an African American superhero, a speculative Alter history. The skater finds refuge in a spaceship, illuminated by halo-like sunshine, is safely welcomed by James Brown and Sun Ra. The spaceship recalls Sun Ra's Ark and Dumas's 'ark of bones': they are both 'arkives' of the past and the future, with redemptive qualities for the protagonist skater who may be able to fetch his past

Fig. 3. Robert Pruitt's comic interior

to make sense of his future. For these purposes, he engages specifically with known African American ancestry. The Transformer superstructure stands side by side with a Dogon totem pole, advising Sun Ra to 'walk with the men', to which Sun Ra replies 'I regard them as kin', which I consider to be a comment on denouncing individualism in favour of communitarianism.

In the next page of the comic, Octavia Butler enters the frame donning a sweater emblazoned with the Black Panther Party logo. Jamal Cyrus's speculative record cover collage, where the image of Black Panthers carrying the coffin with a superimposed galaxy, is invoked here. This image emphasizes the proximity of Black life to death; the skater laments to Butler: 'had some tragic nights recently', referring to police brutality. The poetics around 'kin' as expressed by Sun Ra in the comic foreshadow the introduction of Butler in the next frame through associations with her novel *Kindred* (1979). It is a revolutionary novel that spans the land of the living, the living dead in the antebellum American south, and the future. It is expressive of the onto-triadic sense of being in the context of the diaspora.

The Dogon totem pole invites this past to go beyond the Middle Passage, to Africa. As a response to the protagonist's 'tragic nights', Butler offers, 'till our departure from life we struggle hard', projecting 'golden dreams beyond heaven's door'. The frame in which she articulates this is populated with a painting of Nat Turner as background, assembling with his kin to plot a revolt. This history of slave revolts is mined to inspire the future of resistance – just as slave revolts function in *Kindred* – in this juncture of the twenty-first century where a young boy has just been shot for being Black while wearing a hoodie and walking. While 'walk with the men' is androcentric, Butler intervenes as a matriarchive, holding the past and the future, potentiating endings and beginnings, rebirth and naming. The position of Turner 'behind' her and the Black Panthers as depicted on her chest represent an arc of history that must now shape the African American revolutionary resolve in the contemporary moment. She is soothsayer and holds the vision for an African American futurity, witnessed in the cult status she enjoys today. To the African American grievance with 'tragic nights' she might have added, 'our destiny is to take root among the stars' (Butler 1993: 75).

The abolitionist Nat Turner believed himself to be a prophet and became a fiery preacher and leader of the enslaved on his master's plantation in Southampton Country in Virginia. The narrative about his plans for an insurrection are marked by cosmological phenomena and cosmic shifts surrounding the sun. In February 1831, there was a solar eclipse, which Turner took as a sign that the time for the insurrection had arrived. He and his fellow rebels planned to stage their rebellion on 4 July. On that date, Turner fell so ill that they had to postpone their plans. On 13 August 1831, the sun appeared bluish-green. For Turner, this was the final sign. At two in the morning, Turner and his men set out to the Travis

Fig. 4. Robert Pruitt's comic interior ii

household where they slaughtered the white master and his household. They continued to raid and kill their oppressors on other plantations in a rampage that resulted in a total body count of fifty-five white people. In October of the same year Turner was captured, tried, and sentenced to execution. He was hanged in November 1831. Pruitt locates Turner, Octavia Butler, Kgositsile, the Black Panthers, and Sun Ra in a historical continuum, as prophets, soothsayers, and time travellers. And, most importantly, the three men in the art collective creatively construct an alternative history of thought from which to redirect their own lives, to think from the position of the unthought, and to wage a liberatory practice of their time drawn from known history. Similar to the work undertaken by the editors of *Octavia's Brood*, Turner's and the Panthers' social justice work and Butler's and Kgositsile's imaginative work are brought into dialogue as gospels of social justice for future Black communities, driven by forces of Love and Care.

Future Memory in Africa, Afrofuturism in Diaspora

To conclude this discussions, I offer my reflections on the artistic work fashioned from elsewheres of Southern African cosmologies that are coupled with lived history, storied lives of mythological and philosophical bearings, embodiment and enlivenment rituals and ceremonies, and conceptions of being and becoming. In this chapter, we saw the complexity that required to read/reed these works through the deeper analysis, from a visual perspective, of Kgositsile's 'Towards a Walk in the Sun', as depicted by African Americans in the twenty-first century. I view these translations and adaptations as productive in the ongoing discourses on Afrofuturism, futurity, and surrealism. What might they offer us in thinking about Africa's relationship with its diaspora, about the past in relation to the future in the present, and about space, in its multiple conceptions?

The burning question is: what is the future of Blackness in a perennially anti-Black world? This debilitating and existential question is communally experienced in the Black world, and in this chapter I have argued that we approach it, as Kgositsile and the art collective do, from our specific positionalities. The New World Black experience is troubled by genealogical deracination, natal alienation, and social death. Historicism marked that future with history 1, in which the future absents Blackness precisely because of the evacuation of Africans from the genesis of that history. However, an impressive body of work has been and continues to be produced that is characterized by what Kgositsile calls dreamkeeping and a practice he calls reeding and riting: evident in the work of Henry Dumas and Zora Neal Hurston, in Kgositsile's summation. In this chapter, the lives and works of Octavia Butler, Sun Ra, James Brown, Nat Turner and the Black Panther Party are exemplar par excellence of disordering and rupturing the continuous forward march of history 1. In both instances, history

1's unrelentless and violent trudging forward can be exploded by alternative histories of thought, conceptions of temporality, and space to assert a different form of the human.

We see the different artists in this chapter grapple with this question and challenge. The combination of a cosmocentric perception of being and knowing and Eshun's assertion about indigenous knowledges as the only pathway to worthwhile futures are foundational to Kgositsile's project in 'Towards a Walk in the Sun'. OJ&A understandably fashions speculative futures from their own lived and known archive of Black revolt, Black creativity, orality/aurality, and intellectual tradition. In their search, they enfold Africa in expressing this futurity as the continent is a part of their past, albeit not lived and known/knowable. Kgositsile's production of temporal zones such as the coil of time, NOW, future memory, and pastpresentfuture reflects a cosmology characterized by the totality of being between the past, present, and future, and affirmed by the principle of movement and continuity that enfolds the future and the past in the present. This enfolding also sutures the cosmos and the earth through the principle of *terrafirmament*.

In 'Towards a Walk in the Sun', the sun and the wind command the son to be born again, to lie in the west like the sun, and to rise again with fire that burns white settler occupation and oppression in Southern Africa, the continent, and the larger Black world. Starting out from *Motswasele II* as a source, Kgositsile inspires this revolt with the real-life rebellion and usurpation of King Motswasele by Moruakgomo, backed by the people. He draws a historical arc from Moruakgomo's insurgency to uMkhonto we Sizwe, the military wing of the ANC. His yearning for endings is accompanied by desires for beginnings, a death that must give birth to new life, and one that must be pursued NOW. The language of the poem sounds Setswana from the page through the mythic and poetic turns, the sibilance, and the rhythms that culminate in rupture: the dance and song, the *toyi toyi* that leads to engaging the enemy. In OJ&A's work, they deploy the image of the son raised through the 'ways of the gun' in the 'slum'. He ends his state-sanctioned abjection by occupying an Alter-reality, in the cosmos, where he finds his ancestors. Pruitt draws an arc of history from Nat Turner, while Cyrus's arc/ark is from the Mississippi arkive; but both arcs lead into their current struggle, which foreshadowed Black Lives Matter.

These are the productive differences observed, that echo both Mohale Mashigo and Nnedi Okorafor: the seamless blend of available and existing spiritualities, mythologies, and cosmologies with the imaginative and technological, the culling of lived, known, and knowable histories, indigenous languages, folklore, and urban legends to shape future imaginations. Both writers from the different geographies do this, relevant to their locales. In the case of diaspora, they imaginatively engage with Africa through speculative memory accessible in reading history, fashioning 'prosthetic memory' (Landsberg 2004), to stitch together the found, unlived history of the Dogon people to construct a futurism that is also shaped by a part of their identity as Africans. While both confront the need to divest from white supremacist societies, Kgositsile's work asserts another world, an elsewhere that exists within the paradigm of white totalitarianism, from which he culls these symbolisms, images, and codes to wage political resistance and assert return. In Pruitt's and Cyrus's interpretations, the otherworld is a literal walk towards the sun. Their diasporic experience is ruptured by the heinous Middle Passage that purportedly constituted a border of time. In the absence of material land to return to, the rupture acutely pronounces the absence of a lived past that is a precondition for creating the future, hence their reaching 'towards' Kgositsile as well as Dogon cosmology.

It is therefore inappropriate to term what is happening on the African continent 'Afrofuturism'. The objective is not to discredit Afrofuturism or deny its importance as a radical aesthetic in the Black diaspora. It is to say that it is precisely relevant in the specific context of the diaspora because of particular historical processes and aesthetic legacies. Not unlike the Black arts era's search for a Black aesthetic leading to the recovery of African and African American mythology, ideologies pioneered and propagated by Sun Ra became vital in the artistic expression of twenty-first-century movements such as Black Lives Matter. The writer Lavelle Porter contends that 'in the refrain #BlackLivesMatter, I hear what Sun Ra referred to as The Alter-Destiny, a new way of thinking and being that diverges from the destructiveness of life as it exists on the planet now' (2015). Furthermore, our archives of radical traditions attest to how Black radical imaginations and revolt are intergenerational and mutually reinforcing. In the present day, we saw Afrofuturism's theories of Black mythmaking adapted and transformed by the Black Lives Matter movement in 'creating alternatives to the iconography, culture and thought of white supremacy' (ibid). Afrofuturism is as vital to the Black diaspora at the frontlines of a protracted, centuries-old struggle in which 'the *not yet here*' (Crawford 2017) of the Harlem Renaissance, converges with the *not yet here* of the Black Arts Movement and the *not yet here* of early twenty-first-century African American literature and visual arts. It is a lineage with its own historical particularities.

We need different names for practices coming from the Africans living in Africa imagining futures or reimagining the present: 'whatever you do, do not go and call it something obnoxious like 'Motherland Futurism' – asseblief tog!', Mashigo (2018b) warns, tongue-in-cheek. As stated above, Okorafor calls her practice Africanfuturism, the prefix 'African' signalling her position as a Nigerian living in the States. In this crucial moment in our collective struggle, it will enrich us if we learn to locate and harvest our own archives to forage what our elders on the frontlines of these practices have languaged, conceptualized, and deposited in our collective archive. For those purposes, I draw from Kgositsile to name this practice 'future memory', the texturalities of which I investigate further in the next chapter.

Places: Black Consciousness Ecologies of Futurity 5

This chapter investigates political powers of the erotic in order to open ecologies of futures beyond the dominant culture's anti-Black linear progress narrative. It centres around the death of a revolutionary that gives others the will to live. It is about death rituals ferried from Tswana customs and funeral rites, whose import across the Atlantic soothes the hearts of African Americans. It is about grief and embracing its underside, finding love as a propulsive force towards engaging in purposeful action. This affective poetics is studied in this chapter as it is manifested in Kgositsile's personal life and work and rendered in his short story 'The Favorite Grandson' (*Black World*, November 1972), which revisits and transmutes feelings surrounding the death of his grandmother. He translates that context into the political context of Malcolm X's death in his essay 'Brother Malcolm and the Black Revolution' (*Negro Digest*, November 1968), republished as 'Malcolm X and the Black Revolution: the Tragedy of a Dream Deferred' in another crucial BAM text *Malcolm X: The Man and His Times* (1969), edited by John Henry Clarke.

I frame this chapter with a lesser-known medium from Kgositsile's literary corpus, a short story which, in its personal nature, reveals the world of interiority, interrogating his devastation and grief. The story, which includes a letter written by the narrator when he was only a child, recreates intimate dialogues between beloved grandma and grandson, in which the elder matriarch offers comforting wisdom that becomes salve and guidance, in turn giving the boy a will to live. She reminds him of the dualities of being: life and death, destruction and construction, and beginnings and endings, all within a dynamic of continuity. The boy writes:

> Mami, I do not know what has happened to me since a few days after they took you to the village graveyard. I do not understand it any more than I understand some of the things you have told me. Once, for instance, you said that every natural loss results in some gain; the way of nature's balance, you said it was. Is death such a loss? If it is, what gain results from it? And what then is life? (1972: 57)

This wisdom of loss and gain as intertwined draws from the cosmology of the land and becomes the baseline in Kgositsile's oeuvre. But more pertinent for this chapter, Kgositsile transplants his grandmother's wisdom to the Black world. Madikeledi's words and the principle they enshrine become the nucleic message in his essay 'Brother Malcolm and the Black Revolution', an offering to the African American community in the throes of loss and grief. Further, in his short story Kgositsile introduces us to death rites in the village of Dithakong, as they were carried out during his grandmother's funeral. Therein, a 'Motswana doctor' performs cleansing rituals. This inspires him to place a Motswana doctor at the heart of his essay who performs death rites over Malcom X's death. In the essay, the doctor divines with a Setswana proverb that couches this wisdom of duality as communal wisdom, echoing grandma Madikeledi. The proverb is deployed in its original language and in translation, a decision made by Kgositsile to emphasize the sonic features of the rhythms and sibilance and the music and tonality of the proverb. Kgositsile employs these rhythms to channel wisdom from the matriarchive and redirects it towards his *Negro Digest* readership, whose energies he wishes to inject with a will to live and to continue their collective liberatory mission after their collective loss of Malcolm. He inspires them to derive meaning and purpose from Malcolm's death, just as he has from his grandmother's death.

Curiously, retaining the Tswana proverb in the essay played an unintended, historical role. The magazine *Negro Digest* found its way into South Africa in the late 1960s during the burgeoning of the Black Consciousness Movement, where it made it into the hands of poet and visual artist Lefifi Tladi. He was enthused by the proverb in Kgositsile's essay and adapted it as the title to his body of visual work. His encounter with the political currency of the Tswana proverb deeply inspired him, seeding in him an appreciation of the importance of writing in his own language, of deriving a visual aesthetic from indigenous languages and ritual practices. Secondly, Tladi was moved to harness the musicality and symbolism of the language, as displayed in his visual interpretation of the proverb, in an aesthetic that has been called abstract expressionism. Operating in the matrix of *malopo*, a healing tradition that incorporates song, dance, drumming, divining, and healing reveals, as I will argue, that the vernacular and frequencies of his visual work derive from elsewhere, necessitating another way of seeing and reading his work, outside the given frameworks of western art history.

Invested in magic and poetry as tools to liberate the unconscious, surrealists saw/felt in poetry 'the fundamental experience, the root of all knowledge, the most certain guide to action' against 'the rationalization of the unlivable' (Franklin Rosemont in Keeling 2019: x-xi). We observe something critical in Kgositsile's use of the Tswana proverb as poetic language in his essay: that the Tswana proverb he adapts is a poetic that breaks out of the Europatriarchal legibility and frame of intelligibility; that the proverb is part of storying forms of being that depart from the category of human as dictated by the Europatriarchy. Tladi's adaptation of the Tswana proverb as employed for political ends by

Kgositsile offers Tladi a countercultural aesthetic that functions against 'the rationalization of the unlivable' in apartheid South Africa. Kgositsile's essay situates the proverb as future memory: the deployment of a Tswana proverb in dialogue with Malcolm X was revelatory for Tladi, who was awakened to see anew the practice of poetry as a social force for revolutionary action. This poetry, as was clearly demonstrated to him, inheres in the languages of the people, in their ritual and spiritual practices, and must be approached as potential weapons to explode white settler geography. This was in line with the Black Consciousness Movement philosophy.

This marked a turn in Tladi's evolving consciousness, and what he subsequently achieved in his aesthetic vitalizes the argument made in the previous chapter: I demonstrate how, as a Tswana speaker, he grasped the 'powerful images from our history, legend and art' (Achebe 1987: vi) that are enshrined by the proverb used by Kgositsile and which in turn called up the whole image in Tladi's imagination. Black Consciousness, when successful, harnessed this poetic knowledge rooted in the deepest, strongest, and richest parts of us, and used it as a resource. This is the power of the erotic, and as Audre Lorde argues, 'in order to perpetuate itself, every oppression must corrupt or distort those various sources of power within the culture of the oppressed that can provide energy for change' (1984: 87). The use of the Tswana proverb in this political context of Black internationalism brought into focus the power of poetic knowledge and the erotic. It also enthused Kgositsile's BAM comrades.

In Kgositsile's deft hands, the Motswana doctor freights the proverb with psychic, emotional, and spiritual currency as social forces that gear towards political action. The erotic, as Lorde argues, 'is the nurturer or nursemaid of all our deepest knowledge' (1984: 56), and Kgositsile draws from his storied life, from the wisdom and praxis of the matriarchive, to derive this deep knowledge. Nthabiseng Motsemme (2018) argues that taking the complexity of Blackwomen's lives serviously would have to give earnest consideration to how African women express their spirituality through the church and practices of African traditional beliefs and rituals. This chapter demonstrates that the ritual archive, with Kgositsile's mothers as custodians, are a formative and foundational knowledge. Kgositsile's excavation of his grandmother's wisdom, the *mythos* and *cosmogeny* (Wynter 1984) that storied his being, in his search for the root of all knowledge against the prevailing order, is a type of gathering work that re-members him to other forms of being antecedent to colonial modernity. These are located in the matriarchive.

My interest here lies in Kgositsile's philosophical wandering in the Black world that in turn gifted Tladi with a philosophical contravening of white settler geography. It was crucial for Tladi to know at the time that one could break out of that grid into another world. As I will demonstrate, Tladi's transformation thanks to Kgositsile's essay illustrates that while the Black Consciousness

Movement in South Africa was inspired by the Black Power Movement in the States, there were South Africans that constituted the Black Power Movement, thus complicating any readings in which influence purely moves from North to South, or in which Black South Africans simply emulated African American culture.

Kgositsile: South African 'Negro' in the *Black World*

It is vital here to highlight an important relationship between Kgositsile and Hoyt Fuller, the editor of *Negro Digest/Black World*. This magazine was a mouthpiece for Kgositsile's voice in the Black Arts and Black Power milieu, which saw him as a bridge between Black Africa and Black America even before the publication of his debut collection of poetry. Founded in 1943 in Chicago by John Johnson publishers, the magazine served as a critical vehicle for political thought during the civil rights movement and would be the mouthpiece of the Black Power Movement and its cultural wing, the BAM.[1] The editor, Hoyt Fuller, is considered 'the "midwife" or "dean" of the Black Arts Movement' (Fenderson 2011: v), at the helm of *Negro Digest* (*Black World*) from 1961 to 1975. If the genesis of the Black Arts Movement is marked by Malcolm X's death, then its conclusion is considered to be related to 'John Johnson's decision to stop the production of *Black World* magazine and termina[tion of] its editor, Hoyt Fuller' (ibid.), in 1976. Incidentally, the end of 1975 also marks the end of Kgositsile's exile period in the United States of America and his return to the African continent.

Fuller roused (inter)national sensibilities among Black intellectuals, artists, and activists, 'much like the position granted to Alain Locke by scholars of the Harlem Renaissance' (Fenderson 2011: v). In these early days of *Negro Digest*'s transitioning to a more radical magazine, Fuller took a liking to Kgositsile, who brought to the nascent Black Arts Movement a specific (Southern) African experience. Kgositsile's work first appeared in the *Negro Digest* as early as 1967, in an edition dedicated to defining the burgeoning Black aesthetic that would inform the Black arts ethos. Fuller formed a camaraderie with Kgositsile, based on the unique (Southern) African tenor in the writing of the latter, whom the former published with great enthusiasm. Fuller wrote of him, '[…] Kgositsile is a refugee

---

[1] *Negro Digest* was founded by the same publishers of *Ebony* and *Tan* magazines and was issued on a monthly basis between 1942 and 1951, when it was discontinued. Publisher John H. Johnson wanted to renew the magazine and 'join in the presentation of "negro" news, covered increasingly in periodicals with international circulation' (Lewis 2010: 19). The magazine was revived in 1961 and, until 1965, 'specialized in popular articles digested and reprinted from other magazines, many of them white in orientation. […] In both intention and tone, *Negro Digest* of the early 1960s was integrationist' (ibid.). 1965 marked a radical change in the magazine, with the emergence of militant writing in the Black arts.

from South Africa. [...] Mr Kgositsile has the advantage of being familiar with many African writers unknown in America, but he also is very much a part of the contemporary Black writers' scene in America' (*Negro Digest*, January 1968: 18). Kgositsile's work in his capacity as a short story writer, essayist, poet, book reviewer, and interviewer made frequent appearances in the *Negro Digest*. He was a regular contributor to the magazine, and its covers regularly carried his name as a point of attraction for readers. Natalie Crawford records that, by 1968, Kgositsile 'had become one of the central poets of the Black Arts Movement' (2007: 113).

Kgositsile's first collection of poetry, *Spirits Unchained*, was published in 1969 by Dudley Randall's Broadside Press, which positioned itself to publish the outpouring of poetry by Black writers in that milieu. Kgositsile has already concretized his position in the BAM and that year won the *Negro Digest*-administered second Conrad Kent Rivers Award – named after the poet, who had died the previous year. The award was in the form of prize money amounting to $500. The first Conrad Kent Rivers Memorial Fund Award had been won by Carolyn Rodgers of Chicago in 1968. The judges took some convincing at the time to choose a South African native as the winner of a poetry prize that honours African American poetry. According to literary scholar and writer Sterling Plumpp, 'Fuller made sure [Kgositsile] got the Conrad Kent Award',[2] supported by Chicago poet laureate Gwendolyn Brooks.

These unfolding events, alongside African Americans' repudiation of the label 'negro', motivated the change of the magazine's name from *Negro Digest* to *Black World* in 1970, based on 'Fuller's view that the magazine ought to be a voice for Black people everywhere' (Salaam 1991). Kgositsile had conducted the interview and published 'Black Consciousness in Brazil: Interview with Abdias do Nascimento, A Third World Artist' in the *Negro Digest* of May 1969, bringing the politics of the larger Black world, of Latin America, to the BAM and Black Power context. Further, he had published the poem 'Lumumba Section', dedicated to Patrice Lumumba in the 1968 edition of that magazine. In *The Black Arts Movement Enterprise and the Production of Poetry*, Howard Rambsy II argues: 'The appearance of Kgositsile's poem on Lumumba reveals *Negro Digest*'s commitment to addressing the struggles and injustices on the African continent. Further, the publication of Kgositsile's poem anticipates *Negro Digest*'s developing focus on "Black world" issues beyond the United States' (2013: 31). Kgositsile's incisive essays on third-world matters and on the politics of decolonization in the global south pushed for that periodical's renaming to *Black World* in 1970. The name change communicated Fuller's vision of reflecting 'the widespread rejection of "negro" and the adaptation of "Black" as the designation of choice for people of African descent and to indicate identification with both

---

[2] Author interview with Sterling Plumpp, Chicago, September 2014.

the diaspora and Africa' (Salaam 1991). This name change is emblematic of the adaptations of African-language names by BAM proponents who sought to fashion identities that reflected their ties with the African continent, beyond American soil.

The dialects and languages of the millions in Africa were celebrated in the Black community of the *Black World*, as uniquely witnessed in the January 1975 edition of the magazine, which published Kgositsile's poem 'Places and Bloodstains: Notes for Ipeleng' in English, followed by its Setswana translation, 'Mafelo Le Dilabe Tsa Madi (Ya ga Ipeleng)' (1975b: 62–5). Fuller adds an editor's note at the end of the English version of the poem: 'on the following pages, "Places and Bloodstains" appears in the poet's native language. Mr Kgositsile was born in Azania (South Africa)'. This was a characteristically bold editorial decision by Fuller. Publishing Kgositsile's poem in Setswana as well as English supports Brent Hayes Edwards' assertion that 'it is not possible to take up the question of diaspora without taking account of the fact that the great majority of peoples of African descent do not speak or write in English', and that as such 'the cultures of diaspora can be seen only in translation' (2003: 7). Therein we witness Kgositsile bringing a culture and cosmology of other locations into conversation with his BAM contemporaries. The publication of 'Mafelo Le Dilabe Tsa Madi (Ya ga Ipeleng)' shows how the existence of other worlds in the diaspora were considered by Fuller as productive, not problematic. It emphasizes the reinforcement of a necessarily Black aesthetic in the Black power milieu, grounded in African languages, spiritualities, and cosmologies, which Kgositsile physically and ideologically stood for. The significance of his presence in the Black America and *Black World* during that era cannot be overemphasized.

In 1971, Doubleday published Kgositsile's third collection of poetry *My Name is Afrika*. The collection was initially submitted to Columbia University as part of the requirements for the fulfilment of a Masters' Degree in Arts. In manuscript form, it carried the dedication, 'For Malcolm and Frantz Fanon'; the published version that circulates today, however, is dedicated 'to Hoyt W. Fuller'. The introduction to the collection is written by Gwendolyn Brooks, who by now had formed a solid friendship and literary camaraderie with Kgositsile. Brooks had been part of an older generation of writers who saw the 1960s Black liberation movements as positively turbulent. As Plumpp told me, Brooks 'was not afraid of the possible chaos that could arise from these young poets'.[3] Brooks 'wrote about Black people with great eloquence' (ibid.), and in her *Family Pictures* (1970), she pens three poems dedicated to 'Young Heroes', Kgositsile being one of them. This way, Kgositsile became a permanent feature in the family album of the Black arts era. 'Young Heroes: Keorapetse Kgositsile

---

[3] Author interview with Sterling Plumpp, Chicago, September 2014.

(Willie)' became the introduction to *My Name is Afrika*. The three-part poem 'Young Heroes' was further published in another seminal Black arts anthology, *The Black Poets* (1971), edited by Dudley Randall.

A firm advocate of Kgositsile's work, Brooks highly recommended the inclusion of his poetry in the anthology, *The Poetry of Black America: Anthology of the 20th Century* (1973), which was introduced by Brooks. In her introduction, she writes: 'many applauders of Black poetry have never heard of the searching New York poet Raymond Patterson, or of the carefully rich technics of Audre Lorde and Keorapetse W. Kgositsile' (1973: xxx). These textual circuitries that are deemed anthologies of 'Black America', 'Afro-American writing', and 'negro digest' are complicated by Kgositsile's presence therein. They task us to rewrite the historiography of the Black arts era in the States to expand its geographies towards South Africa. The BAM book culture represents not only imagined communities but real and lived communities that continue to shape the production of Black arts and politics on both sides of the Atlantic. Fuller's *Negro Digest* and the seminal BAM anthologies provide an ideal site to study these communities and Kgositsile's participation and transformational power therein.

Poetic Divinations

Imagine you are a reader of *Negro Digest*, leafing through its November 1968 edition that carries the face of recently assassinated Black leader Malcolm X on the cover. The first article published therein after the contents page is penned by Keorapetse Kgositsile. This would not have struck any regular reader as particularly peculiar, especially as the name of the magazine suggests that there would be 'negro' writing therein. Kgositsile was a regular contributor to the magazine, his name often appearing on the cover – as it did on this particular edition – to attract the magazine's readership. When you read his essay 'Brother Malcolm and the Black Revolution', you are taken aback by the poem that prefaces his musings: Langston Hughes' iconic 'Harlem', cited in its entirety. You prepare for the intellectual throes promised by a conversation between Kgositsile, Malcolm, and Hughes and are hooked by the first line of the essay: 'I write this with something bordering on fear' (1968: 42). It sets the tone. The subject matter is shrouded by dread: the relationship between the death of Malcolm and the deferred dream prophesied by Hughes might become apparent at this point. Kgositsile brings in a fourth party to convene this conversation: a Motswana doctor, who 'throws his bones' to divine over the dream's deferral, the processing of Malcolm's death.

The fourth interlocutor, the Motswana doctor, speaks another language in his divination. He comes from another world with its sets of signs and symbols, codes and visions. It throws the idea and image of Kgositsile you have always had into a mystery, operating between familiar and strange. As a regular reader of *Negro Digest* you are thrown by Kgositsile into a world *other* to yours even in your commitment to pan-African Blackness, bringing this world closer and perhaps even invoking something familiar. Kgositsile writes:

> [...] running through my mind are the following words of Setswana wisdom; a Motswana doctor throws his bones and when they tell him of an irretrievable loss he will say:
>
> '*Se ileng se ile*
> Se ile mosimeng, motlhaela-thupa
> Lesilo ke moselatedi'
>
> Loosely translated, this says, 'what is gone is gone / it has gone down the hole, the-unreachable-by-rod / the irrational (i.e. the unwise and ill tempered) is he-who-follows-it'. (42)

In this critical period of social change that makes demands on a people, in the face of collective shock, loss, and grief, Kgositsile draws from ancient wisdom to find a way forward. He revisits the emotions around Madikeledi's death, her own advice drawn from communal Tswana wisdom, that 'every natural loss results in some gain; the way of nature's balance' (1972: 57). In the essay, he enshrines her words as sacred, uttered by a healer and seer. Notably, a Motswana doctor also appears in *Motswasele II* – the doctor is commonplace as intercessor for the family or community in its time of crisis. Following the lead of the Batswana, of his grandmother, and of his literary predecessors, Kgositsile calls on the wisdom of the ancestors through the 'Motswana doctor', a productive nomenclature which, instead of 'traditional doctor', modernizes and rallies that medicinal science as productive in this context. This signals how poetic knowledge in the form of a Setswana proverb is deployed as an alternative philosophical and historical thought culled from a Southern African medicinal practice older than colonial modernity to operate in America, in the *Negro Digest*. Such is the nature of the knowledge systems Kgositsile deploys to intercede in these grave matters; he cloaks himself with priestly robes to function as seer and diviner in the tradition of gifted orators and healers of his land. He speaks from elsewhere, outside colonial modernity's parameters of being and knowing, outside its frame of intelligibility and legibility. He hacks/hexes its restrictive borders of logic and registers of realism with spiritual practices from Southern African cosmologies.

The Tswana proverb utilized by Kgositsile may be read as what Sylvia Wynter calls 'a new science, a hybrid science: a science of the Word' preconditional to rewriting/resounding and producing knowledge beyond the machinations of Euromodern 'Man' (McKittrick & Wynter 2015: 17). What is noteworthy here is that Wynter deems Aimé Césaire's notion of 'poetic knowledge' as constituting that science. Poetic knowledge constitutes the stories, mythologies, cosmologies, indigenous languages, proverbs, and songs that break with the limits and strictures of the dominant order and its categories of being and knowing. The presence of the traditional doctor disrupts western medicinal science, while his sound knowledges rendered in the proverb form depart from the exclusionary episteme towards collective and communal knowledges. Kgositsile's *gathering work* coalesces acoustemologies and epistemologies through interweaving the oral/aural and literary African traditions with African American literary (Hughes) and political (Malcolm X) traditions to adapt the elsewhere to the context of Black America. By so doing, he upholds the cultures and knowledges from below, from the body and collective internetworked bodies, from the collective, from the matriarchive, routing them to impact Black international politics.

Was Kgositsile exposed to African spiritual practices in his formative years? We learn about this in 'The Favorite Grandson', which addresses his grandmother's passing and funeral rites; here, a Motswana doctor is invited to cleanse the family, according to custom. In his essay, Kgositsile invites the Motswana doctor into the context of Black America for a ritual of cleansing, re-routing that custom. Conversing with Paule Marshall's work of 'poets of the kitchen', Mandisa Harhoff argues that 'Black womxn's talk, conversations, prayers, and recollections are sites of literary inspiration, living and embodied archives that we must uphold more deliberately and intentionally' (2021: 91). This present book's method of diligently looking to where the women are sounded attends to these embodied archives, erotics, gnosis, and poetic knowledges, the prayers and spiritual practices which are a science. They unmake the ongoing march of the colonial narrative of progress and its assumed universality: they recast the erotic as worldmaking. Further, this science comprises poetics of aliveness against the death machine of nonbeing and thingification. These elements in Kgositsile's essay do not belong to him but are communal cultural heirlooms: he is practising what he has lived, producing a philo-praxis that formulates a generative space for his Black diaspora counterparts as well as Tladi. The erotic sciences require what Maria Lugones calls 'faithful witnessing' (2003), an honest re-evaluation and overturning of our value system regarding what constitutes knowledge, resistance, politics, and revolution.

Kgositsile's reimagining of Tswana proverbs in the context of Black internationalist politics is a practice of an elsewhere science, but this science must first and foremost be recognized as a scientific offering. As Francis B. Nyamnjoh states, not only are proverbs

> [...] universal in their use to express emotions, thoughts, experiences and challenges, they are also universal in the very fact of the mobility of humans, ideas and language across geographies. The power of the proverb lies in its eternal incompleteness of mean-

ing, that constantly opens itself up to improvisation and creative innovation in usage with and across cultural communities. (2021)

This beautiful meditation on proverbs informs us of the incompleteness of proverbs, always reaching out and forward, rooted/routed in a living past. Proverbs enshrine future memory: an imagining of the future that couches the sensibility of their collective makers in the past; these collective makers issue an invitation to never foreclose meaning nor stop transmitting the incomplete heirloom, improvising upon it to issue forth its innate gesture of hope, purpose, and desire to impact the future. The proverb is felt ('emotions'), thought ('thoughts'), and lived ('experienced'), putting forward forms of being, knowing, and doing that point to particular beliefs and worldsystems. In retrieving these sound knowledges, Kgositsile acknowledges his own incompleteness, fostering continuities between past, present, and future, while also enlivening himself and proponents of the BAM with the open-ended and mutable dance, with meaning and comprehension of himself, them, and their collective fears, loss, grief, desires, and dreams. The proverb traverses new contexts across the Atlantic to produce 'new' significations, meanings, and comprehensions of history and geography, of kinship with others, becoming the basis of solidarity and conviviality in their mutual incompleteness.

As the proverb travelled back to South Africa freighting new political and revolutionary currencies, it shifted Tladi into a new understanding of himself through what was already there, urging him to fix his eyes to hear/feel the science of the word of his people in the proverb: what the Black Consciousness Movement was all about. In employing the lens of future memory to read Tladi's work, as opposed to surrealism or Afro-surrealism, I propose renewed ways to *reed* and *rite* about art fashioned from these otherworlds and their ritual archives. Toyin Falola's offering of 'ritual archives' attends to the active, physical, and metaphysical cultural expressions from those worlds, their erotics, science, and cosmologies. It underscores 'the metaphorical and mystical sense of "archive" […] that dimension of archive that is never (fully) collected but retains power and agency in invisible ways' (Falola 2017: 913). These archives – felt but unseen – shape and inform the work of some African artists such as Tladi, worlds that are governed by incompleteness, totality, continuity, erotics, sciences, and sound knowledges. We must overturn our co-opting and capturing cosmological orders to hear and feel their art as much as we 'view' it.

BAM and the Search for Erotics of Revolution

The sonics in the sibilance of the Motswana doctor's proverb, the communitarian currency embedded in his intercession, and the trenchancy of his wisdom rooted in Setswana remain outside the full grasp of the *Negro Digest* readership. These aspects of the text constitute what Brent Edwards calls *décalage* – 'the trace or the residue [...] of what resists or escapes translation' (2003: 13). However, Kgositsile marshals the prophecy of Hughes's poem to operate within the prophetic signification of the Motswana doctor's bones, while citing the poem – by now an anthem in Black America – to facilitate ritual through incantation. The image of the Motswana doctor is brought closer to comprehension; the conceptual and experiential fissure among Black world readers is sutured, assisted by Kgositsile's reframing through his bridging work to draw from their own contexts. The reader is assisted by personal or literary encounters with shamans, healers, vodun priestesses, and soothsayers in Black diaspora spiritual practices; figures that might have been conjured in the narratives of Frederick Douglass, Harriet Tubman, Jean Toomer, Zora Neale Hurston, and Henry Dumas, among others. These figures become knowable to the Black diaspora through their spiritual practices routed to and transformed into the New World setting, but with roots in Africa. Spiritual practices remain a mainstay in tracing continuities and forging relationalities and kinship between these two geographies on both sides of the Atlantic.

Kgositsile's essay in this edition of *Negro Digest* is critical, as the Black arts era was in search of Black aesthetics grounded on invoking the 'powers of magic, song, divination, theology, and ancestral Blackness as weapons in a holy war for righteousness and justice' (Wright 2003: xi). As one of the figureheads of the movement, Larry Neal explains:

> behind much of the Black Arts Movement's strident literary nationalism lay a more quiet and contemplative but no less intense search for harmonious values, ontology, and self, a search that perceived Blackness as ultimately 'embracing the Universal in man', and which employed the language of religious reform and the symbolism of ritual experience and spiritual transcendence'. (cited in ibid: xiii)

Proponents of Black arts agitated and hungered for aesthetic uses of African and African American cosmologies, iconographies, and mythologies to achieve that quest. Kgositsile's work was a great example in this regard, receiving what might read as superlative praise by BAM-era poets, scholars, publishers, and literary critics alike: Sterling Plumpp wrote of Kgositsile's poetry: 'this is the work of a poet hearing his own muse and inventing an original expression as medium for the oracle' (cited in Kgositsile 2002: 7). Tom Dent argues that Kgositsile's 'voice contains an innate, almost divine authority, as if he is participant in a privileged conversation about the nature of life' (1976: n.p.). George Kent writes: 'In Kgositsile's poetry, you hear a true and distinguished voice. It is the voice of the African priest speaking directly to your soul [...] whether he is talking about ancestral things or contemporary nerve failures [...]' (cited in Kgositsile 1974: i). In an article for the *Negro Digest* in September 1968, Don Lee (later known as Haki Madhubuti) counsels his compatriots to heed Kgositsile's characterization of Black poetry: 'brother Kgositsile is more than accurate when he calls his poetry "love poetry"; it's the love of one's people that is embodied in his poetry, the will to survive as a nation of Black people' (1968: 29). Eschewing the labels peddled in that era – protest poetry or resistance poetry, or even Black poetry – Kgositsile offers us an apt appellation – love poetry – for the root of anger and resistance against oppression is love.

Rage and revolt assert, affirm, and articulate that we come from love, that we know and have lived by something else that is not the lovelessness and spiritual death of colonial modernity and white supremacy. Kgositsile's poetry embodies this and invokes, as John Wright writes, 'one ancestral Blackness as weapons in a holy war for righteousness and justice' (2003: xxvi). In his 'Poet's Credo', Kgositsile writes: 'I frantically believe in the supremacy of Spirit'. He continues: 'I am a part of the world – a release of the greater force [... than] the white world's denial of the supremacy of Spirit; because of the white world's denial of love' (1968: 42–3). A politics of resistance is a politics of love; resistance poetry is love poetry. Revolt built upon love is a holy war for it fights for the supremacy of spirit. In his 1968 essay 'Brother Malcolm and the Black Revolution', Kgositsile foregrounds *love* as the connective tissue between *politics* and *spirit*.[4] He writes:

> To talk of a revolutionary ideology is to talk about the *spirit* of a people. And Malcolm [...] was our spiritual thrust. Many people who have written about Malcolm have overlooked, deliberately or unwittingly, the importance of his *inner landscape*, his spirit. [...] what did not die, what cannot die [...] Malcolm's *inner landscape* informed his movement, the practical manifestation of his abstract energy [...] This was, and will always be, the godly power in Malcolm, his energy, spiritual (1968a: 6, emphasis in original).

The ties that bind the four interlocutors in his essay become evident: Kgositsile is invested in Malcolm's 'inner landscape', viewing Malcolm as one who possesses and channels something Kgositsile recognized in the orators of his native land, characterized by 'the distilled voice of the community' that casts the orator as 'a kind of receptacle of the feelings and the spirit of the community', 'partly historian, partly philosopher, partly the consciousness of the community,

---

4   As also argued by Audre Lorde: 'The dichotomy between the spiritual and the political is also false, resulting from an incomplete attention to our erotic knowledge. For the bridge which connects them is formed by the erotic – the sensual – those physical, emotional, and psychic expressions of what is deepest and strongest and richest within each of us, being shared: the passions of love, in its deepest meanings' (1984: 89).

and partly a singer and entertainer' (1978: 37). These qualities were inherent in Malcolm. They are also qualities of a poet-orator in traditional Southern African society. To Kgositsile, Malcom's power was larger than himself, the release of a greater force possessing him in his moment of oration, channelling spiritual energy that points to the propulsive forces of love and spirit. This is what Kent, Plumpp, Dent, and Madhubuti observed in Kgositsile's work: his inner landscape. In bringing the Motswana doctor into contact with Hughes, Malcolm, and himself, Kgositsile writes a treatise on the power of the erotic and its potential to shift the felt and embodied of the inner landscape – the depthoffeeling and collective desires – to the mind of the people, who would subsequently use it to produce political thought that ultimately 'explodes', in the Hughesan sense, into revolutionary action.

Love bridges emotional and spiritual realms with psychic and political ideology or expression, transforming it to inform collective action. At the heart of this is the matriarchive – Kgositsile's first experience and comprehension of love. Anna Malaika Tubbs' book *Three Mothers: How the Mothers of Martin Luther King, Jr., Malcolm X, and James Baldwin Shaped a Nation* (2020) recasts Malcolm's mother Louise Little in his politics of love. Indeed, as Malcolm himself said: 'The mother is the first teacher of the child. The message she gives that child, that child gives to the world'. The book I have written and that you are reading also seeks to bring from the shadows the role of Blackwomen in building the rich inner landscapes of Black leaders who led their people with love and purpose. As bell hooks taught us, those same leaders could not have learnt love outside the homeplace in the white supremacist environments in which they lived; it was in the home, often created by women, that they could be 'be subjects, not objects', and where 'they had the opportunity to grow and develop, to nurture [their] spirits' (1990: 384). The matriarchive attends to this labour by Blackwomen, tasking us to re/think of Black liberation through the framework of family and community beyond the cult of personality, and as intergenerational work.

Proponents of the Black Arts Movement and their quest for Black aesthetics must be read as a search for this inner landscape, for a science of the erotic which is the grammar of depthoffeeling, and for ritual archives to break with the strictures of the prevalent order of white domination and its oppressive structures. This world limited their experience to survival – a denial of the supremacy of spirit – reducing their lives to the everyday desolation that surrounded them, thereby precluding any form of self-actualization. According to Toyin Falola, ritual archives are

> The conglomeration of words as well as texts, ideas, symbols, shrines, images, performances, and indeed objects that document as well as speak to those religious experiences and practices that

> allow us to understand the African world through various bodies of philosophies, literatures, languages, histories and much more. (2017: 913)

I wrote of these ritual archives earlier as sciences of the erotic, where Kgositsile in his essay is consciously practising gathering work by interweaving those symbols and images from Southern Africa with those of African America, their sound worlds and knowledges, and their literatures and histories. Placing Hughes alongside the Motswana doctor opens the sound worlds of these two geographies to co-exist and co-constitute meaning on both sides of the Atlantic. But it is also a recognition and nod to Hughes' deployment of African American sound knowledges and ontological bearings in his poetics of the communal. Critically, literary scholar and writer Sterling Plumpp finds Kgositsile's reverence of Hughes' work fascinating, and he believes there are stark similarities between the two poets. He states:

> Oddly enough there is great similarity between Langston Hughes and Kgositsile in their efforts to forge a relationship with a commitment to the African American community of the Harlem Renaissance and the Black Arts Movement. Hughes arrived in New York in the early 1920s from Mexico City to attend Columbia University ostensibly to become an architect. [...] Hughes becomes enthused with blues and Black music and adopts and adapts blues verse as a basic stanzaic block to give authenticity to citizens of Harlem. His imagination as an artist reflected his commitment to the people of Harlem and their history and culture and struggles. Kgositsile, on the other hand, arrives in Harlem/New York City in the early 1960s to receive training at the New School. He ventures to Harlem and adopts its people as his own. He brings with him a fully developed imagination regarding his people's history and culture and struggles. He extends that imagination to communicate with Harlem and Black America. Jazz, blues and gospel are as natural to him as any Setswana folk song or proverb.[5]

If the BAM is the second wave of the Harlem Renaissance, as some critics have argued, then Plumpp is here arguing that Kgositsile is to the BAM what Hughes was to the Harlem Renaissance. By extending his imagination to communicate with Harlem and Black America, Kgositsile aligns himself with Hughes, positioning his work as polyvocal, speaking with Hughes in solidarity with the collective struggles of African Americans in all directions of time. This strategy

---

5   Author interview with Sterling Plumpp via email exchange, April 2015.

is informed by gathering work, and we saw it manifest in Kgositsile's deployment of Richard Wright's *Native Son* in the previous chapters, as a vehicle to address the hearts and collective desires of Black America. Hughes's work is emblematic of the tradition within which he works: Hughes's commitment to the people of Harlem and their history, culture, and struggles mirrors Kgositsile's own commitments. They are driven by a politics and a poetics of love. In his pursuit of social cohesion, Hughes looked to Black music to find the 'current vernacular of the African American people' and presented the authenticity of the citizens of Harlem.[6] Similarly, Kgositsile's preoccupations with communitarian values and collective action was articulated through harnessing Black music.

Through the universalism of the proverb, Kgositsile opens a space of incompleteness in which African Americans in their own search for the 'language of religious reform and the symbolism of ritual experience and spiritual transcendence' (Neal cited in Wright 2003: xiii) can find meaning and relation. Tladi, however, listens into these worlds and, being Tswana himself, is moved in specific ways by the rituality of the proverb and Motswana doctor, their orbit in political and intellectual formations of the Black diaspora, which in turn inspires him to interpret them into a visual language that dances and sings. The motion, movement, and action of his paintings resist the rigidity and stasis of Euromodern art worlds, while also sounding rhythms of a new day brought about by ritual.

A Dialogue Across the Ocean: Black Consciousness and Black Power

Kgositsile demonstrates that the universal can be claimed from any cultural position. His transformation of Tswana sound knowledges into Black internationalist contexts powers his mission and grants his work a latent charge, opening multiple locations of spacetimes and universals from which to reject western universalism. The multiplicity is enriched by the bridging qualities of his work and its masterful interweaving of African American vernacular, literary, political, and spiritual practices with those of Southern Africa. This way, he asserts a logic of solidarity and flow between these geographical loci that challenges the directions of flow from north to south in the archives of Black internationalism in the twentieth century, demonstrating complex routes of exchange that exceed movements of people, even in the heightened surveillance of the white supremacist regimes of both countries. This essay, alongside the poem published in the January 1975 edition of *Black World* titled 'Mafelo Le Dilabe Tsa Madi (Ya ga Ipeleng)' and discussed earlier, illustrate the polyglottic nature of the black diaspora beyond colonial languages, and the variegated

---

[6] Ibid.

cosmologies, spiritualities, and worlds that shape diasporic culture, politics, relationalities, and sensibilities. It enriches the tapestry of Black diaspora work that pushes us beyond thinking in Anglophonic terms.

Kgositsile's essay on Malcolm X found its way to South Africa into the hands of Black Consciousness (BC) visual artist and poet Lefifi Tladi, mentioned earlier in this chapter, who was so immensely moved that he produced a body of work inspired by the Tswana proverb as it sounded new political contexts. Filling the vacuum of literary elders left by post-Sharpeville exile, imprisonment, banning, and censorship, Tladi was excited and energized by getting his hands on the work of a South African in exile. The transoceanic movement of the *Negro Digest* copy recorded here is of a different kind: of South Africans living, writing, rioting, and publishing in the States, while their work, banned in South Africa, found its way across the border through underground structures. Andries van der Vlies coins the phrase 'textual Atlantic' to account for 'South African-American-European identification' through print cultures, adding that,

> attending to text and print cultures in the textual Atlantic, to the material fates of texts in print and in constant physical and metaphorical movement, allows us to cast light on the processes by which writing from South Africa and the United States circulates and is transformed in transnational spaces of exchange and appropriation (2007: 53).

The fugitivity that marks underground movements of texts by banned writers back into their own countries is largely unaccounted for precisely because of the covert and clandestine nature of the texts' movements, which require a different type of tracing and mapping.

Tladi read Kgositsile's essay in the 1960s, a decade that commenced with the dragnet of apartheid security and surveillance functioning under the banner of The Suppression of Communism Act of 1950, and tightening control through the passage of various acts. The vacuum of the 1960s was compounded by the ongoing effects of the Bantu Education Act (1953) in the previous decade, which essentially prepared Blacks for manual labour and servitude by designing subpar curricula for Black schools. The Publications Act of 1963 declared the publication, printing, or distribution of 'undesirable' materials produced both locally and abroad a statutory offence, punishable by prison sentences (McDonald 2009: 33). The underground became the only feasible route through which alternative political education could be obtained, pronouncing similarities between apartheid in Southern Africa, colonialism on the continent and its diasporas, and the fight for civil rights in America.

While reading Kgositsile was banned in South Africa,[7] the younger generation who became leading Black Consciousness writers and artists within the country attest to having accessed and read his work via the robust underground routes established at the time. Tladi shares an anecdote of accessing intel on books that were banned in that milieu:

> Our guru Geoff Mphakati thought 'we need to get these books that are banned', but we did not know the names of those books or their authors. So we went to Van Schaik's [bookstore] and informed the manager that we were responsible citizens who loved reading, but we heard there were books that are banned, and we did not want to read them by mistake and get arrested, so we need a list of the entire collection. The manager printed out the list and gave it to us. When we left the bookstore Bra Geoff instructed us to go search for those books.[8]

By issuing a list of banned authors and their titles, the apartheid surveillance apparatus unwittingly became complicit in its own subversion. State security entities provided intelligence for the acquisition and circulation of undesired fugitive texts in the underground movement. Mongane Serote also recalls how an English teacher at his high school in Alexandra taught European literature, but always told them that Black literature by South Africans existed, and that it was banned. He planted a seed in those who were curious, like Serote, who had already started writing and hungered for the work of their literary ancestors, to go in search of these texts. Serote recalls:

> By the time we were on the grounds of Morris Isaacson Secondary School in Soweto in 1968, we had already started going outside of South Africa to look for books that were banned in our country. We knew that there was a very important bookshop in Botswana, and another one in Swaziland, and we visited them and later some of our people even went to Mozambique to look for books. That created a group of us who really explored, because we got all the banned books into the country. We even began to explore Afro-

---

[7] In July 1962, the apartheid government passed the General Law Amendment (or Sabotage) Act, 'silencing 102 anti-apartheid activists [...] and forcing the closure of most of the leading oppositional periodicals of the time. Following the terms of the Suppression of Communism Act, this new "gagging clause" banned various writers and journalists as persons, removing their rights of association [and] making it illegal for them to be quoted in public' (McDonald 2009: 33).

[8] Author interview with Lefifi Tladi, Mabopane, Pretoria, April 2014.

American literature, Caribbean literature, and African literature. So we created our own circumstances of education.[9]

Within this dynamic, the nascent radical group of artists called MDALI (an umbrella organization whose name is an acronym from Music, Drama, Arts & Literature) was founded in 1972 in the township of Alexandra. Young Mongane Serote was part of this outfit, whose motto was to write prideful Black poetry and 'to combat exploitation by white impresarios' (South African History Online 2011). MDALI aligned themselves with 'prideful Black poetry' which 'added African percussion instruments', and their 'virile' poetry resounded 'African strength and anger; they liked to talk of *spears pivoting in the punctured marrow of the villain*' (Wylie 2006: 43, my emphasis). Their mood of combat was evidently fuelled by Kgositsile's poem, 'Towards a walk in the sun', whose poetic line is italicized in this quotation, and which they presumably accessed within the country. Read within cultural configurations of sound, these musical formations were not divorced from the developments in the Black world of music troupes such as The Last Poets and Gil Scott-Heron, no matter the desires of the security police branch. They were parallel and had more in common than not.

Efforts by Geoff Mphakati and other cultural foot soldiers to access contraband literature led to magazines such as *Negro Digest* finding their way into the country. Tladi recalls with relish the first time he read Kgositsile's essay on Malcolm X in the early 1970s via the underground. He deems that essay 'the most prolific work from Kgositsile' made unique and notable by Kgositsile's creative use and transformation of a Tswana proverb into African American literary and political culture: 'we thought if this guy can write in such pure Setswana while in America, so can we. Then we began to understand the importance of thinking in our own languages'. There was a dire need for representation at the time, for the youth coming up to see the use of their languages in contexts of revolution. 'From this essay', he continues, 'I made an exhibition as a tribute to that concept called 'Mosima Motlhaela Thupa'.[10] The eponymous body of work was created around 1973 and exhibited at the National Museum and Art Gallery, Gaborone, Botswana in 1980. It was in dialogue with Kgositsile, and by association, the plight of African Americans all the way from across the Atlantic through a proverb that accrued textual Atlanticism, and that now functioned in Black internationalist contexts. The potency of Tladi's visual language ascribes the proverb with modernist or even avant-garde aesthetics to articulate this transformation.

There is a possibility that Tladi might have never thought of the Tswana proverb as enshrining revolutionary qualities had it not first made a turn across

---

[9] Author interview with Mongane Serote, Johannesburg, May 2014.
[10] Author interview with Lefifi Tladi, Mabopane, Pretoria, April 2014.

the Atlantic. This was certainly the case for Kgositsile. In his interview with Charles Rowell, when asked about his literary influences during the era of Black arts, Kgositsile offered:

> Baraka made or fertilized the ground [...] to be receptive immediately to people like Malcolm, Fanon, and others. What that did, too – which is interesting, because *it might not have happened if I had not come here* – was to open up in me memories of earlier wisdom during my young years in South Africa (Rowell 1978: 30, my emphasis).

Kgositsile affirms that, had he not sojourned to the States, perhaps he might not have tapped into the wisdom inherent in his indigenous languages and its liberatory possibilities. It might not have happened if he had not left South Africa. Being removed from the immediate context of the proverb made it sound differently, out of its everyday use. We could also surmise that Tladi's encounter with the Tswana proverb in its context of textual Atlanticism, used to preface and frame an elegy for the death of a popular revolutionary leader such as Malcolm, was revelatory to him. He recognized then the value of the intergenerational wisdom of his people, treated it as a ritual archive from which he could harness a Black conscious politics of a particularly Southern African tenor and orientation.

Crucially, the historiography of the BCM clearly articulates the influence of the Black Power Movement on the former's formation. It is paramount to rewrite this history wherein the identity of Black Power that influenced the BCM is not composed solely of African Americans and is not exclusively Anglophonic. Further, because this historiography is scripted before the transnational turn in academia, within

Fig. 5. Lefifi Tladi's 'Mosima Motlhaela Thupa'

spatial-bound and nationalist frameworks of Area Studies and South African Literature and Political Science, Kgositsile's work has never found an easy home. His itinerant career reveals the limitations of these disciplines and of institutional memory that would locate BCM poetry within the national borders of South Africa. Currently, his work is neither read/taught as Black Consciousness nor as American Black arts poetry, rendering it exiled in its own way. What happens when we situate his work in Black Studies, in both America and Southern Africa? This book seeks to address these lacunas by reconfiguring Black political geographies. I advocate his work finding its rightful position in the Black arts corpus, but also in the Black Consciousness body of literature, for these are not two distinct historical moments, but parallel, overlapping, coeval, and convivial in many other ways. Reading his work within the context of Black internationalism and Black studies offer a prismatic lens which positions the engagements of radical movements and political thought within dynamic and multivalent circuitries staged on variegated terrains.

Mosima Motlhaela Thupa

Tladi's encounter with Kgositsile's work shaped the philo-practical turn of the Black Consciousness Movement – the turn towards using lived experience and quotidian languages, vernaculars, idioms, and sound knowledges to produce philosophical thought. This environment underscored the formation of collectives such as MDALI, who wove music, drama, arts, and literature together to bring this philo-praxis into performance. Tladi founded Dashiki with other musicians, poets, and painters in the Pretoria region; and this troupe founded itself on aesthetics rooted in the traditional sounds of *malopo*, visual art that captured 'an inner vista of ourselves' (3rdEarMusic n.d.), and indigenous languages poetry. They grounded their aesthetics and sound in *malopo* cosmology, *malopo* comprising the matrix of healing, song, dance, drum, and ritual in the likeness of *ngoma*.

Malopo and *ngoma* both operate in the respective healing traditions of the Bapedi and the Nguni people and attend to the human as tridimensional. Dashiki proponents rooted their artistic production in the sound worlds of *malopo*. As alluded to in the previous chapter, the *ngoma* or *malopo* healing traditions are contingent on sound and ritual to not only heal ailments but divine the affairs of the living by collapsing the barriers between living and dead, seen and unseen, spirit and material, past and future, and the cosmos and the earth. Practitioners within these healing traditions are gifted 'seers' in the likeness of the Motswana doctor invited by Kgositsile to divine over Black world politics. Tladi and his contemporaries sought to bring the ritual, rhythms, and movements of the *malopo* matrix, the totality of those worlds and continuity of their people's traditions and culture in their work, to assert a knowledge of self pooled from ritual archives. This was central to the objectives of the Black Consciousness Movement.

The *malopo* complex of totems, drum, dance, song, names, and land are harnessed in Tladi's body of work 'Mosima Motlhaela Thupa' (see above image) to imbue the figures in his painting with spirit. The musical horns are actively transmitting breath, air, wind, and spirit – *moya* – as they contort the bodies and faces of their

Fig. 6. Lefifi Tladi's 'Mosima Motlhaela Thupa' ii

blowers. The characters in the painting are not fixed or static; there is life, movement, and sound in this piece. In viewing the painting, the viewer is engaged and feels moved by listening to the image. *Malopo* is a healing practice, and Tladi freights the horns from jazz practice with spi/ritual properties – they signify *dinaka*, a set of wind instruments ranging from horns of bucks to whistles and reeds, central to *malopo*. The transformation of these *dinaka* to modern jazz instruments is paradigmatic of Kgositsile's transformation of the Tswana proverb to Black internationalist contexts. Both are concerned with drawing continuities between the past and the present to shape decolonial futures and sounding the names-songs-places dynamic. Through jazz horns, Tladi asserts contemporary struggles as related to the revolt waged by his predecessors, whilst also affirming belonging to the larger Black world, with the masks pointing to other geographies and cultures on the continent. The figures in his work are depicted in African masks as a technology to collapse those geographical borders, mitigate alienation, and transgress the psychic limitations set by the ruling order.

The masks also bridge the living with the living dead and the not-yet-here. This affirms the living and imbues them with aliveness, situating them in transgenerational belonging in a pastpresentfuture. It also affirms the rich and substantial gifts of poetic knowledge, ritual archives, and wisdom of the ancients and their capacity to generate and shape a Black radical imagination required for political philosophy and action. The proverb remodelled by Kgositsile enables Tladi to position himself in a coil of time that gathers together Malcolm's message of love with that of Batswana elders and ancestors, akin to the manifestation of ancestral presence in the healing practice of *malopo* and *ngoma*. Engagement with these worlds, as Tladi learnt, can and must happen through philo-practical return, for continuity; return is possible, one that does not celebrate or claim purity but adapts to the historical imperative. The jazz aesthetic represents this contemporaneous ritual-making marked by continuity. Tladi was also awakened to the intimate dance between the continent and its diaspora, where the emerging intellectual and political projects in the Black world were not new or emergent to him but continuous with what was happening on the continent. This sensibility opens a space of solidarity capacious enough to accommodate geographical specificity and differences.

Crucially, Tladi's aesthetic gives us another facility through which to listen to a tenor of South African jazz, one that sounds a vocabulary of the healing practices of the land, from *bongoma* to *malopo*. It is a vernacular of spirit drawn from the rituals, sonicscapes, and healing ceremonies in which the dynamics of community – the human community and that of the larger living world – are reconstituted by totality and continuity. These rituals animate spirit and enhance participants' sense of self and community through reconnecting them with the memories, value systems, and desires of their predecessors. A poet or painter, and Tladi is both, who aligns their word-images with the collective songs and aspiration of the people seeks to articulate, connect to, and express that spirit. This imbues their poetry-image with the revitalizing qualities of aliveness enshrined by indigenous languages, which in turn generates the possibility to name disenchantment with the terms of order, combusts the communal dance (*toyi toyi*), and explodes into political action. We observe this enlivenment in Tladi's painting, quivering with spirits that refuse to be contained, that refuse their own captivity by motioning forward, dancing to the tune of the collective drum and song. We must understand the vernacular of South African jazz and so-called abstract expressionism to emerge from this *ngoma-malopo* matrix: they are fanned by the conception of self as incomplete, operating in the realms of improvisation as a practice of wandering and co-creating with the living dead and larger non-human world, and thereby finding meaning in being-with or being with-ness.

Performance in the context and dynamic of the *malopo* or *ngoma* matrix is characterized by what Bayo Akomolafe (2019) calls *with-nessing*: when we participate in ritual, we wander into the unknown, but we are knowable to this unknown; when we call our ancestors' names, they are always-already-there, yearning for us and calling our names in return; when we embrace our ancestors, they are already embracing us. In witnessing we are in turn being witnessed; in embarking upon ritual, we are responding to their invitation: it is an entanglement of the elsewhere with the here. There is mutual and co-constitutive participation and transformation of all presence. In his analysis of Zim Ngqawana's practice, musician and scholar Asher Gamedze captures this aptly:

> Through the music Zim blurs the traditional and the avant garde and challenges their opposition, suggesting that the latter is not far out because of its rooting in, and familiarity with the former. Playing free music is an extension and improvisation of the traditional's

being in community, at home and sharing and celebrating. Without rehearsal, it is a permanent state of readiness, the spontaneity of performance which *isn't a performance but rather a sonic elaboration*, a celebration of being together, and eating together, a mediation on breathing together – the basis of funeral gatherings, prayer meetings and other ceremonies which require preparation and organisation but not practice or rehearsal. (2021: 44, my emphasis)

This collapse of the border between the traditional and avant-garde is observed in Kgositsile's work, in his situating of words uttered by a Motswana doctor in relation to Langston Hughes' poem, or as poetic elaboration of Malcolm X's politics. It is the struggle of artists entangled in the manifolds of historical and modern being, fashioning an imagination that seeks to move in between multiple cosmologies and worlds. It is a question of consciousness, of awakening the traditional and historical, and denouncing that which deems it primitive, barbaric, or backwards. The struggle calls for gathering work, to work from the cultural world by viewing it as actively materializing as opposed to antiquated or ossified. This lesson was evident and impactful for Tladi. In previous chapters, I worked through the politics and poetics of breathing together, of breath, air, wind, spirit, and *moya*. We will recall Kgositsile's disavowal of the notion of citizen, opting rather for *moagisani*: 'building together', or 'in the same breath'. That is from the ways of his people, the traditional's being in community, at home and sharing and celebrating together. Gamedze beautifully reminds us of traditional Black life as the basis that informs continuous movement in a state of readiness, present for moments that might demand of us to operate within a sonic elaboration and collaboration without practice or rehearsal.

When we view Tladi's work, and that of other (Southern) Africans deemed abstract expressionists or surrealists, we must be attentive to the sounded communion of the onto-triad, to existence without boundaries, to temporalities of elsewhere, and to the motions and rhythms of a Black consciousness fashioned from that elsewhere. Gamedze continues: 'through improvisation's insistence [...] on being existence, it configures itself as boundary-less and prepares for the possibilities of rupturing realms. When the communion sounds, the communion that is the music that is also the existence which has no boundaries, when did it start? (When and where) does it stop?' (2021: 44). This is future memory – when did it start, and when and where does it stop, when existence is experienced as boundary-less? Black geographies attend to this reconfiguration of space, the experiential poetic and politic culled from elsewhere, 'engendered by wandering terrains outside the recognized Enlightenment's governing system of meaning' (McKittrick 2006,:17). Bodies of work from this cosmology call for a shift and perhaps even a complete break from western art history's ways of seeing and methods of reading.

Legacies of Black Conscious Erotic Elaboration

In his seminal book *Freedom Dreams*, Robin D.G. Kelley writes that 'the *dream of a new world*, my mother's dream, was the catalyst for my own political engagement' (2003: 5, emphasis in the original), attesting to his personal relationship to the matriarchive. He points to Black nationalism, Marxism, communism, surrealism, and Black feminism as social movements that enabled participants to imagine different futures, to imagine life after the revolution (6, 9). The everyday oppressions and experiences of survival in Black life make it 'difficult to see anything other than the present', as he argues, and it has been poets who lit the fires by whose light we could see possible futures. Kelley cites the words of 'the great poet' Kgositsile, 'when the clouds clear / we shall know the color of the sky' to speak to the ability of poets to imagine the colour of sky (11). He writes: 'when movements have been unable to clear the clouds, it has been poets […] who have succeeded in imagining the color of the sky' (11). He calls this ability the radical imagination, able to see 'there' before others do. The lines cited by Kelley are from a Setswana proverb – *'fa maru a apoga / re tla itse mmala wa loapi'* – translated by Kgositsile in his poem 'When the Clouds Clear', from his eponymous 1990 collection. Kgositsile cited this proverb to express his *dream of a new world* right on the cusp of South African democracy in 1990.

Elsewhere, Tladi pushed his generation of writers to look to their cultural archive in producing a Black aesthetics and consciousness. As Mphutlane wa Bofelo writes, 'the presence of writers of the [BCM] era who wrote in African languages and their commitment to the development of indigenous African languages [influenced] many writers [who] have observed the fact that many musical groups and artists started writing in their own languages more in the 1970s' (2008: 199). Tladi's drive was inspired and fuelled by Kgositsile, this poet he had not met, but who could write in such pure Setswana such a long way away in America, sowing in him a personal challenge: he began 'experiment[ing] with proverbial and idiomatic expressions' (ibid.). Tladi continues to proclaim this message today:

> I was telling my young students that we need a new generation that is going to write poetry that draws from African proverbs, and which is able to translate to our contemporary setting. I used as an example these few lines of a poem: 'Gophuthulla metsweditswedi ya hlago kego ngatholla masedi a sedimosang ditoro', which means something like 'unfolding the oasis of nature is to share *the light that makes dreams visible*'. The beauty and depth of this is that for any person to see anything, you need light, but what kind of light is it that makes dreams visible? (cited in ibid., my emphasis)

Tladi uses the beautiful proverb to sow seeds that encourage dreaming, that will help a radical imagination to flourish, because without the structures of the imagination we cannot dream a new society into being. The notion of 'the light that makes dreams visible' recalls Kelley's reading of the Tswana maxim translated by Kgositsile, that when the clouds clear we shall know the colour of the sky. Is Tladi talking about dreams of freedom? The Tswana lines he cited above can clearly be interpreted into political contexts. Sharing the light that makes dreams visible is not unlike the role of poetry, as perceived by Kelley, to grant us maps to another place, to see this place beyond our current desolation. Tladi directs us to the generative role of proverbs in ongoing contexts of the political imaginary in our unfinished struggle. This wisdom, or communal riches, is grounded in a cosmology that strives for attuning our inner ear to our inner worlds, to what is deepest and strongest and richest within us, to bring into being a new world. The dream begins in the inner landscape, as seen in Kgositsile's appraisal of Malcolm X.

Kodwo Eshun's statement from the last chapter, 'no futurism is worthwhile unless it includes indigenous knowledges' (2017a) finds further expansion in this chapter. In Kgositsile's essay we see the capacity of Southern African cosmologies enshrined in the Tswana language, its literatures, and indigenous healing practices of the land, used to speak power to and shape futurity. If the thesis of ahistory enshrined by colonial modernity absents Africans, then there are no Africans in historicism's future. Elsewhere cosmologies that coagulate pastpresentfuture, the onto-triad, and *terrafirmament* in the lived experience of Africans are antithetical to the colonial thesis. The ritual technologies fashioned by Kgositsile through the bones used by the Motswana doctor, and by Tladi through the masks, all speak to the collapsing of boundaries erected by Europatriarchy, barriers that sow alienation and a sense of exile caused by severance from indigenous cosmologies and their knowledges. The retrieval of those cosmologies and their storied forms of being, their sound knowledges, and their intersubjective sense of being and becoming enliven and locate Blackness in a larger arc of history, time, and enfolded geographies and ecologies of being. An awakening to this consciousness is a re-membering of that which is already there. It is, as Kgositsile advocates, continuity, not return.

Coda

There is a throughline of continuity that Kgositsile aims to draw from the cultures, customs, and sense of community instilled in his homeplace by his mothers and bring to the cultures and politics of Johannesburg and those of the larger Black world. This is a non-linear line that he conceptualizes as a coil. The coil enables his poetics and politics to operate within cosmologies of Southern Africa and their conceptions of the human, temporality, spatiality, knowledge, and intersubjective relationality. The coil, harnessed for its etymology – to 'gather together' –, locates the aspirations and objectives of Kgositsile's life and work in an ongoing intergenerational interlocution contiguous with the structuring of the human as an onto-triad comprising of the living dead, the living, and the not-yet-born. This coil has been fashioned to suture Black America to Black South Africa, their oral/aural and literary traditions, histories, and politics. In his work, he devised several working terms and phrases that I have tasked myself with developing as critical theories from elsewhere with which we can disrupt and rupture the dominant, dehumanizing, hierarchical, gendering, differentiating, and mechanizing Europatriarchal terms of order. I have termed these poetics of possibilities. Much ink has been spilled pontificating on the crucial need for decolonial theory and concepts, but very few worlds, archives, vocabularies, practices, tools, material steps, processes, procedures, and approaches have been offered as interventions in these discourses.

My book has brought these poetics to the surface as an offering at this critical juncture in which the field of Black studies is preoccupied with imagining the human and the world anew to upend anti-Blackness and challenge the dominant paradigm of western civilization and its cosmologies of being, knowing, and doing. Kgositsile's work and the poetics of possibility it offers are crucial on many levels. This book draws from his work written in the 1960s and 1970s, critical decades that occasioned mass decolonization in Africa and the rest of the third world. Even though South Africa was not one of those countries that witnessed independence, I contend that Kgositsile, due to the internationalist nature of his work, should be read in the canon of decolonial theorists and poets of this era who sought to provide critical analysis of imperialism, culture, and liberation. To be clear, although this long overdue book on his life and work is coming out in the twenty-first century, in the third decade of South Africa's flag-democracy, his oeuvre that surfaces and encapsulates decolonial theories, poetics, and praxis as conceptualized in the critical moment of independence in most countries in the Global South is in conversation with, and should be read alongside other postcolonial texts such as Edward Said's *Orientalism* (1978), Ngugi wa Thiongo's *Decolonizing the Mind* (1986), and Amilcar Cabral's *Return to the Source* (1973).

Further, as this book has shown, his work teaches us that it is not only scriptural texts that reflected on and theorized that critical moment, but also oral and sonic texts harnessing communal knowledges of the collective. He demonstrates that poetry and the fields of the imagination at large are able to attend to both epistemologies and acoustemologies, to a multiplicity of cosmologies, and to forms of being and relationalities that decentre otherwise singular, ocularcentric, monolithic, and binary modalities of being and knowing enshrined in coloniality. Reading it alongside what we call first-generation post-independence literature, as a literature of decolonization in conversation with Patrice Lumumba, Léopold Senghor, Skunder Boghossian, and Ayi Kwei Armah, Kgositsile's work offers us another entry point into Kgositsile's practices of Pan-Africanism[1] beyond the frameworks of Black Arts, Black Consciousness, and Black Power bodies of work. The publication of this book within an atmosphere of decoloniality in South Africa today, one that found Black world resonance and opened dialogue,[2] ties the first-generation intellectual tradition of the 1960s to the twenty-first century.

Within this frame, Kgositsile's work intervenes in crucial ways in the corpus of decolonial texts: he contributes modes of knowledge that disrupt the exceptionalism of the new independence leader and his national liberation movement, the heroes of the nation, as always male. He does so by attuning us to the community in its totality. He resacralizes the 'son' who was desacralized through Christian colonial morality, disembodiment, and Enlightenment inauguration of western man and rationality as supreme, severed from the body of the mother. For Kgositsile the body of the mother forms material, biological, and spiritual links that tie him to the soil or land beneath which his navel is buried through birth rites, and which subsequently inform his placemaking, belonging, and revolt. He re-enchants 'the son' into the 'sun' to situate himself simultaneously in a lineage of human and non-human community, in which the cosmos informs cycles of being through and with the world. The sun sets and rises daily, a metaphor that makes revolution and return to the land a certainty. The cyclic poetic disorders linearity of temporality from which he produced

---

[1] Apropos Brent Edwards's *Practices of Diaspora* (2003).
[2] I am thinking here of the #RhodesMustFall protests that called for the removal of a monument commemorating colonialist Cecil John Rhodes at the University of Cape Town, which symbolized the decolonization of colonial and Eurocentric curricula in higher education. The toppling of the statue gave rise to the call for decolonization at Oxford University, as well as universities and public spaces in urban areas of the States.

four temporal concepts in his work: coil of time, future memory, NOW, and pastpresentfuture. The coil/cyclical poetic crucially dis/locates the land and the body to exist outside colonial-capitalist interpellations as commodities and extractable units of labour. To the existing post-colonial library Kgositsile recentres ecosomatics-geopoetics, the bodies that produce knowledge as not only those of men, but also women's bodies, land, celestial bodies, and bodies of water. We will return to this later.

Kgositsile's approach to his work and its circulation reveals his intention to participate in decolonial developments on the continent, culturally and politically. It is prudent to discuss some of his participation and contributions that offer a deeper understanding of his work as a bridge between Black America and Black Africa. He attended Léopold Senghor's First World Festival of Negro Arts (1er Festival Mondial des Arts Nègres, or FESMAN) in Senegal in 1966 in order to have his finger on the pulse of transition and independence on the continent. He reported on the festival in an essay published in the July 1966 edition of the New York-based African American periodical *Liberator*. There, he trains a critical eye on the elitist nature of the festival, a rude revelation to him that he used as a basis to issue a warning on the necessity of performing class suicide. He warned of the Senegalese masses having been locked out from the festival's proceedings: 'the hungry fisherman and the tubercular mine laborer will lose their naïve faith in any agency that perpetuates their condition'; 'beware. It will be millions of unpretentious ex-natives and ex-negroes ready to slit God's own throat' (1966: 11). This essay and others published in African American periodicals of the time contain political and economic analyses that can be read together with Walter Rodney's *How Europe Underdeveloped Africa* (1972), Aimé Césaire's *Discourse on Colonialism* (1955), and Frantz Fanon's *Wretched of the Earth* (1961), among others. It inaugurates his body of work as an essayist of great political acumen; his clarity of vision with respect to politics, social change, and struggle reveals his possession of a deep understanding of the global process of decolonization.

Kgositsile also contributed some of his earliest poetry written in the States to nascent magazine and periodicals in newly independent Uganda and Nigeria: *Transition*, *Okike*, and *Black Orpheus*.[3] In 1965, he published two poems in the

---

[3] These magazines were notoriously funded by the U.S. Central Intelligence Agency (CIA) and are a site to study the intersection of the Cold War, anti-apartheid movements, and decolonization. For instance, it later emerged that the U.S. Information Agency that offered Kgositsile a scholarship in 1961 to study at Lincoln University was also a concerted effort by the States' surveillance machinery aimed at curbing 'communism'. The magazines and scholarship were, however, not so one-dimensional. They enabled mobility, collaborations, Black internationalism, political solidarities, and gatherings across the Black and red worlds, beyond their initial intention. See my paper 'Of Worlds Black and Red: South Africa's Poet Laureates and Their World-Making Networks' (2019).

Uganda-based magazine *Transition*, edited by Rajat Neogy and co-edited by Lewis Nkosi and Christopher Okigbo. At the helm of founding modern African literatures in European languages, *Transition* and *Black Orpheus* (co-edited by Wole Soyinka and Ezekiel Mphahlele) represented an imbrication of modern national literatures of Nigeria with South African modern deterritorialized national literatures by exiles. After *Transition* published Kgositsile's poem, Okigbo wrote to Kgositsile to solicit a manuscript that he wanted to publish with Mbari (they had previously published Alex La Guma's *A Walk in the Night and Other Stories* in 1962 and Dennis Brutus' *Sirens, Knuckles and Boots* in 1963). Kgositsile obliged and sent off a collection of poems to Nigeria in 1967. The eastern provinces of Nigeria's secession as independent Biafra threw the country into civil war, bringing those plans to an abrupt stop. When Kgositsile ran into Lindsay Barrett – a Jamaican poet/novelist/essayist whom he had met at FESMAN in Dakar in 1966, who had decided to remain in West Africa, where he became, from 1966 to 1967, secretary of the Mbari Artists Club –, Barrett told Kgositsile he had seen some of Kgositsile's scattered poems floating here and there in the yard at Mbari. That was the end of what would have been Kgositsile's debut collection.

In their discussion of small magazines, Christopher Ouma and Madhu Krishnan write:

> These magazines became mid-century platforms of Pan-African imagination, continental internationalism and diaspora practice. As they enabled the movement of ideas, indeed of imagination across the continent, they also became exchange platforms from which the raging civil rights in the US intersected with anti-apartheid imagination in Africa as well as the continental project of decolonisation. (2021: 202)

Kgositsile's poetry was also published in Dakar/Paris-based *Présence Africaine* in 1967, an opportunity made possible by Mauritian poet Edouard Maunick, who translated Kgositsile's poems into French. Maunick conducted an interview with Kgositsile during the 1966 FESMAN in Dakar, which prefaces the three-poem-suite. The interview and poems situate Kgositsile's work published in and from the States within Anglophone and Francophone worlds, and function as practices of diaspora. As Tsitsi Jaji notes, the 'interview reveals how Kgositsile's very presence was essential to the work he did in linking geographically dispersed Black intellectual communities' (2014: 108). Maunick presented Kgositsile's poems as 'hosties noires', or 'Black sacrifices', echoing Léopold Senghor's 1948 poetry collection, which can be read as Maunick's 'attempt to bring Francophone and Anglophone African worlds in closer intimacy' (ibid.). Maunick's labour of bringing Kgositsile's work in the Black Arts and Black Power Movements into dialogue with the Francophone world is akin to Kgositsile's interview with Brazilian Abdias do Nascimento in the *Negro Digest*, which brought the Lusophone world of Brazil into close contact with the Anglophone Black world.

Kgositsile also edited *The Word is Here: Poetry from Modern Africa* (1973), where he anthologized contemporary poets from the continent, a feat he accomplished from the States. He was possibly drawing from the extensive work undertaken by his literary colleagues and fellow poets on the continent, who would have assisted him in compiling lists of poets from various regions. With this anthology he sought to bring the voices of a modern Africa, a Black modernity that shaped the continental project of decolonization, to the BAM. He sought to bring the BAM into dialogue with a contemporary Africa, rather than one of an exclusive 'glorious past' and ancient civilizations. The anthology is 'dedicated to the memory of Magolwane [Jiyane], Langston Hughes, Zora Neale Hurston, Chris Okigbo & Can Themba – dream keepers & weaverbirds all'. The act of collating an anthology of African poetry while in exile in the Black diaspora can thus be thought of as Kgositsile's way of weaving a pastpresentfuture celebration of 'the word' as technology for geographical, ontological, epistemological, and cosmological suture. Interweaving himself into the tapestry woven over deep time and disparate histories by Jiyane, the 'greatest Zulu poet', along with Hughes, Hurston, Okigbo, and Themba, defines weaving and dreamkeeping: they sound the generational song as a praxis of care, repair, community, belonging, and ontological affirmation for all involved.

Kgositsile is also anthologized in major African poetry anthologies of the day, including *Modern Poetry from Africa* (1970), edited by the German scholar Ulli Beier and the British scholar Gerald Moore, and *Poems of Black Africa* (1975) edited by Wole Soyinka. All of this is detailed to locate Kgositsile's work in a larger Black cartography of circulation, collaboration, and exchange, and to place him in the heart of literary imaginaries of Black modernity, post-independent nationalisms, Pan-Africanism, and Black internationalism.

Continuities: Rural *Roots-en-Route*

As a manner of concluding this book's preoccupation with Kgositsile's impact on the Black Arts Movement, I focus on his relationship with Tom Dent, the founder of BLKARTSOUTH in New Orleans. Kgositsile completed his Masters in Fine Arts at Columbia University in 1971, and officially installed himself in the American academy as writer in residence and professor. At the time he traversed the American south as a teacher and humanities consultant for the Institute for Services to Education (ISE) at Tulane University and the Southern University of New Orleans. There he met activist and writer Tom Dent, who has since emphatically written about their encounter, with Kgositsile acting as mentor and advisor. Kgositsile encouraged Dent to adopt a Black aesthetic of the American south in his work and activism. Having been reared in rural South Africa and its rich cultural world and cosmology, he always thought of the rural American south as a key generative and transformative site of a living and embodied culture of Blackness crucial for recovering Black aesthetics.

He motivated and inspired Tom Dent, who had been born and was now living again in New Orleans, to return, poetically, politically, and ritually, to his New Orleans 'roots'. In his work Kgositsile had always celebrated literature by African American writers with a 'southern orientation' in their work: Jean Toomer (*Cane*, set in Georgia), Zora Neale Hurston (*Their Eyes Were Watching God*, set in Florida), and Henry Dumas (whose Arkansas roots reoriented his potent mythmaking), whose corpus continues to be indelible and generative in the African American literary present-futures. This is important as it redresses the balance between the so-called advanced urban metropoles and the 'backwards' rural countryside. Kgositsile's sensibilities recast rural knowledges as Black intellectual and imaginative traditions. He situates them and sutures them with progressive urban Johannesburg politics, and in the States, during the period of the Black Arts and Black Power Movements, encourages the politics and imaginaries of 'progressive' New York to be moulded and transformed by the 'backwards', 'countrified' South. This, in his view, is how we hear the spirit of Black people and deploy it towards practising affective epistemologies in the service of a liberatory Black tradition.

Dent credits Kgositsile's influence and mentorship on Dent's education as a writer-teacher-community organizer, and Dent's subsequent mentoring of African American southern writers. When Dent decided to enrol in a creative writing programme at Goddard College, he sought Kgositsile to be his dissertation mentor, even when Kgositsile was based at another institution. It is clear from the recommendation letters Kgositsile wrote for Dent's application to graduate programmes in creative writing that this was an unusual request, but that Dent was adamant to have Kgositsile on board. In a letter addressed to Goddard College, dated 15 June 1973, Kgositsile writes from Greensboro, North Carolina:

> I was glad to learn recently that [Dent] decided to join your program and use most of his talent to write more poetry. He has discussed what he wants to do with me and I am eager and anxious to work with him on this project. Hoping that this application meets your approval, I would like to know, at your earliest convenience, what my responsibilities as a field faculty member would be.[4]

---

4 Archive material from the Amistad Center, New Orleans.

'This project' in question is Dent's collection of poetry, *Magnolia Street*, and Kgositsile cites one of Dent's poems in his recommendation letter, demonstrating a prior engagement with Dent's work in progress. A year later, in a letter dated 10 June 1974, Kgositsile recommends Dent for The National Fellowship Fund, in which he also commits to working with Dent on *Magnolia Street*.[5] *Magnolia Street* was eventually published in 1976, and carries glowing missives to Kgositsile, which I will discuss shortly. It is vital to follow Dent's trajectory from New York City, where he was member of both Umbra and the Black Arts Movement, to his founding BLKARTSOUTH in New Orleans, and to also map his evolving consciousness on the links between arts praxis and academia, the American south and the African Caribbean, and African American-centred Black nationalism and broader diasporic consciousness, all entwined with his engagements with Kgositsile.

Dent lived in New York between 1962 and 1965 and was part of the literary formation founded in Manhattan's Lower East Side, Umbra, that was the precursor to the Black Arts Movement. Umbra's members included writers such as Jayne Cortez, Askia Toure (formerly Roland Snellings), Ishmael Reed, Stephen Henderson, Rashida Ismaili, and Sun Ra. Dent moved to New Orleans to form a chapter of the Black arts in the south, where he joined the Free Southern Theatre and founded the Congo Square Writers' Union in 1965, which he ran until 1970. Dent credits Kgositsile's presence in New Orleans and his caring, nurturing, and passionate approach to Black arts, politics, and Black life for his own impactful role in the organizational mentoring of African American writers from the south (1976: n.p.).

In the preface to *Magnolia Street*, Dent maps his movements in chronological order to signal an impasse in his being when he returned to New Orleans after his work in Umbra and the BAM in New York:

> whenever I think of the poems in *Magnolia Street* I am reminded of that time, the early 1970s, when I expended quite a bit of energy on new poems, poems which attempted to come to terms with the New Orleans I found myself rather permanently domiciled in after school years, army years, and six crucial years in New York City. (1976: n.p.)

In New York, the Lower East Side taught him, as he later reflected, 'an appreciation for the diversity of voices within our "we-ness" as a way of absorbing and interpreting the times, which were deeply imbued with the struggle for diasporan and anti-colonial political liberation, and the emerging sense of Black cultural identity' (Dent 2006: 597). Dent reaches a deadlock

---

[5] Ibid.

within himself when he attempts to make sense of the 'elusive and multifaceted' city of New Orleans, which 'has been the focus of some of the finest [white] American writing'; emboldened by his experience in Umbra, and 'being Black, I thought it important to portray the city's Black community and culture, which has been so brilliantly rendered through music, but almost totally ignored in literature' (1976: n.p.). He had a formidable task ahead of him, to use the spirit of Black arts in New York as inspiration for establishing and nurturing a similar community in the deep south. In his preface to *Magnolia Street*, Dent emphasizes the importance of Kgositsile's influence as key to unlocking the deadlock post-New York:

> I could feel this place reverberating with the presence of a living past that jogged my own sense of memory, my desire to learn and retain as much as I could if I was ever to comprehend the present, knowledge without which it is impossible to understand the present. [...] My perspective achieved focus when I began to conceive of Black New Orleans in terms of African remnants, which provided even more extraordinary depth to its living memories. [...] I saw Black New Orleans as more crucially related culturally to the Caribbean diaspora and the mother continent than to mainstream America. About this time I met and became close friends with South African poet Keorapetse Kgositsile, who was living and working in the United States, work which often brought him to New Orleans. Kgositsile is a powerful poet whose voice contains an innate, almost divine authority, as if he is participant in a privileged conversation about the nature of life. More than any other writer or friend Kgositsile encouraged me in the pursuit and validity of my purpose, and I needed encouragement. (1976: n.p.)

Dent's experience of New Orleans was in flux, revealing many facets to him. He needed direction. At the time the work that 'often brought [Kgositsile] to New Orleans' was his work for Tulane University and the Southern University of New Orleans. While there, Kgositsile spent sustained periods of time with Dent and Kalamu ya Salaam (Val Ferdinand) with whom he found community, comradeship, and deep friendship. It was during this time that Kgositsile encouraged Dent – 'more than any other writer or friend' – to pursue the validity of his purpose. This is crucial, and I want to tie this encouragement to find a purpose to Kgositsile's possession of what Dent refers to as his 'innate, almost divine authority', his 'participation in a privileged conversation' (1976: n.p.).

What Dent writes about Kgositsile in these superlative terms, that his voice possesses an 'almost divine authority', is grounded in what I have theorized in this book as the onto-triadic state of being within Southern African cosmologies.

According to this, the human being is understood to comprise the living, the living dead, and the yet-to-be-born. This is what informed Kgositsile's aims and objectives in his poetry, to write poems that are 'ritualistic and inspired' (1975a: 17), to sound and resound the multiplicity of his being. To achieve this, his poems strove to draw from the 'African worldview', its 'philosophical orientation' and 'music or sound patterns' that reflect his 'connectedness to the collective circle without sacrificing the realities of the present' (1975a: 16). The collective circle is the cycle of the multiplicities of life and lifeforms that have been, are, and will be. In pursuing '*continuity*, not *return*', connectedness, and collectivity, he is invested in hearing and feeling the sound knowledges of his beginnings, in being accompanied through the notion of 'guided mobility' in his wanderings both in exile and in his writing practice of jazz improvisation. That is, he is deliberate in his work as a dreamkeeper to sound the intergenerational and ancestral song, echoing in his work the wisdom of his people to shape decolonial futures. This fuelled his purpose as a poet of the revolution, and this is what Dent witnesses in Kgositsile's work, seeking it for himself.

This voice in Kgositsile's poetry that is in dialogue with a divine authority is also observed by Sterling Plumpp, who dubs it 'an inner-ear sensitivity to Setswana' orality and aurality, although one that is not essentialist or tribalist: 'Kgositsile is not into his South Africanness; I can say that Wole Soyinka is in his Yorubaness. Kgositsile takes off those garbs, retains the essence of it, so that his voice becomes more universal. And I think the blues and jazz makes him more universal'.[6]

Plumpp's summation of the sonic and auditory worlds of Kgositsile's work reveals Plumpp's close study and appreciation of the acoustemological orientation under investigation in this book. He reveals the 'subconscious act' of retaining Setswana in the aesthetic of his poems as inextricably related to Kgositsile's self-assuredness of history, culture, family, and language, resulting in a becoming that is closely tied or tethered to particular circumstance. I have read Plumpp's sophisticated conception of an 'inner ear sensitivity' biologically, to evoke the cochlea. I borrowed from Kgositsile and reimagined the 'spiral shaped cavity' in the ear as a coil gathering together his history, culture, and language to operate in the pastpresentfuture enfoldment of his becoming. Any danger or damage to the cochlea threatens disorientation to the body, a lack of balance that results in vertigo and nausea. I have read Kgositsile's conception of the coil of time as a metaphor for reorientation in a world whose social reality is invested in throwing his identity and humanity into crisis. It is his poetic manufacturing of an inner compass with which to navigate the world. The same

---

[6] Author interview with Sterling Plumpp, Chicago, September 2014.

regaining of equilibrium and reorientation are what Dent needed as he sought to re-enter the New Orleans of multi-layered geographies and cosmologies.

Further, if the coil that Kgositsile gathers together with 'the essence of Setswana', with 'the autonomy of his mother tongue', were to be damaged, this could cause philosophical and aesthetic catastrophes in his life, which would evacuate the suturing and interweaving in his work. In many ways the coil of the inner ear is a central organizing element of relation with Black America, its spirit. He is conscious of these associations, and in his poem 'Mystique' (1974) addresses the loss of collected step and dance that situates one in harmony with the collective circle. The inability to step/walk as a result of a loss of balance is presented in the poem as encumbering the 'soildance' that constitutes the 'thread through and around our soul'. The collected step, moving together in a collective dance, is the principal modality of solidarity. This dance is the 'toehold of the coil / through and around / our soul and soil' (1974b: 9). The soil and the land, the capaciousness of its meaning produced by the connection between his umbilical cord buried in the soil, the same soil that buries his mother, and his access to it through his navel, all require the thread to be unbroken from the soil that entangles the toe, moving through the soul like a coil, gathering them together. If the cochlea contains nerve endings essential for hearing, then the burial site of the umbilical cord is the beginning/point of departure that enfolds any articulation of his aesthetic that aspires to ritual or 'writing as riting', that is essential to performing continuity and relationality in the collective circle of the immediate family, community, and the larger Black world.

I have called this dynamic the names-songs-places matrix, grounded in the praise poetry of the Southern African tradition. According to this concept, one's names are expressive of the *where consciousness*, tying birth and land and spirit – toe, soil, and soul – together in a coil, encoded in the song, dance, and rhythms of the lineage or generations. It is an articulation of ontological belonging framed by ecosomatics, rooted not only in the rhythms of the family lineage, but also of the larger living world: the trees, wind, bodies of water, and celestial bodies. The roots of the names-songs-places matrix are also routes: they not only gesture towards a grounding (point of departure), but are also inherently invested in the enfolding qualities of a continuously moving world in constant becoming. Hence the dance is imperative to this movement – complimentary movement with the larger whole implies solidarity with all that is.

These are the poetics of relations and solidarity that Kgositsile embodied in Black America, ones sung in his paeans in *Spirits Unchained* in which he sings the names of revolutionaries in the Black Atlantic, distorting place between Harlem and Sophiatown, Watts and Sharpeville, with the Mississippi and Limpopo Rivers converging, and where Amiri Baraka is Can Themba, Nina Simone echoes his mothers, and Malcolm X is with the brothers on Robben Island. He deploys spirit/breath/wind in the poetics of citizenship articulated in Setswana as *moagi*, which means 'building together' and 'in the same breath'. Breath, spirit, wind, air, or, as it is signified in Southern African languages, *moya* – is the unifying factor that brings the dismembered and deranged white settler geography into wholeness. He imparted this on Tom Dent, whose comprehension of the New Orleans geography shifted fundamentally, to understand New Orleans as part of the Caribbean and Africa and to harness the African remnants and the extraordinary depth of its living memories.

Kgositsile awakened in Dent a *where consciousness*, a coming into being and ontological affirmation fashioned through the names-songs-places matrix which located him in deeper history and alternative cosmologies. Dent re/oriented to the knowledges archived by the bodies of people, bodies of land, bodies of water, and celestial bodies, as can be observed in *Magnolia Street*, which is dedicated to Kgositsile, among others.[7] Dent was able to hear/feel the spirit of Blackness, redirecting the activities of the Free Southern Theatre into more experimental and experiential Black theatre. James Smethurst writes that Dent became chairman of the theatre's board and facilitated its move from 'an integrated civil rights institution, […] to a more self-consciously Black theatre with a strong nationalist bent' (2021). Under Dent, Smethurst chronicles, the Free Southern Theatre transitioned 'from civil rights to Black Arts, from Negro to Black, from serving the folk of the Black South to being emphatically southern in a Black modality' (ibid). Dent proclaimed: 'Blacks already have the richest, most viable, most complex and rewarding culture in this potpourri of America. The battle is not of bringing culture to Black people, but of us learning to value, and affirm, the culture we already have' (cited in Thomas 2006: 232). Dent became preoccupied with a revivalist project, encouraging an active cultural archaeology and archiving.

Through his workshops, he mentored other writers to tell their stories to each other using their unique vernaculars and idioms, and tapping into the substantive Black archive of New Orleans and African American oral/aural and literary traditions. Dent in turn impacted the orientation of the BLKARTSOUTH movement. He groomed a cohort of artists and writers, one of which, Quo Vadis Gex Breaux, wrote a commemorative paper titled 'Tom Dent's Role in the Organizational Mentoring of African American Southern Writers: A Memoir' after Dent's passing.[8] Breaux declares:

---

[7] The dedication of Dent's *Magnolia Street* reads, 'especially for roberta / for willie k. / for albert w. & jessie c. / with love from the hull of the ship …'

[8] When Dent died in 1998, Kgositsile, Amiri Baraka, former U.N. Ambassador Andrew Young, and singer Germaine Bazzle were the assigned dignitary pallbearers at his funeral in New Orleans.

> Thomas Covington Dent left a legacy larger than his published works. He left a legacy of caring, nurturing, passionate involvement in the grooming of writers and the organizations that support them. His work with the Umbra Workshop in the New York of the early 1960s, his efforts to sustain Free Southern Theatre writing workshop that became Blkartsouth in the late sixties and seventies, and his Herculean efforts to keep a group of Black writers workshopping in New Orleans through the Congo Square Writers' Union in the 1980s all speak to a passion he expressed best in the closing lines of the preface to his book of poetry, *Magnolia Street*. Invoking both his mentor and friend, South African poet Keorapetse Kgositsile, and his own passion for writing, Tom wrote, 'Maybe someday I can pass on to someone else struggling to gain confidence in this passionate work something of what Kgositsile has bequeathed to me'. As peers, protégés, and friends readily attest, Tom succeeded in sharing his passion and bolstered many a floundering confidence. (2006: 339)

Kgositsile's conceptual poetics of dreamkeeping are evinced here. He is witness to and celebrant of his people's cultures and languages, their ways of being, relating, and knowing. He espoused them as his own, echoing them in his work and forms of community-making with others encountered on his journey. What he imparted upon Dent is what was imparted upon him. In this way, the lessons live through past, present, and future. He demonstrates what we understand today to be a love ethos central to fostering community with others on the basis of care and generosity. What he bequeathed to Dent in his time of need, when his confidence floundered, is a gift of a *moagi*, building together towards the same dream of Black liberation. This work can only be done within contexts of interdependence, interconnection, and interrelation: there are no revolutionary soloists. As a committed cadre of a liberation movement, he belonged to all communities that shared a vision of dismantling all oppression. As a dreamkeeper, a visionary working to end the world of white domination and western imperialism, he also functioned in the realm of imagining the world anew. He placed value in literature and culture as repositories of languages and cultural worlds generated by communities, their aesthetics, worldviews, songs, cosmologies, and folklore imperative in rebuilding a just world. This new vision of the world is built upon a living past, a future memory.

The Black Arts Movement Archive: Pro/Creation

The poetics of death and birth, creation and destruction, endings and beginnings in relation to Kgositsile's poetry have been explored in this book. The potency of

'Towards a Walk in the Sun', which was published in *Black Fire: An Anthology of Afro-American Writing* (1968), spotlighted the incendiary nature of his work in that milieu. He was asked by editors Ahmed Alhamisi and Harun Kofi Wangara to write the introduction to the canonical BAM text *Black Arts: An Anthology of Black Creations*, published in 1969. Here, Kgositsile highlighted the voice of Mari Evans as ground from which the seeds of social transformation in Black America can and must sprout. He writes: 'Mari Evans, the echo of whose voice you should seek in the depths of your spirit, has said [...]' (1969b: 15). In these opening lines, Kgositsile locates the echo of Evans's work as entryway to elsewhere: 'we start off where the silence is, the silence of the moment of inner tension or peace, the point where death and birth, or destruction and construction, meet and follow the line of the rhythm of another beginning' (1969b: 15). It is this other beginning, this elsewhere with otherwise possibilities, that shapes and propels a way forward, that informs purposeful action, and that is rooted not in individualism, but in collective consciousness. In his introduction, he casts Mari Evans as the propulsive force of the matriarchive.

He continues: 'the solid coil that unifies the products of creative activity in this anthology is the force, the spirit that mothers this activity' (1969b: 15). In the depths of the Black spirit is a strong hunger for and inclination towards the collective, to its songs, dances, stories, mythologies, rituals, and ceremonies that define its spirit. These, as Kgositsile emphatically demonstrates in his work and seeks to reveal in Black America, are sound knowledges that are inherited, learnt, and practised at the hands of mothers. They are the erotics of being and becoming that are the core ingredients for choreographies of gathering, gestures of belonging, rites of relation, registers of repair, and poetics of accompaniment which suture the individual with the community, and the present with the past and the future. Practising and living these erotics become antidotes to alienation, disenchantment, and Black melancholy produced by living in coloniality. This spirit is what Kgositsile calls upon to mother the activity of Black liberation; this struggle is one that 'follow[s] the line of the rhythm of another beginning' (1969b: 15), beginnings that are not the inauguration of history by New Worlding forces or colonial contact that do not follow the rhythms of linear progressive time. The modality of knowing and hearing/feeling these other beginnings happens through deep listening: to the rhythms and its knowledges, to its erotics everpresent in the blood ('names, songs, / places we only remember / in the blood like everpresent melodies', 1971: 22) and in the gut ('gut it is will move us from the gutter', 1969c: 17). These erotics transport and enshrine possibilities and aliveness against social death.

As seen in Chapter 2, in prying his heart open to the strong fabric Madikeledi wove there, 'for us', and in heeding Galekgobe's eye that is stronger than any faith in some god, he listens into, feels, and follows rhythms of another beginning. They are his internal compass – 'my consciousness and conscience' (1968b: 42)

– moving him so he may charge us with his words into collective movement towards revolutionary action. The internal compass, the inner ear, the spirit, are intricately connected to another beginning that is tied to the matriarchive and, in this introduction to *Black Arts*, Kgositsile seeks to offer this rhythm to his contemporaries in the Black world. This anthology, as he writes in its introduction, contains work that is 'informed and molded by the grasp and caress of the energy that issues from Love and Care, both collective and personal; the authentic energy that informs our sense of mission, the creative vision probing and exploring that reservoir of energy in us' (1969b: 15). Love and Care are erotic politics that are counterpoint to the loveless white settler culture; they are antidotes to its violence, coercion, control, and spirit of domination. This Love and Care could never be learnt outside of the homeplace in white supremacist cultures; it is learnt in the home, as bell hooks (1990) reminds us. It is that spirit that should inform the purpose and mission of Black liberation – never should it devolve into the same self-indulgence and megalomania of what it seeks to eradicate.

A revolution whose *raison d'etre* is exclusively a negation of white supremacy is one at risk of losing sight of its own internal organizing force, of that which makes us revolt, that which makes us refuse the domineering and coercive terms of humanity and relationality set by the ruling class. For Kgositsile, Black liberation's purpose is not simply a matter of usurping white power so the Black male may lead the new Black nation onwards. The goal is 'linking together our yesterdays and our tomorrows' (1969b: 16) – gathering together, in a coil, memory and desire, the past and the future, and the individual with the community. This, he argues, 'will bring us new strength of personality' (1969b: 16). In this treatise Kgositsile brings Mari Evans, Agostinho Neto, and Ho Chi Minh into dialogue with one another in a similar manner to the seamless way in which he has come to locate Madikeledi in dialogue with Frantz Fanon, Malcolm X, and Amiri Baraka. In the world he seeks to bring into being, when the people's collective efforts end the white colonial world, there is only culture that will grant the people their sense of being; he was of the Amilcar Cabralian school of thought, in which, as Kgositsile sums it up, 'in the beginning it's culture, in the end it's also culture' (1978: 15). And this culture is intergenerational, one invested in collectivism, custodianship, interdependence, and interrelation. Its aim is, among other goals, class suicide and the elimination of relations built on domination. It is a culture that must be used to overthrow any other culture of separation, hierarchies, and binaries. At the core of this, of the liberation struggle, should be culture – the force that will mother this act. Any independence *fathered* exclusively by a Black liberation movement erases women's erotic power and other labour and renders these invisible, running the risk of perpetuating the culture of colonialism.

Culture is the force that mothers an ethos and futurity of Black liberation committed to the community as a whole: living and living dead, seen and unseen, human and more-than-human. We need politics to exist alongside culture and spirit; as Gwendolyn Brooks diligently observes in the introduction to Kgositsile's *My Name is Afrika*, 'He sees pretty flowers under blood. / He teaches dolls and dynamite' (1971: 11). Here 'flowers' and 'dolls' are the erotics of revolution necessary to mother the act of armed struggle, not just the machinery and hard power of guns, dynamite, and war. His works ask us to revise our historiography, to revisit the history of the Black Arts Movement and listen into the work of women in the realm of the erotic, to see Nina Simone as a central figure as important as Rap Brown, Max Stanford, A.B. Spellman, and Lindsey Barrett, as internationalist as Aimé Césaire, David Diop, and Malcolm X. Kgositsile is not able to write liner notes for Pharoah Sanders's works, which are 'moved by rhythms of another beginning' (1969b: 15), without finding Sanders' South African wife Thembi as a central figure in it. Nor can he sing the virtues and valency of his comrades in his debut collection, historical figures who have become 'men of history', without locating as the beginning Gloria House, known in the movement as Aneb Kgositsile – his comrade with whom he organized in the Student Nonviolent Coordinating Committee (SNCC) in the early 1960s – and concluding with his then-wife Melba Johnson. The point of departure is the point of return.

James Smethurst asserts that the Black Power and Black Arts Movements were 'so twinned and joined at the hip that it is impossible, really, to tell where one begins and the other ends' (2021). Kgositsile's work, as explored in this book, asks us to rethink the principal agents and proponents of these movements as we rewrite their history. In our restorying, t becomes imperative to pay attention to the erotics localized in that hip as connective tissue, that enjoined the gut's intuition and 'natural instinct which teaches a man to be free' (1969c: 10),[9] that birthed a language of the gut/hip informing the artistic, intellectual, and political activity of the era. Nina Simone is a figure of the Black Arts and Black Power Movements as much as Miriam Makeba is. They provided not only the music for the generation, but also the rhythms of another beginning. They are also thinkers and fighters – what Kgositsile has previously called lover-warrior-revolutionists.

He tasks us to consider musicians such as Aretha Franklin who were active in this movement but are not included in its historiography. When he elucidates his use of 'spirit' in his interview with Charles Rowell, he offers: 'It is spirit that makes Aretha Franklin, John Coltrane, Malcolm X, and President Julius Nyerere sound the way they do and do the things they do, the way they do them' (Rowell 1978: 31). Kgositsile is very deliberate in his words; he mentions Aretha Franklin 'in the same breath' as a gesture of shared citizenship through shared breath/

---

[9] A line from 'When Brown is Black' (1969), dedicated to Rap Brown.

spirit. Aretha is 'building together' 'in the same breath' with Malcolm, Coltrane, and Nyerere; he seeks to locate her in the throughline of Black political thought and radical traditions.

Kgositsile's work also pushes us to reframe the Black Arts Movement beyond the period of 1965 to 1975 by insisting on tracing the genealogies and lineage that makes the BAM possible. Here we begin to bring into focus the roles of Gwendolyn Brooks, whose revolutionary work Kgositsile reads in the same instantiation as Ghanaian post-independent novelist Ayi Kwei Armah and Guyanese Pan-African activist Eusi Kwayana.[10] In his work, Brooks is presented as the solid coil that unifies the creative activity of BAM with the force and the spirit that mothers their political activity. He also emphasizes the role of Zora Neale Hurston in the BAM, whom he writes of as a dreamkeeper, singing and resounding the intergenerational song and holding the ritual archive of the American south needed to mother the culture of Black liberation. He sings her name in his work, and as stated earlier, he extols her as keeper of the word, of wisdom, as griot and prophet, dedicating *The Word is Here* (1973), an anthology of modern African poetry, 'to Langston Hughes, Zora Neale Hurston, Chris Okigbo & Can Themba'. She is the matriarchive, and the dynamic of rural *roots-en-route* are evinced in her work.

I deployed the methodology of hearing where the women are sounded in Kgositsile's poetry and his larger work, which I also deploy to listen to women in the Black Arts Movement. What could the method and practice of *diligently looking for where women are sounded* in Kgositsile's Black arts era poetry reveal for our approach of the Black Arts Movement historiography? Who will write of Miriam Makeba as lover-warrior-revolutionary operating within the formations and logics of the Black Power and Black Panther movements? What potentials to hear women of the Black arts surface when we pay attention to the erotics of these social movements?

These are the poetics of pro/creation: the coming into being of any life, rebirth, movement, new dawn, as seen throughout the book, are the purposeful acts of the collective mothered into reality through the female principle – there is no birth without blood! This, too, is pro/creation: the continuous digging of Black arts archives by future generations in the twenty-first century strives to unearth aesthetics, poetics, and politics from which to cull and engage in intergenerational dialogue. Pro/creation is characterized by poetics of suture and gathering, and these are maternal, contingent on creation and creativity – the imperative of Black liberation is to remake the world anew, to resacralize and rebirth an interdependent existence with the larger environs; this requires the feminine principle.

---

[10] See the poem 'For Eusi, Ayi Kwei & Gwen Brooks' in *My Name is Afrika* (1971: 73).

Gathered

In an obituary published in the *Sunday Times*, Kgositsile's comrade and close friend Mandla Langa wrote in heart-rending terms about the influence exercised by the women who raised Kgositsile on his personhood and politics:

> [Kgositsile] had it in him to write in any of the languages he spoke fluently. From the Setswana he had suckled from the breast of his mother, Galekgobe Mary Kgositsile, the woman who set him on this long and returnless journey to self-knowledge. It is a language that gives rise to empathy [...] in telling the story of his children, of the children of this country, as well as the story of the children of the workers and peasants, the underclass of Africa, Asia and Latin America. Bra Willie [Kgositsile] was drawing on his own childhood. (2018)

I am enthused by Langa's language, brought together from the cosmological archive of Southern Africa, which has strong orientations towards the matriarchive. When speaking of the mother's breast in this context, he is translating from the parlance of the Tswana maxim, '*o e nyantse letsweleng*', or 'the child suckled it from the breast', implying that the child first encounters the culture and language of the family and larger society at a mother's breast. That is, the child's first comprehension of the world system they are born into is at the mother's bosom. In this cosmology, it is understood that the foundations of a child's identity are transmitted through breast milk. Further, what is transmitted through the breast fortifies the child, is everpresent in the blood, nourishing their becoming. Through breast knowledge and matriarchival knowledge, the child will always know their name, their origin or lineage, and their home or belonging. What is transmitted through the breast signals that from which one cannot easily wean oneself, that which cannot be easily abandoned or taken away.

These are the myths that constitute symbolic life, whose entanglement with biological life produce the hybrid human in the Wynterian sense, characterized by both the corporeal being born of the womb and the stories that shape their onto-epistemological becoming. Kgositsile wages an oppositional politics from the subject position of these stories, mythologies, spiritual practices, and cosmologies, recalibrating the coordinates of western liberal humanism to assert and affirm other forms of being-in-becoming, untethered to colonial ways of being and becoming. Kgositsile takes the position of custodian, of dreamkeeper stewarding 'the spontaneous song and the dance / pulsating with the force of my people's ethos' (2002: 102). These are the words of guidance to his son Thebe Kgositsile, counsel he has sought in his own life, and that he passes on to the next generation. This is the place of Setswana, its song and dance, its wisdoms and rhythms, and the matriarchive in Kgositsile's life that Langa captures in this elegy, echoing the arguments made in this book regarding the central figure of the body in Kgositsile's poetics and politics of intimacy, relation, solidarity, and belonging. As quoted above, Sterling Plumpp finds that Kgositsile 'has an assurance of a self born out of superior knowledge of his history, culture and family'. This assurance is what Langa calls a 'returnless journey to self-knowledge' and attributes to the matriarchive.

This is a gesture that generates radical empathy through an ethics of personhood, governed by accountability to self and others, underwritten by an ethos of interdependence and intersubjective kinship that is durable and expandable to hold the pain and stories of 'the children of the workers and peasants, the underclass of Africa, Asia and Latin America'. Langa is a faithful witness: 'Kgositsile was drawing from his childhood'. In his obituary, Langa pronounced: 'his mother's name could be the key to Kgositsile's journey into writing poetry' (2018). Throughout this book, I have sought to theorize that key and use it to unlock the elsewhere from which Kgositsile's powerful imagination is derived. May the treasures unlocked here offer us worlds of vocabularies, theories, frameworks, methodologies, and mythologies to lighten our journeys as dreamkeepers, fortifying our gathering work, igniting our resolve, and returning us to a dynamic of contiguity with all our bodies – of knowledge, water, land, and cosmos.

Bibliography

Primary Sources

Kgositsile, K. (1969a). 'The Ab/Original Mask', *Black World*, 18(12), 54–60.
——. (1974a). 'An Excerpt from a Work in Manuscript, I KNOW MY NAME', *Nkombo*, 9, 41–4.
——. (1968a). 'Brother Malcolm and the Black Revolution', *Negro Digest*, 18(1), 4–10.
——. (1991). 'Crossing Borders without Leaving', *Staffrider*, 4(2), 5–10.
——. (1978). 'Culture and Liberation in South Africa', *Lotus: Afro-Asian Writing*, 11(1), 10–15.
——. (1992). 'Culture as a Site of Struggle', *Staffrider*, 10(4), 47–64.
——. (1970). *For Melba* (Chicago: Third World Press).
——. (1980). *Heartprints/Herzspuren* (Schwifting: Schwiftinger Galerie-Verlag).
——. (1973a). 'I Know My Name', *The Black Position*, 3, 60–9.
——. (2002). *If I Could Sing: Selected Poems* (Cape Town: Kwela Books).
——. (1969b). 'Introduction', in: A. Alhamisi and H.K. Wangara (eds), *Black Arts: An Anthology of Black Creations* (Detroit: Black Arts Publications), 15–16.
——. (2023). *Keorapetse Kgositsile: Collected Poems, 1969–2018*, ed. by P. Devilliers and U. Phalafala (Lincoln: Nebraska University Press).
——. (1993). 'Language, Culture and Visas to the 21st Century', *Southern African Review of Books*, 7(7), n.p.
——. (1970). 'Malcolm X and the Black Revolution: the tragedy of a dream deferred', in: J.H. Clarke (ed.), *Malcolm X: The Man and His Times* (New York: Collier), 27–36.
——. (1971). *My Name is Afrika* (New York: Doubleday & Co.).
——. (1975a). *Places and Bloodstains* (Oakland, CA: Achebe Publications).
——. (1975b). 'Places and Bloodstains: Notes for Ipeleng', *Black World*, 24(9), 62–5.
——. (1968b). 'Poet's Credo', *Negro Digest*, 17(9), 42–3.
——. (1969c). *Spirits Unchained: Paeans* (Chicago: Broadside Press).
——. (1972). 'The Favorite Grandson', *Black World*, 22(1), 54–8.
——. (1974b). *The Present is a Dangerous Place to Live* (Chicago: Third World Press).
—— (ed.). (1973b). *The Word is Here* (New York: Doubleday & Co.).
——. (1995). *To the Bitter End* (Chicago: Third World Press).
——. (1990). *When the Clouds Clear* (Johannesburg: Congress of South African Writers).

Personal Interviews by Author

Gwen Ansell, Johannesburg, April 2018.
Ipeleng Kgositsile, Oakland, October 2014.
Keorapetse Kgositsile, 2012–2018.
Muxe Nkondo, Pretoria, March 2013.
Abiodun Oyewole, New York, August 2014.
Sterling Plumpp, Chicago, September 2014.
Mongane Serote, Johannesburg, May 2014.
Lefifi Tladi, Mabopane, Pretoria, 2014.

Secondary Sources

Achebe, C. (1987). *Anthills of the Savannah* (Oxford and Johannesburg: Heinemann).
Alexander, M.J. (2005). *Pedagogies of Crossing: Meditations on Feminism, Sexual Politics, Memory, and the Sacred* (Durham, NC: Duke University Press).
Alhamisi, A. and Wangara, H.K. (eds). (1969). *Black Arts: An Anthology of Black Creations* (Detroit: Black Arts Publications).
Baderoon, G. (2014). *Regarding Muslims: FromSslavery to Post-Apartheid* (Johannesburg: Wits University Press).
Barad, K. (2007). *Meeting the Universe Halfway: Quantum Physics and the Entanglement of Matter and Meaning* (Durham, NC: Duke University Press).
Baraka, A. (1969). *Black Art* (Newark, NJ: Jihad Productions).
——. (2002). *Blues People* (New York: Perennial).
——. (1988). 'The Works of Henry Dumas—A New Blackness', *Black American Literature Forum*, 22(2), 161–3.
Baraka, A. and Neal, L. (eds). (1968). *Black Fire: An Anthology of Afro-American Writing.* (New York: Morrow).
Biko, S. (1978). *I Write What I Like* (London: Bowerdean Press).
Bofelo, M. wa. (2008). 'The Influences and Representations of Biko and Black Consciousness in Poetry in Apartheid and Postapartheid South Africa/Azania', in: A. Mngxitama, A. Alexander, and N.C. Gibson (eds), *Biko Lives! Contesting the Legacies of Steve Biko* (New York: Palgrave Macmillan), 191–212.
Bogues, A. (2016). *Black Heretics, Black Prophets: Radical Political Intellectuals* (New York: Routledge).
Brooks, G. (1971). *Family Pictures* (Detroit: Broadside Press).
——. (1973). 'Introduction', in: A. Adoff (ed.), *The Poetry of Black America: Anthology of the 20th Century* (New York: Harper & Row), i–vii.
——. (1971). 'Young Heroes', in: K. Kgositsile, *My Name is Afrika* (New York: Doubleday & Co.), 11–13.
Brown, J. (2021). *Black Utopias: Speculative Life and the Music of Other Worlds* (Durham, NC: Duke University Press).
Butler, O. (1993). *Parable of the Sower* (New York: Four Walls Eight Windows).
——. (1979). *Kindred.* (New York: Doubleday).
Campt, T. (2019). 'Black Visuality and the Practice of Refusal', *Women & Performance:*

A Journal of Feminist Theory, 29(1), 79–87.
Cabral, A. (1973). *Return to the Source: Selected Speeches of Amilcar Cabral* (New York and London: Monthly Review Press).
Cervenak, S. (2014). *Wandering: Philosophical Performances of Racial and Sexual Freedom* (Durham, NC: Duke University Press).
Cesaire, A. (1955). *Discourse on Colonialism* (New York: Monthly Review Press).
Clarke, C. (2006). 'After Mecca': *Women Poets and the Black Arts Movement* (New Brunswick, NJ: Rutgers University Press).
Chakrabarty, D. (2000). *Provincializing Europe: Postcolonial Thought and Historical Difference* (Princeton, NJ and Oxford: Princeton University Press).
Chrisman, L. (2004). 'Du Bois in Transnational Perspective: The Loud Silencing of Black South Africa', *Current Writing: Text and Reception in Southern Africa*, 16(2), 18–30.
——. (2002). 'Postcolonial Studies and Black Atlanticism.' Talk given to African Studies and English Departments, University of Kansas at Lawrence, 28 March.
——. (2000). 'Rethinking Black Atlanticism', *The Black Scholar*, 30(3–4), 12–17.
——. (2012). 'Whose Black World Is This Anyway', in: B. Ledent and P. Cuder-Domínguez (eds), *New perspectives on the Black Atlantic: Definitions, Readings, Practices, Dialogues* (Bern and New York: Peter Lang), 23–57.
Collins, L.G. and Crawford, M.N. (eds). (2006). *New Thoughts on the Black Arts Movement* (New Brunswick, NJ: Rutgers University Press).
Comaroff, J. and Comaroff, J. (2015). *Theories from the South: Or, How Euro-America is Evolving toward Africa* (New York: Routledge).
Crawford, M.N. (2017). *Black Post-Blackness: The Black Arts Movement and Twenty-First-Century Aesthetics* (Urbana: University of Illinois Press).
——. (2007). 'Productive Rites of "Passing": Keorapetse Kgositsile and the Black Arts Movement', *Black Renaissance Noir*, 7(3), 112–20.
Crawley, A. (2016). *Blackpentecostal Breath: The Aesthetic of Possibility* (New York: Fordham University Press).
——. (2020). 'Stayed Freedom Hallelujah', in: T. King, A. Smith, and J. Navarro (eds), *Otherwise Worlds: Against Settler Colonialism and Anti-Blackness* (Durham, NC: Duke University Press), 27–37.
Cromartie, V. (2018). 'Black Social Movements Past and Present: A Comparative Analysis of the Black Arts Movement and the Hip Hop Movement', *Journal of Pan African Studies*, 11(6), 77–148.
Debela, A. (2004). 'A Jewel of a Painter of the 21st Century (1937–2003)', Prepared for Arts Council of the African Studies Association Conference: 13th Triennial Symposium on African Art, April 2004.
Dent, Tom, (1982). *Blue Lights and River Songs* (Detroit: Lotus Press).
——. (1976). *Magnolia Street* (New Orleans: T. Dent).
De Villiers, P.Y., Ferrin-Aguirre, I. and Xiao, K. (2010). *No Serenity Here* (Beijing: World Knowledge Publishers).
Dubey, M. (1994). *Black Women Novelists and the Nationalist Aesthetic* (Bloomington, IN: Indiana University Press).
Du Bois, W.E.B. (1898). *Some Efforts of American Negroes for their Own Social Betterment* (Atlanta, GA: Atlanta University Press).

Dumas, H. (1970). *Ark of Bones and Other Stories* (Carbondale: Southern Illinois University Press).
——. (2003). *Echo Tree: The Collected Short Fiction of Henry Dumas* (Minneapolis, MN: Coffee House Press).
——. (1974). *Play Ebony Play Ivory* (New York: Random House).
Edwards, B.H. (2017). *Epistrophies: Jazz and the Literary Imagination* (Cambridge, MA: Harvard University Press).
——. (2003). *The Practice of Diaspora: Literature, Diaspora and the Rise of Black Internationalism* (Cambridge, MA: Harvard University Press).
Eshun, K. (2017a). 'The Algorithmic Poetics', in: Research Center for Proxy Politics (ed.), *Proxy politics: Power and Subversion in a Networked Age* (Berlin: Archive Books), 21–36.
——. (2017b). 'Ceddo in the Future of 1976', In: *Angazi but I'm Sure*. Raw Academy, Dakar, Senegal 21 April 2017.
Falola, T. (2017). 'Ritual Archives', in: A. Afolayan and T. Falola (eds), *The Palgrave Handbook of African Philosophy* (Austin, TX: Palgrave Macmillan), 703–28.
Fanon, F. (1952). *Black Skin, White Masks* (New York: Grove Press).
Feld, S. (2015). 'Acoustemology', in D. Novak and M. Sakakeeny (eds), *Keywords in Sound* (Durham, NC and London: Duke University Press), 12–21.
——. (2012). *Sound and Sentiment: Birds, Weeping, Poetics, and Song in Kaluli Expression*. 3rd edn. (Durham, NC: Duke University Press).
Gayle, A. (ed.). (1971). *The Black Aesthetic* (Garden City: Double Day).
Gillespie, M.A. (2008). *The Theological Origins of Modernity* (Chicago: University of Chicago Press).
Gilroy, P. (1993). *The Black Atlantic: Modernity and Double Consciousness* (Cambridge, MA: Harvard University Press).
Gordimer, N. (1984). 'Something Out There'. *Salmagundi*, 62, 118–92.
Grillo, L. (2018). *An Intimate Rebuke* (Durham, NC and London: Duke University Press).
Gumbs, A.P. (2020). *Undrowned: Black Feminist Lessons from Marine Mammals* (Edinburgh: AK Press).
Gumbs, A.P., Martens, C. and Williams, M. (2016). *Revolutionary mothering: love on the frontlines.* (New York: PM Press).
Haraway, D. (2016). *Staying with Trouble: Making Kin in the Cthulucene* (Durham, NC: Duke University Press).
Harhoff, M. (2021). '"Umthandazo": Black Womxn's Prayers and the Recollections of the Everyday', *Imbiza*, 1(2), 91–7.
Hartman, S. (2007). *Lose Your Mother: A Journey along the Atlantic Slave Route* (New York: Farrar, Straus and Giroux).
——. (2002). 'The Time of Slavery', *The South Atlantic Quarterly*, 101 (4), 757–77.
——. (2019). *Wayward Lives, Beautiful Experiments: Intimate Histories of Social Upheaval* (New York: W. W. Norton & Co.).
Hartman, S. and Wilderson, F. (2003). 'The Position of the Unthought: An Interview with Saidiya V. Hartman conducted by Frank B. Wilderson III', *Qui Parle*, 13(2), 183–201.

Head, B. (1984). 'A Period of Darkness', *The Iowa Review*, 14(2), 123–8.
——. (1971). *Maru* (London: Gollancz).
——. (1968). *When Rain Clouds Gather* (London: Heinemann).
Heitner, D. (2013). *Black Power TV* (Durham, NC: Duke University Press).
hooks, b. (1990). 'Homeplace (a Site of Resistance)', in: *Yearning: Race, Gender, and Cultural Politics*. (Boston: South End Press), 41–9.
——. (2004). *The will to change: Men, Masculinity, and Love* (New York: Atria Books).
Jaji, T. (2009). 'Sound Effects: Synaesthesia as Purposeful Distortion in Keorapetse Kgositsile's Poetry', *Comparative Literature Studies*, 46(2), 287–310.
Keeling, K. (2019). *Queer Times, Black Futures* (New York: New York University Press).
Keller, M. (2002). *The Hammer and the Flute: Women, Power, and Spirit Possession* (Baltimore, MD and London: Johns Hopkins University Press).
Kelley, R.D.G. (2003). *Freedom Dreams* (Boston, MA: Beacon Press).
——. (2000). 'Introduction', in: C. Robinson (ed.), *Black Marxism: The Making of the Black Radical Tradition* (Chapel Hill: University of North Carolina Press), xxvii–xxxiii.
Kent, G. (1974). 'Introduction', in: K. Kgositsile, *The Present is a Dangerous Place to Live* (Chicago: Third World Press), i–iii.
Laclau, E. (1995). 'The Time Is Out of Joint', *Acta Philosophica*, 16(2), 109–23.
Landsberg, A. (2004). *Prosthetic Memory: The Transformation of American Remembrance in the Age of Mass Culture* (New York: Columbia University Press).
Langa, M. (2018). 'Ode to a Poet', *Sunday Times*, 7 January 2018.
Lee, D.L. (1968). 'Black Poetry: Which Direction?', *Negro Digest*, 17(11–12), 27–32.
Lorde, A. (1993). *Poetry is not a Luxury* (Osnabrück: Druck- & Verlagscooperative).
——. (1984). *Sister Outsider: Essays and Speeches* (Berkeley, CA: Crossing Press).
——. (1978). *The Uses of the Erotic* (New York: Out and Out Books).
Luchembe, C. (1977). 'An Interview with Mazisi Kunene on African Philosophy', *Ufahamu*, 7(2), 3–28.
Lugones, M. (2003). *Pilgrimages/Peregrinajes: Theorizing Coalition against Multiple Oppressions* (Lanham, MD: Rowman & Littlefield).
——. (2010). 'Towards a Decolonial Feminism', *Hypatia: A Journal of Feminist Philosophy*, 25(4), 742–59.
Lynskey, D. (2011). *33 revolutions per minute* (London: Faber).
McDonald, P. (2009). *The Literature Police: Apartheid Censorship and its Cultural Consequences* (Oxford: Oxford University Press).
Mackey, N. (2018). 'Breath and Precarity: The Inaugural Robert Creeley Lecture in Poetry and Poetics', in: M. Mi Kim and C. Miller (eds), *Poetics and Precarity* (Albany: SUNY Press), 42–9.
Madhubuti, H. and Mitchell, G. (eds). (1998). *Releasing the Spirit* (Chicago: Third World Press).
Mangharam, M.L. (2013) 'The Universal is the Entire Collection of Particulars: Grounding Identity in a Shared Horizon of Humanity', *College of Literature*, 40(3), 81–98.
Marechera, D. (2009). *House of Hunger* (Harlow: Heinemann).

Marshall, P. (1983). 'From the Poets in the Kitchen', *The New York Times*, 9 January 1983.
Mashigo, M. (2018a). *Intruders* (Cape Town: Pan Macmillan SA).
Mavhunga, C. (2014). *Transient Workspaces: Technologies of Everyday Innovation in Zimbabwe* (Boston, MA: MIT Press).
Mavimbela, V. (2018). 'Tribute to Keorapetse Kgositsile', *The Star*, 19 January 2018.
M'Baye, B. (2003). 'The Representation of Africa in Black Atlantic Studies of Race and Literature', in: I. Hoving, F. Korsten, and E. van Alphen (eds), *Africa and Its Significant Others: Forty Years of Intercultural Entanglement; Thamyris/Intersecting: Place, Sex and Race* (Leiden: Brill), 151–62.
Mbembe, A. (1992). 'Provisional Notes on the Postcolony', *Africa*, 62(1), 3–37.
McKittrick, K. and Wynter, S. (2015). 'Unparalleled Catastrophe for Our Species? Or, to Give Humanness a Different Future: Conversations', in: K. McKittrick (ed.), *Sylvia Wynter: On Being Human as Praxis* (Durham, NC: Duke University Press), 9–89.
Morgan, J. (2021). *Reckoning With Slavery: Gender, Kinship, and Capitalism in the Early Black Atlantic of Being* (Durham, NC: Duke University Press).
Morrison, T. (1987). *Beloved* (New York: Alfred A. Knopf Inc.).
——. (2019). *Mouth Full of Blood* (New York: Random House).
Moten, F. (2003). *In the Break: The Aesthetics of the Black Radical Tradition* (Minneapolis, MN: University of Minnesota Press).
Mphahlele, E. (1959). *Down Second Avenue* (London: Faber and Faber).
——. (1979). 'The Voice of Prophecy in African Poetry', *English in Africa*, 6(1), 33–45.
Mthembu, I. (2012). 'Working Class Hero: TUMI', *MindMap-SA*, 5, 19.
Musila, G.A. (2019). 'Desire and freedom in Yvonne Vera's fiction', in: M. Adenjunmobi and C. Coetzee (eds), *Routledge Handbook of African Literature* (London: Routledge), 323–38.
Ndikung, B. (2018). 'Corpoliteracy', in: S. Angiama, C. Butcher, and A. Zeqo (eds), *aneducation, documenta 14* (Berlin: Archive Books), 107–15.
Neal, L. (1969). 'Any Day Now: Black Art and Black Liberation', *Ebony Magazine*, August 1969.
Nuttall, S. and A. Mbembe (eds). (2008). *Johannesburg: The Elusive Metropolis* (Durham, NC: Duke University Press).
Nyamnjoh, F.B. (2021). 'Being and becoming African as a permanent work in progress: inspiration from Chinua Achebe's proverbs', African Literature Association (ALA) Lecture, Cape Town, 23 January 2021.
Okiji, F. (2018). *Jazz as Critique: Adorno and Black Expression Revisited* (Stanford, CA: Stanford University Press).
Olver, T. and Meyer, S. (2004). 'Introduction: African Shores and Transatlantic Interlocutions', *Current Writing: Text and Reception in Southern Africa*, 16(2), 1–17.
Ouma, C.E.W. and Krishnan, M. (2021). 'Small magazines in Africa: ecologies and genealogies', *Social Dynamics*, 47(2), 193–209.
Oyewole, A. (2014). *Branches of the Tree of Life: The Collected Poems of Abiodun Oyewole, 1969-2013* (New York: 2Leaf Press).
Oyěwùmí, O. (1997). *The Invention of Women: Making an African Sense of Western*

Gender Discourses (Minneapolis: University of Minnesota Press).
Patel, J. (2003). 'Jungle brothers: Straight Out the Jungle, Done by the Forces of Nature, De la Soul: 3 Feet High and Rising, De La Soul Is Dead, Buhloone Mindstate, A Tribe Called Quest: People's Instinctive Travels and the Paths of Rhythm, The Low End Theory, Midnight Marauders', in: O. Wang (ed.), *Classic Material: The Hip-Hop Album Guide* (Toronto: eCW Press), 97–104.
Phalafala, U. (2020). 'Decolonizing World Literature Through Orality', in: S. Helgesson, B. Neumann, and G. Rippl (eds), *Handbook of Anglophone World Literatures* (Berlin and Boston: De Gruyter), 193–208.
———. (2017). 'Home is where the music is: an interview with South African poet laureate Keorapetse Kgositsile', *Journal of the African Literature Association*, 11(2), 246–53.
———. (2019a). 'My Name is Afrika: Keorapetse Kgositsile in the "Black World"', in: M. Berthet, F. Rosa, and S. Viljoen (eds), *Moving Spaces: Creolisation and Mobility in Africa, the Atlantic and Indian Ocean* (Leiden: Brill), 161–76.
———. (2019b). 'Of Worlds Black and Red: South Africa's Poet Laureates and Their World-Making Networks', *Research in African Literatures*, 50(3), 116–35.
Philip, M.N. (2014). *She tries her tongue, her silence softly breaks* (Middletown, CT: Wesleyan University Press.)
Peterson, B. (2019). 'Spectrality and inter-generational Black narratives in South Africa', *Social Dynamics*, 45(3), 345–64.
Plaatje, S. (1916a). *A Sechuana Reader* (London: University of London Press).
———. (1930). *Mhudi* (Alice: Lovedale Press).
———. (1916b). *Native Life in South Africa* (London: P.S. King and Son Ltd.).
———. (1916c). *Sechuana Proverbs* (London: K. Paul, Trench, Trubner and Company).
Powell, C. (1991). 'Rap Music: An Education with a Beat from the Street', *Journal of Negro Education*, 60(3), 245–59.
Quashie, K. (2021). *Black Aliveness, or A Poetics of Being* (Durham, NC: Duke University Press).
Raditladi, L.D. (1970). *Motswasele II* (Johannesburg: Witwatersrand University Press).
Rambsy, H. (2013). *The Black Arts Movement Enterprise and the Production of Poetry* (Ann Arbor: University of Michigan Press).
Ramose, M. (2003). 'The Ethics of Ubuntu', in: P. Coetzee and A. Roux (eds), *The African philosophy reader* (New York: Routledge), 324–33.
Redmond, E. (1976). *Drumvoices: The Mission of Afro-American Poetry; A Critical History* (New York: Anchor Press).
Redmond, S. (2014). *Anthem: Social Movement and the Sound of Solidarity in the African Diaspora* (New York and London: New York University Press).
Robinson, C. (ed.). (2000). *Black Marxism: The Making of the Black Radical Tradition.* (Chapel Hill: University of North Carolina Press).
———. (2012). *The Terms of Order.* (Chapel Hill: University of North Carolina Press).
Robolin, S. (2012). 'Black Transnationalism: 20th-Century South African and African American Literatures', *Literature Campus*, 9(1), 80–94.
———. (2015). *Grounds of Engagement: Apartheid-era African American and South African Writing* (Urbana: University of Illinois Press).

Rodney, W. (1972). *How Europe Underdeveloped Africa* (London: Bogle-L'Ouverture Publications).
Rowell, C. (1978). '"With Bloodstains to Testify": An Interview with Keorapetse Kgositsile', *Callaloo*, 2, 23–42.
Sarr, F. (2019). *Afrotopia* (Minneapolis: University of Minnesota Press).
Said, E. (1978). *Orientalism* (New York: Pantheon Books).
Salaam, K. ya. (1991). 'Interview with Keorapetse "Willie" Kgositsile', *BBB*, 1(8), 75–81.
Salami, M. (2020). *Sensuous Knowledge: A Black Feminist Approach for Everyone* (London: Zed Books).
Serote, M. (1983). *To Every Birth its Blood* (London: Heinemann Educational Books).
——. (1972). *Yakhal'inkomo* (Johannesburg: Renoster Books).
Sharpe, C. (2016). *In the Wake: On Blackness and Being* (Durham, NC: Duke University Press).
Shringarpure, B. (2019). *Cold War Assemblages: Decolonization to Digital* (New York and London: Routledge).
Sithole, T. (2018). *The Life and Music of Zimontology* (London: Poetry Printery).
Smethurst, J. (2014). 'The Black Arts Movement', in: J. Bracey, S. Sanchez, and J. Smethurst (eds), *SOS—Calling All Black People: A Black Arts Movement Reader* (Amherst: University Massachusetts Press), 1–10.
Stewart, E. and Duran, J. (1999). 'Black Essentialism: The Art of Jazz Rap', *Philosophy of Music Education Review*, 7(1), 49–54.
Stratton, F. (1994). *Contemporary African Literature and the Politics of Gender* (London: Routledge).
Taylor-Guthrie, D. (1996). 'Conversation with South African Poet Keorapetse Kgositsile', *African Issues*, 24(2), 36–7.
Thiong'o, N. wa. (1986). *Decolonising the Mind: The Politics of Language in African Literature* (London: James Currey).
Thomas, L. (2006). 'The Need to Speak: Tom Dent and the Shaping of a Black Aesthetic', *African American Review*, 40(2), 325–38.
Tladi, L. (1980). *Mosima Motlhaela Thupa* (Gaborone: National Museum and Art Gallery).
Toomer, J. (1923). *Cane* (New York: Boni & Liveright).
Tubbs, A.M. (2021). *The Three Mothers: How the Mothers of Martin Luther King, Jr., Malcolm X, and James Baldwin Shaped a Nation* (New York: Flatiron Books).
Van der Vlies, A. (2007). 'Transnational Print Cultures: Books, -scapes, and the textual Atlantic', *Safundi: The Journal of South African and American Studies*, 8(1), 45–55.
Wacquant, L. (2001). 'Deadly Symbiosis: When ghetto and prison meet and mesh', *Punishment & Society*, 3(1), 95–133.
Walker, A. (1983). *In Search of Our Mothers' Gardens: Womanist Prose* (New York: Harcourt).
——. (2005). 'Zora Neale Hurston: A Cautionary Tale and A Partisan View', in: *In Search of Our Mothers' Gardens* (London: Orion Books), 83–92.
Walser, R. (1995). 'Rhythm, Rhyme, and Rhetoric in the Music of Public Enemy', *Ethnomusicology*, 39(2), 193–217.

Weheliye, A.G. (2005). *Phonographies: Grooves in Sonic Afro-Modernity* (Durham, NC: Duke University Press).
Willan, B. (2018). *Sol Plaatje: A life of Solomon Tshekisho Plaatje 1876–1932* (Auckland Park: Jacana Media).
Wright, J. (2003). 'Introduction', in: H. Dumas, *Echo Tree: The Collected Short Fiction of Henry Dumas* (Minneapolis, MN: Coffee House Press), ix–xxxvii.
Wright, M. (2004). *Becoming Black: Creating Identity in the African Diaspora* (Durham, NC and London: Duke University Press).
——. (2015). *Physics of Blackness: Beyond the Middle Passage Epistemology* (Minneapolis: University of Minnesota Press).
Wright, R. (1998). *Native Son* (New York: Harper Perennial).
Wylie, D. (2006). *Art + Revolution: The Life and Death of Thami Mnyele* (Johannesburg: Jacana).
Wynter, S. (2015). 'The Ceremony Found: Towards the Autopoetic Turn/Overturn, Its Autonomy of Human Agency and Extraterritoriality of (Self-)Cognition', in: J.R. Ambroise and S. Broeck (eds), *Black Knowledges/Black Struggles: Essays in Critical Epistemology* (Liverpool: Liverpool University Press), 184–252.
——. (1984). 'The Ceremony Must Be Found: After Humanism', *boundary 2*, 12(3)–13(1), 19–70.
——. (2003). 'Unsettling the Coloniality of Being/Power/Truth/Freedom: Towards the Human, After Man, Its Overrepresentation—An Argument', *CR: The New Centennial Review*, 3(3), 257–337.

Discography

A Tribe Called Quest. (1991). *The Low End Theory*.
Baraka, A. (1972). *It's Nation Time*.
Black Forum. (1970–73). *Free Huey*.
Gamedze, A. (2020). *Dialectic Soul*. With sleeve notes by Robin D.G. Kelley.
Giovanni, N. (1971). *Truth is on its Way*.
Roach, M. (1960). *Freedom Now Suite*.
Mankunku, W. (1968). *Yakhal' Inkomo*.
Mbulu, L. (1996). *Not Yet Uhuru*.
Mhlongo, B. (1999). *Urban Zulu*.
The Last Poets. (1993). *Holy Terror*.
——. (1970). *The Last Poets*.
——. (1971). *This is Madness*.

Unpublished thesis

Gamedze, A. (2019). 'It's in the out sides: An investigation into the cosmological contexts of South African jazz' (Masters Dissertation, University of Cape Town).

Web-based sources

Akomolafe, B. (2019). 'Making sanctuary: hope, companionship, race and the emergence in the anthropocene', https://www.bayoakomolafe.net/post/making-sanctuary-hope-companionship-race-and-emergence-in-the-anthropocene [Accessed 28 February 2023].

Aku, T. (2018). 'Review of Some Rap Songs', Pitchfork, https://pitchfork.com/reviews/albums/earl-sweatshirt-some-rap-songs/ [Accessed 14 October 2018].

Among the Believers. (2010). 'Among the Believers', News24, https://www.news24.com/citypress/entertainment/news/among-the-believers-20100410 [Accessed 16 May 2019].

Baderoon, G. (2018). 'The creation of Black criminality in South Africa', AfricaIsACountry, https://africasacountry.com/2018/12/the-creation-of-Black-criminality-in-south-africa [Accessed 16 December 2018].

Bradley, R. (2019). 'Regard for One Anther: A conversation between Rizvana Bradley and Saidiya Hartman', *LA Review of Books*, https://www.lareviewofbooks.org/article/regard-for-one-another-a-conversation-between-rizvana-bradley-and-saidiya-hartman/ [Accessed 12 March 2020].

brown, a.d. (2015). 'Afrofuturism and #Blackspring', https://adriennemareebrown.net/2015/05/02/afrofuturism-and-blackspring-new-school-afroturismtns/ [Accessed 11 July 2021].

Castro, L.M. (2010). 'Phonic Substance, Jamal Cyrus', https://artpace.org/exhibitions/phonic-substance/ [Accessed 1 February 2023].

Coates, T. (2003). 'Keepin' it Unreal', *Village Voice*, https://www.villagevoice.com/2003/06/03/keepin-it-unreal/ [Accessed 1 February 2023].

Creativetime. (2023). 'Otabenga Jones &Associates', http://creativetime.org/projects/Black-radical-brooklyn/artists/otabenga-jones-and-associates/ [Accessed 1 February 2023].

Francis, S. (2012). 'Art of this World: Robert Pruitt', *Futuristically Ancient*, https://futuristicallyancient.com/2012/05/08/art-of-this-world-robert-pruitt/ [Accessed 5 July 2019].

Hutchings, S. (2020). 'We need full integration of Black perspective in the telling of history', *Big Issue*, https://www.bigissue.com/latest/social-activism/we-need-full-integration-of-Black-perspective-in-the-telling-of-history/ [Accessed 30 July 2020].

Jenkins, C. (2018). 'Earl Sweatshirt Fights Off Bad Vibes', *Vulture*, https://www.vulture.com/2018/11/interview-earl-sweatshirt.html [Accessed 27 October 2019].

Jordan, P. (2006). 'Inauguration of KW Kgositsile as Poet Laureate', South African Government Website, https://www.gov.za/p-jordan-inauguration-kw-kgositsile-poet-laureate [Accessed 1 February 2023].

Lowndes, J. (2017). 'Linton Kwesi Johnson and Black British Struggle', *AfricaIsACountry*, http://africasacountry.com/2017/05/linton-kwesi-johnson-and-Black-british-struggle/ [Accessed 6 February 2018].

Lucas, P. (2016). 'Glasstire's Best of 2016', *Glasstire*, https://glasstire.com/2016/12/21/glasstires-best-of-2016/ [Accessed 17 September 2020].

Mabandu, P. (2014). 'I Fuck with Every Record', *The Con Mag*, http://www.theconmag.co.za/2014/06/05/i-fuck-with-every-record/ [Accessed 1 February 2023].

Madondo, B. (2010) 'Among the Believers', *City Press*, https://www.news24.com/citypress/entertainment/news/among-the-believers-20100410 [Accessed 16 May 2019].

Mashigo, M. (2018b), 'Afrofuturism is not for Africans living in Africa', *Johannesburg Review of Books*, https://johannesburgreviewofbooks.com/2018/10/01/afrofuturism-is-not-for-africans-living-in-africa-an-essay-by-mohale-mashigo-excerpted-from-her-new-collection-of-short-stories-intruders/ [Accessed 4 November 2019].

Mazaza, S.M. (n.d.). 'Return of the King: Tumi Molekane Reflects On 10 Years In Hip-Hop', https://www.okayafrica.com/tumi-molekane-return-of-the-king-interview/ [Accessed 1 February 2023].

Morrison, T. (1993). 'Nobel Lecture', *The Nobel Prize in Literature*, https://www.nobelprize.org/prizes/literature/1993/morrison/lecture/ [Accessed 21 May 2020].

Moten, F. (2018a). 'Left of Black with Fred Moten', YouTube, https://www.youtube.com/watch?v=fFTkoZTFd1k&t=1351s, *YouTube*, [Accessed 21 November 2019].

———. (2018b). 'To refuse that which has been refused to you', *Chimurenga*, https://chimurengachronic.co.za/to-refuse-that-which-has-been-refused-to-you-2/ [Accessed 22 April 2020].

Motsemme, N. (2018). 'On Death, Desire and Spirituality: Reimagining the African Women's Archive', YouTube, https://www.youtube.com/watch?v=kXCUjhokJUM [Accessed 7 May 2021].

Murph, J. (2002). 'Q-Tip/Kamaal Fareed: Jazz, Blues and the Abstract Truth', *Jazz Times* 32(2), 38. Available at https://jazztimes.com/archives/q-tip-jazz-blues-and-the-abstracts-truth/ [Accessed 1 February 2023]

Okorafor, N. (2019) 'Africanfuturism Defined', *Nnedi Blogspot*, http://nnedi.blogspot.com/2019/10/africanfuturism-defined.html [Accessed 8 July 2021].

Otabenga Jones & Associates, (n.d) 'Otabenga Jones &Associates', Tumblr, https://ojandassociates.tumblr.com/ [Accessed 1 February 2023].

Pearce, S. (2019). 'Earl Sweatshirt Does Not Exist', *Pitchfork*, https://pitchfork.com/features/profile/earl-sweatshirt-does-not-exist/ [Accessed 10 October 2020]

Porter, L. (2015). 'Dry Bones Breathe', *The New Enquiry*, https://thenewinquiry.com/dry-bones-breathe/ [Accessed 24 April 2020].

Raache, H. (2019). 'Crystal Bridges Send Art Up, Up & Away into Outer Space', *KNWA*, https://www.nwahomepage.com/news/crystal-bridges-sends-art-up-up-away-into-outer-space/ [Accessed 4 August 2021].

Ramaphosa, C. (2018). 'Eulogy at Official Funeral of Prof Keorapetse Kgositsile', https://www.gov.za/speeches/deputy-president-cyril-ramaphosa-eulogy-official-funeral-prof-keorapetse-kgositsile-16-jan [Accessed 12 February 2019].

Sanneh, K. (2011). 'Where's Earl', *The New Yorker*, http://www.newyorker.com/magazine/2011/05/23/wheres-earl [Accessed 1 February 2023].

Smethurst, J. (2021). 'The Black Arts Movement's Revolution in the South', *The Nation*, https://www.thenation.com/article/society/james-smethurst-black-arts-movement/ [Accessed 12 November 2022].

Snyder, G. (2005). 'Life's Truth Aesthetically Interpreted: Greg Snyder Talks with Keorapetse Kgositsile,' *Bulletin*, http://www.newschool.edu/tcds/twenone.htm [Accessed 4 February 2013].

South African History Online. (n.d.). 'Black Consciousness Movement Timeline 1903–2009', *SAHO*, https://www.sahistory.org.za/article/Black-consciousness-movement-timeline-1903-2009 [Accessed 1 February 2023].

Tippett, K. and Perel E. (2019). 'The Erotic Is An Antidote to Death', *On Being*, https://onbeing.org/programs/esther-perel-the-erotic-is-an-antidote-to-death/ [Accessed 27 June 2021]

Whitney Biennial. (2006), 'Jamal Cyrus', *Whitney Biennial*, https://whitney.org/www/2006biennial/artists.php?artist=Cyrus_Jamal [Accessed 1 February 2023].

Zulu, Z. (2015). 'The African Cosmic Knowledge – Part I', https://zulumathabo.com/2015/08/03/the-african-cosmic-knowledge-part-i/ [Accessed 1 February 2023].

Index

AAPSO 54
AAWA 54
Abdur-Razzaq, Abdullah 51
African Americans 10, 52
   BAM 11
   identity 52
   The Last Poets 107
   uMkhonto we Sizwe 101
   vanguards of Black modernity 10
African languages
   change of opinion on use of 57
African poetry
   anthology 177
Afrofuturism 25, 31, 117, 127–9
   analysis of application of 145
   cosmologies 138
   diaspora 145
Ailey, Alvin 111
Amandla! cultural ensemble 56
ANC 47
   'Backwardness' towards culture 47, 55–6
   banning 48
   joining of 47
   messenger for detained members 48
ANC Women's Section 55
Angelou, Maya 13, 80
   Blacks, Blues, Black! 13, 30, 80–1
anti-apartheid 48
   CIA 51, 175n3
   detention of dissidents 48
   struggle 68, 110
anti-Blackness 2, 26, 62, 93, 134, 143, 173
apartheid 31, 48
   culture 47
   decolonization 64

   Sharpeville massacre 48
   tribalism 47
   various acts 162
appendectomy 42–3

Babu, Ahmed Mohammed 51
BAM 10, 80
   African American centrism 10
   African Americans 11
   anthology 99
   black aesthetics 157, 159
   coil 188
   decolonization 177
   Dent, Tom 13
   depthoffeeling 159
   diaspora 52
   Harlem 160
   history 187
   Hurston, Zora Neale 188
   Kgositsile's place in 12
banned books 162, 163
Bantu education 40, 162
Baraka, Amiri 6, 38, 186
Barrett, Lindsey 176
BCM 101
   Biko, Steve 101–2
Benga, Ota 129–130
Berlin Wall fall 56
Bigger Thomas 101, 114, 118
Biko, Steve 102, 109
   Black consciousness 102–3
   Black man 101–3
birth rituals 66, 67, 91
   names-songs-places 75
Black aesthetics 11
Black American culture
   Black consciousness 80

Black arts   6
Black bodies   18, 89
　carceral cast   135
　police brutality   135
　suffering   26
　trans*formations   124
　white supremacy   36, 41
Black consciousness   54
　Biko, Steve   102–3
　Black American culture   80
　third world consciousness   54
Black diaspora *see* diaspora
black geography   62
Black liberation   30, 61, 88, 117, 118, 123, 134, 184, 188
　movements   6, 152
　mission   186
　relationship with Black arts   88
Black internationalism   88, 149, 161, 164, 166
Black Lives Matter movement   30, 121, 123, 134, 144, 145
Black man   6, 102
　Biko, Steve   101–3
　leaders   13
Black music   26, 84
　Black sonic cultures   123
　Cyrus, Jamal   130
Black nationalism   6
Black Panther Movements   8, 188
Black Panthers   13, 123, 143
　breakfast for school children programme   129
Black sonic cultures   30, 106
　Black music   123
　Kgositsile, Thebe Neruda   112
Black sonics   15, 126, 130, 132
　diaspora   30
Blackness   2, 93
　definition   11
　Dent, Tom   183
　ecosomatics   62
　future   143
Blacks, Blues, Black!   13, 30, 80–1

Blackwomen   6, 63, 87, 88, 149
　matriarchive   77, 79
　native reserves   42
　place in Black history   110–11
　roles   159
BLKARTSOUTH   13, 177, 179, 183, 184
　Dent, Tom   177, 179, 183
bloodsong   70, 75
bodies
　purpose   72
　enslavement   18
　ecosomatics   62
bodies of water   62, 91, 175, 182, 183
Bosman, Gloria   84
Botswana   55
boxing club   44
Boykie   35, 36, 41, 69
BPP   8
　health programme   129
　Party logo   141
Brown, James   123, 129, 143
building together *see* moagisani
Butler, Octavia   123, 129, 141, 143

Carmichel, Stokely   51
Carter, Betty   84
celestial bodies   25, 62, 87, 91, 128, 175, 182, 183
childhood images   65
childhood memoirs   21, 73
children   56
christianity
　denouncement   41
CIA
　young political students   51
citizen
　in Setswana   22, 28, 169
clan names   20
coil   7, 173
　of time   7–8, 23, 144, 175, 181
　as wind   23
　metaphor of inner ear   27, 182
　BAM   188
　gathering work   8, 23, 181

colonial culture   3, 63
colonial history   14–15
colonialism   1, 23, 37, 171
  acculturation   14
  ahistory   171
  settlers   29, 37, 70
  victims of   14
comic adventure   121
  cover   135, 136 fig.2, 137
  Pruitt, Robert   121, 134
  theme   135
comic books   30, 134
Conrad Kent Rivers Memorial
  Award   53, 151
COSAW   56
cosmologies   1, 6
  Afrofuturism   138
  Dogon   137, 139, 145
culture   47, 186–7
  expressive   8, 38, 107, 110, 134
  matriarchive   111
  USA   111
Culture and Resistance conference   55,
  56, 57, 115
Cyrus, Jamal   118, 129
  Black music   130
  collage   130, 132–4
  Pride Records   130, 132, 134

DAC   56
Darwish, Mahmoud   54
Davidson, Peter   51
death rites
  Motswana doctor   148, 155
  Tswana proverb   148
death, 3 January 2018   59
decolonization   12
  Africa   173
  apartheid   64
  BAM   177
  Pan-Africanism   174
  political essays   12, 151
  vision   105, 175
deep hearing   17, 27

NOW   18
Dent, Tom   13, 157, 177
  BAM   13
  Blackness   183
  BLKARTSOUTH   177, 179, 183
  divine authority   53, 157, 180, 181
  legacy   184
  mentorship   178
  New Orleans   179–180, 183
  Umbra   179
  workshops   183
depthoffeeling   8
  BAM   159
  concept   11
  political imaginary   68
  songs   29, 82
diaspora   13
  Afrofuturism   145
  BAM   52
  ecosomatics   63
  matriarchive   13
  metaphor of a tree   26
  spatio-temporality   77
  trees   106
  wind   25
divine authority   53, 157, 180, 181
divorce   54, 57
Doctor of Literature and
  Philosophy   58
Dogon   137
  cosmologies   137, 139, 145
  masks   137, 139
domestic workers   43–5
Dowling Street Martyr Brigade   132,
  133 f.1
  album cover design   132–4
dreamkeepers   74, 190, 184
  Earl Sweatshirt   113
  female musicians   84, 85
  Hurston, Zora Neale   85, 188
  Neruda, Thebe   113, 114
  value   83
Drum   46
Dumas, Henry   129, 133–4

Earl Sweatshirt   13, 30, 57
  see also Kgositsile, Thebe Neruda
  dreamkeepers   113
  rap   30
  The Last Poets   30
ecosomatics   62
  Blackness   62
  bodies   62
  concept   62
  diaspora   63
  geopoetics   62, 103–4
  healing   62
embodiment   72, 143, 174
  definition   72
  expanding into the navel   72
  masks   137
  triad of mind, body and spirit   73
English language
  change of opinion on use of   57–8
erotic   11–12
  poetic knowledge   149
Europatriarchal   22
  boundaries   171
  critique   22
  dominance   173
  limitations and bounderies   66
  realities   68, 69
  spatio-temporality   24
  Tswana proverb   148
Evans, Mari   185, 186
Evans, Medina Kenya   122, 123, 129, 135

family life   57
Fanon, Frantz   6, 38, 186
father see Moagi, Neo
FBI
  Harlem   51
female musicians   84
  future memory   85
Feni, Dumile   54, 55
FESMAN   175
First World Festival of Negro Arts   175
formative years   33–5
Fort Hare University   57

Franklin, Aretha   187–8
future memory   75, 88, 117
  defintion   24, 128
  female musicians   85
  matriarchive   88
  Neal, Larry   88–9
  Tswana proverb   149, 156
  water spirits   87

Galekgobe   3, 4
  death   71, 147
  Johannesburg employment   35
  matriarchive   20
  politics of refusal   42
  servants' quarters   44, 61
  woman-dancer-of-steel   20, 44, 64
gathering work   4, 8, 10, 155, 169, 190
  coil   8
  method   9
geopoetics   61
Ginwala, Frene   50
grandmother see Madikeledi
Gwangwa, Jonas   51

Harlem   51
  BAM   160
  cultural festival   98, 111
  history and culture   160–1
  Hughes, Langston   160–1
  Renaissance   11, 145, 150, 160
  Sophiatown   29, 40, 182
Harlem Cultural Council Poetry
  Award   53
Harris, Cheryl   57, 114
  Kgositsile, Thebe Neruda   112
Head, Harold   51
healing rituals
  names-songs-places   137
heretics   64
  matriarchive   88
  practices   65
hip hop   108, 110
history 1 and history 2   14, 30
Holiday, Billie   84

homemaking   30, 66, 70, 72
Hughes, Langston   113, 153, 169
   Harlem   160–1
   Motswana doctor   157, 160, 169
human zoos   129–130
Hurston, Zora Neale   85, 113, 143, 157, 177
   dreamkeepers   85, 188

Ibrahim, Abdullah   109
Illinois, Chicago   56
indigenous languages   5, 6, 47, 68, 73, 77, 144, 165, 168
inner-ear   27, 181
   Setswana language   27–8

jazz   26, 29, 110
   as modality   126
   influences   46
   Setswana language   46
Johannesburg
   place of birth   76
Johannesburg years   45–51
Johnson, Melba   85, 86
Jordan, Pallo   58

Kain, Gylan   99, 104
Kgositsile, Thebe Neruda
   see also Earl Sweatshirt
   birth   112
   Black sonic cultures   112
   dreamkeepers   113, 114
   Love and Care   115
   mother   112
   rapper   114–15
Kgotsitsile, Galekgobe Mary *see* Galekgobe
Kimberley visit   76, 79
King, Martin Luther   80, 131, 132, 159,
Kotane, Moses   54
Kunene, Mazisi   57, 125–6
La Guma, Alex   47, 54, 176

AAWA   54
   writer-in-residence   54
Langa, Mandla   55
leitmotif   25
   self-reference as 'the son'   62
   wind   25
Lincoln University   51
   CIA   175n3
   scholarship   175n3
Lotus: Afro-Asian Writing   54
Louw, Joe   51
Love and Care   9, 93, 97, 101, 115, 128, 186
love poetry   158
Luciano, Felipe   104
Lumumba, Patrice   77, 151

Madibane High School   46
Madikeledi   2
   death   42, 45, 154, 147
   English language rejection   3, 36, 77
   Europatriarchal refusal   75–6
   funeral   148
   letters written   147
   peripatetic nature   75
   radical mothering   4
   Tswana culture   3
   Tswana literature   38
Mafeking   33, 35
Mahlasela, Vusi   56
Malcolm X   5, 29, 38, 51, 147, 186
   anniversary of death   98
   essay on   31
   Motswana doctor   153
   Negro Digest   153
   Tswana proverb   148
Masekela, Hugh   51, 111, 115
masks   137
   Dogon   137, 139
   embodiment   137
   Tladi, Lefifi   137, 167
trans*formations   137

matriarchive   6
  Blackwomen   77, 79
  characteristics   68
  concept   6, 63
  conceptualisation   66
  culture   111
  diaspora   13
  future memory   88
  Galekgobe   20
  heretics   88
  influences   7
  mining industry   77
  navel   66, 67–8, 174
  point of departure   78
  'sifting and shifting'   69
  spatio-temporality   66
matrilineal influences   4, 6, 67
Maunick, Edouard   176
Mbete, Baleka   55
MDALI   164, 166
medicinal practices   154, 154
Medu Arts Ensemble   55
memories   66, 68
  concept   66
Minh, Ho Chi   54
mining industry   76
  matriarchive   77
  racial capitalism   75, 76, 82, 100
Mnyele, Thami   55
Moagi, Neo   35, 36
moagisani   22, 28, 84, 169, 183, 184
Monyaise, Daniel Philip
    Semakaleng   46, 49
Moruakgomo   95–8, 144
'Mosima Motlhaela Thupa'   164, 165
    fig.5, 166–9
mother *see* Galekgobe
Motswana doctor   137, 149, 154, 161, 171
  death rites   148, 155
  Hughes, Langston   157, 160, 169
  Malcolm X   153
  spiritual practices   157, 166
Motswasele II   95–8, 99, 144
mythologies   1, 6, 119

  sacred   25
  women and water   87

names-songs-places   29
  birth rituals   75
  deployment   69
  female musicians   84–5
  healing rituals   137
  praise poetry   182
  reclamation of land   50
  reeding and riting   73–4
naming rituals   68
National Endowment for the Arts
    Poetry Awards   53
National Poet Laureate   54, 57, 58
Native Land Act, 1913   34, 50
navel   90
  matriarchive   66, 67–8, 174
  placemaking   72
  symbolism   90, 105
Neal, Larry   10, 30, 52, 88
Negro Digest / Black world   12, 83, 150–51, 150n.1, 154
  decolonization   83
  South Africa   148
Nelson, David   98–9, 104
Neruda, Pablo   57
Neto, Agostinho   54
Nokwe, Duma   54
NOW   8, 18
  concept   23
  future memory   88
  pastpresentfuture   120
  'sifting and shifting'   23
  time   23
obituary   189–190
occult   90
Odd Future   112. 114
Ohlange Institute   46
OJ&A's *see* Otabenga Jones & Associates
oral traditions   38–40, 41
Otabenga Jones & Associates   30, 116
  mission   129
  rap   30
Oyewole, Abiodun   98, 104, 105, 106

PAC
  banning 48
Pan-Africanism 174
  decolonization 174
  #RhodesMustFall 174n2
pastpresentfuture 120, 171, 181
  time 23
Plaatje, Solomon 33–4, 47
placemaking 30, 66, 72, 174
  colonialism 70
  navel 72
  rituals 66
poet of the revolution 54
poetic knowledge
  erotic 149
  Tswana proverb 154
police brutality 141
  Black bodies 135
police violence 139
political essays
  decolonization 12, 151
political exile 48
  harrowing passage into 49–51
praise poetry
  names-songs-places 182
praise songs 67
precolonial history 14–15
Pride Records 130, 134
  Dowling Street Martyr Brigade 132
print cultures 7, 12, 162
'pro/creation' 110, 112, 188
proverbs *see* Tswana proverb
Pruitt, Robert 118
  comic adventure 121, 134
  comic first page 139, 140 fig.3, 141
  comic second page 141, 142 fig.4
  Turner, Nat 144
pygmies 129–130

racial capitalism 22, 41, 63, 100
  mining industry 75, 76, 82
radical political imagination 69, 90
Raditladi, Leetile 95–8
rap 8, 106, 110
  beginning of 107

Earl Sweatshirt 30
Otabenga Jones & Associates 30
The Last Poets 52, 106
Rebelo, Jorge 54
reeding and riting 22, 73–5, 124–9, 143
  function of sound 125
  method and praxis of recuperation 126
  names-songs-places 73–4
return to Africa 53–60
Revolutionary Action Movement 77
#RhodesMustFall 174n2
Robben Island 29, 56, 182

SACP 54
Sanders, Pharoah 52, 110, 187
SANNC 35
scholarship 51, 175n3
  Lincoln University 51, 175n3
Serote, Wally 55
servants' quarters 44
Setswana language 22
  change of opinion on use of 57
  citizen 22
  inner-ear 27–8
  jazz 46
Setswana proverb *see* Tswana proverb
Sharpeville 29, 48, 162, 182
  massacre 48
'sifting and shifting' 18, 69, 74
  matriarchive 69
  NOW 23
  writing process 18, 25
Simone, Nina 84, 86, 87
slums 42, 123, 135
SNCC 51, 52, 187
'son' and 'sun' 72, 62, 87, 91, 119
songs 29
  as resistance 29
  Black world 70–1
sound knowledges 6, 8
  black experience 15–19
South Africa 148
  exiles 51
  history 34
  Negro Digest 148

Soviet Union   54, 55, 56
Soyinka, Wole   27, 57, 176, 177, 181
spatio-temporality   18, 25, 173
    diaspora   77
    Europatriarchal   24
'spear of the nation'   50, 94, 97
Spearhead   50
Stanford, Max   77
storytelling   38–40
Sun Ra   121, 122, 127
    Otabenga Jones & Associates   122–3
Suppression of Communism Act, 1962   163n7

Tambo, Oliver   54
Tanganyika   48, 49, 50
Tanzania   54
The Blue Notes   108
The Last Poets   13, 94
    African Americans   107
    debut album   106
    Earl Sweatshirt   30
    fifty-year anniversary   112
    Kain, Gylan   99, 104
    Luciano, Felipe   104
    Nelson, David   98–9, 104
    Oyewole, Abiodun   98, 104, 105, 106
    rap   52, 106
Themba, Can   29, 46–7, 118, 177, 182, 188
time
    boundaries   24
    NOW   23
    pastpresentfuture   23
Tladi, Lefifi   31, 148, 166–9
    masks   137, 167
    transformation   149
    Tswana proverb   148–9, 165, 170–1
to wander is to see   15–16
totems   16, 20, 62
    animal   16, 20
    woman-dancer-of-steel   20, 44, 64
trans*formations   124, 137
    Black bodies   124
    masks   137

Transition and Black Orpheus   176
translations
    different media   30, 118, 121
    French   176
    Setswana   132
Treason Trial   47
trees
    metaphor of diaspora   92, 106
tribalism   47
Tswana culture   3
Tswana literature   38, 39
Tswana proverb   31
    African American culture   164
    Black internationalism   149, 156–7, 167
    death rites   148
    Europatriarchal   148
    future memory   149, 156
    medicinal practices   154
    poetic knowledge   154
    Tladi, Lefifi   148–9, 165, 170–1
    visual interpretation   148
Turner, Nat   123, 141, 143, 144

Umbra   179
uMkhonto we Sizwe   50, 94, 97, 101, 105, 144
    African Americans   101
    ''spear of the nation'   50, 94, 97
University of South Africa   58
USA 1962-75   51–53

vinyls
    fictional   130–1

Washington, Harold   56
water spirits   87
Wayne State University   57
white friends   44
white myths   119
white nurses   42–3
white settler geography   62
white supremacy   42, 186
    Black bodies   36, 41
    revolt against   94

Wilson, Cassandra   84
wind   28
   coil   23
   diaspora   25
   ecosomatics-geopoetics   103–4
   key element   92
woman-dancer-of-steel   20, 44, 64
women writers   13

writing process   18
   'sifting and shifting'   18, 25

youth   164
   colonial alienation   *38*
   culture   108

ZANU   97–8

AFRICAN ARTICULATIONS

ISSN 2054-5673

Previously published

Achebe and Friends at Umuahia: The Making of a Literary Elite
Terri Ochiagha, 2015. Winner of the ASAUK Fage & Oliver Prize 2016

A Death Retold in Truth and Rumour: Kenya, Britain and the Julie Ward Murder   Grace A. Musila, 2015

Scoring Race: Jazz, Fiction, and Francophone Africa   Pim Higginson, 2017

Writing Spatiality in West Africa: Colonial Legacies in the Anglophone/Francophone Novel   Madhu Krishnan, 2018. Winner of the ALA Book of the Year Award – Scholarship 2020

Written under the Skin: Blood and Intergenerational Memory in South Africa   Carli Coetzee, 2019. Winner of the ALA Book of the Year Award – Scholarship 2021

Experiments with Truth: Narrative Non-fiction and the Coming of Democracy in South Africa   Hedley Twidle, 2019

At the Crossroads: Nigerian Travel Writing and Literary Culture in Yoruba and English   Rebecca Jones, 2019. Shortlisted for the ASAUK Fage & Oliver Prize 2020, 'Honorable Mention' for the ALA First Book Award – Scholarship 2021

Cinemas of the Mozambican Revolution: Anti-Colonialism, Independence and Internationalism in Filmmaking, 1968–1991   Ros Gray, 2020

African Literature in the Digital Age: Class and Sexual Politics in New Writing from Nigeria and Kenya   Shola Adenekan, 2021

Newsprint Literature and Local Literary Creativity in West Africa, 1900s–1960s   Stephanie Newell, 2023

Keorapetse Kgositsile & the Black Arts Movement: Poetics of Possibility   Uhuru Portia Phalafala, 2024

Anglophone African Detective Fiction 1940–2020: The State, the Citizen, and the Sovereign Ideal   Matthew J. Christensen, 2024

www.ingramcontent.com/pod-product-compliance
Lightning Source LLC
Chambersburg PA
CBHW070803230426
43665CB00017B/2472